Debates

with

Historians

DEBATES

WITH

HISTORIANS

by PIETER GEYL

A MERIDIAN BOOK
NEW AMERICAN LIBRARY
TIMES MIRROR

MERIDIAN TRADEMARK REG. U.S. PAT. OFF. AND FOREIGN COUNTRIES
REGISTERED TRADEMARK—MARCA REGISTRADA
HECHO EN CHICAGO, U.S.A.

SIGNET, SIGNET CLASSICS, MENTOR, PLUME and MERIDIAN BOOKS
are published by The New American Library, Inc.,
1301 Avenue of the Americas, New York, New York 10019

FIRST PRINTING, SEPTEMBER, 1958

8 9 10 11 12 13 14 15 16

PRINTED IN THE UNITED STATES OF AMERICA

CONTENTS

PREFACE TO THE FIRST EDITION

The essays here collected deal with a variety of subjects, but in all of them the author will be seen at grips with problems belonging to the same order. It is this which must be my justification for presenting them together in this volume.

Of the thirteen essays, eleven were printed before in English, but scattered over several reviews and independent publications. A situation had thus arisen which seemed to me to be in more than one way unsatisfactory. Some of the essays (including the two here published for the first time) are closely linked with others, but apart from that, readers might find some interest in watching my progress among the dangers and delights of history. None of this could be made visible except by complete publication in book form.

In reprinting some of the essays a few corrections were made, certain passages expanded, and several explanatory footnotes added.

Five of the essays already published appeared together in 1952 as number XXXIX of the Smith College *Studies in History* (Northampton, Mass.). I am glad to take the opportunity of once more expressing my gratitude to the History Department of Smith College for having thus honored the lectures which I had delivered before them earlier in the year while holding the W. A. Neilson Research Professorship. The essays on Ranke and Macaulay there included will now be seen to have found a complement in similar ones on Carlyle and Michelet, and the four great historians of the same generation dominating the middle of the nineteenth century are thus presented. The one lecture on Toynbee published in

7

the Smith College volume here reappears as the third in a little series of four, in which the progress of the critic's hostility to the method and the system will clearly appear.

The antecedent history of particular essays is not perhaps of much interest. Nevertheless, some interest will be found in the Note of Acknowledgment.

My thanks are due to the University of Utrecht, which made the present edition possible by including the volume in the *Historiche Studies uitgegeven vanwege het Instituut voor Geschiedenis der Rijksuniversiteit te Utrecht.*

—P.G.

Utrecht, March 25, 1955

PREFACE TO THE MERIDIAN BOOKS EDITION

The present edition is more than a simple reprint of the First Edition. The opportunity has been used, not only to correct a few not very important inaccuracies which it is unnecessary to specify, but also to enlarge and strengthen the last part of the Michelet essay. The passages on Lefebvre, on De Tocqueville, and on Renan have been completely recast.

Utrecht, August 15, 1958

I RANKE IN THE LIGHT OF
THE CATASTROPHE

Agatha Christie, in one of her witty books, *The Moving Finger*, introduces a girl fresh from school and lets her run on about what she thinks of it. "Such a lot of things seem to me such rot. History, for instance. Why, it's quite different out of different books!" To this her sensible elderly confidant replies: "That is its real interest."

Let me remind you of this before everything else. History is infinite. It is unfixable. We are always trying to state past reality in terms of certainty, but all that we are able to do is to render our own impression of it. No book can reproduce more than a part of that reality, even within the confines of its particular subject; and each book contains something else, which gets mixed up with historical truth in an almost untraceable manner—I mean the opinion, or the sentiment, or the philosophy of life, of the narrator; or, in other words, the personality of the historian. The admixture does not necessarily turn historical truth into falsehood, but it does transform it into something different from the simple truth.

This applies also to Ranke.

You may think: naturally. But Ranke stands before us as the great founder of the school of objective history. In the preface to his very first book, written in 1824, when he was not yet thirty, he stated that he did not presume, as did most historians, to sit in judgment on the past; that he only wanted to show "what had really happened." And what, indeed, has always struck his readers, during his lifetime and afterwards, is that he withholds his judgment. An English critic, Lord Acton, a few years after the master's death, put it rather scathingly. He first relates his last meeting with

Ranke, who was then, in 1876, past eighty and had produced an enormous row of large works about large subjects. There was his *History of the Popes,* and his *German History in the Times of the Reformation in Germany;* there was a Prussian History and other works on Germany in the eighteenth century, a *History of France* and a *History of England,* both principally in the sixteenth and seventeenth centuries and each consisting of some five or six volumes. "He was feeble, sunken, and almost blind, scarcely able to read or write," so Acton told his audience at Cambridge afterwards. "He uttered his farewell with a kindly emotion, and I feared that the next I should hear of him would be the news of his death." Instead, there came another rash of volumes, of a *World History,* which was broken off somewhere in the late Middle Ages when the old man died, in 1886, in his ninety-first year.

His achievement commanded universal respect. There is among writers of history hardly a second figure who is equally awe-inspiring. Yet not everybody surrendered, and Acton especially expressed himself in very qualified terms. Ranke's work, unequalled as regards bulk, had also, he admits, exercised unequalled influence. "He is the representative of the age which instituted the modern study of history. He taught it to be critical, to be colourless and to be new. We meet him at every step, and he has done more for us than any other man." But the word "colourless" is not exactly indicative of enthusiasm. And listen to the rest:

His object was above all things to follow, without swerving, and in stern subordination and surrender, the lead of his authorities. He decided effectually to repress the poet, the patriot, the religious or political partisan, to sustain no cause, to banish himself from his books, and to write nothing that would gratify his own feelings or disclose his private convictions.

"To banish himself from his books"—Is Ranke then an exception to what I stated, a moment ago, to be an absolute rule, namely, that in every historical account truth is served up to us mixed with a personal ingredient? There is another question here, to which I shall for the moment only allude in passing, namely, whether Ranke's method of avoiding the expression of a judgment is either good or bad, salutary or dangerous, or, to what extent, either the one or the other. That Acton did not like it is clear enough, and, from a fanatic for moral judgment such as he was, nothing else was to be expected. It is possible, however, to observe this same habit of mind in Ranke and to express admiration instead of contemptuous reprobation. That is, for instance, what Allard Pierson, a Dutch critic, did. Writing in the late seventies, he denied to Macaulay "the crown of all gifts," namely "a complete liberty of mind," because Macaulay in his work obtrudes his own self and continually indulges in valuations according to his personal, that is to say, nine-teenth-century liberal, standards. Over against Macaulay, Pierson then places Ranke, in whose work this liberty "manifests itself in a criticism which does not in the first place approve or condemn, but which characterizes and assigns an order. Between preference and dislike Ranke's criticism seeks its ally in a contact of sentiment."

Pierson here speaks approvingly of the same habit of Ranke's mind which elicited hostile comment from Acton. And indeed his description of it is strikingly different and does not by any means imply the elimination of the historian's personality from his work. For "to criticize, to characterize and to assign an order . . . to establish a contact of sentiment"—all this is not the doing of a robot, but of a human being.

There is no doubt in my mind that Pierson hit the mark, and that Acton missed it. We do meet Ranke in his work, and the history which he has given us in his fifty volumes is no dry statement of facts without sense or intention. If that is what Acton meant to convey, it only proves that he had not understood Ranke. There can be no doubt, however, that, although Ranke *is* to be found in his work, if one cannot attune one's mind to his, one will still miss him.

The mind of Ranke did indeed differ, and was in communication with an entirely different cultural current, from those of the rationalist and radical writers whom, even in his youth, he had criticized with that famous statement about not wishing to play the judge and only setting out to tell what had happened. Of those others, let me mention only the German writer Schlosser, whose popular fame, even in his lifetime, far exceeded that of Ranke. Schlosser looked down on men's follies from the height of his enlightened ideals. To distribute praise and blame was to him the true task of the historian. The example he set himself was that of Dante in his *Divina Commedia;* Schlosser, too, allotted to the great ones of this world, according to their behavior, either the bliss of heaven or the punishment of hell—and by far the greater number Schlosser consigned to hell. In the same spirit a French radical, Laboulaye, criticized Ranke, in 1852, for his detachment. The historian, so he declared, must be a judge (although it is clear that he meant a public prosecutor) in order "to accuse in the name of the oppressed past and in the interests of the future." Macaulay, too, who was so often, in the third quarter of the nineteenth century, bracketed together with Ranke as one of the two greatest European historians, belonged to that school. Progress was his religion, and his attitude toward the past was like that of a schoolmaster putting it through an examination on questions which are highly unfair to the candidate because they are so exclusively bound up with the examiner's range of interests and experience.

Ranke's different conception of history is rooted in a different philosophy of life. To a certain extent the difference was conditioned by the period. Romanticism is a notion which eludes exact definition, but the word is indispensable. The reaction against eighteenth-century rationalism is an essential part of the Romantic attitude of mind. But on tracing the forms in which that reaction could realize itself, one finds a diversity which sometimes obscures the common origin. There were illusionist possibilities as well as realistic ones, egotistical as well as social. There was the tendency to lose oneself in ideals or fantasies, the preoccupation with the inmost stirrings of one's own soul, the surrender, too, to all passions. But no less essentially part of Romanticism was the breaking away from the generalizations or the abstractions constructed by the reasoning faculty and the desire to open the mind to reality in its manifold manifestations and appearances. It is in this latter aspect that the Romantic movement has become so exceedingly stimulating to scholarship, nowhere more than in Germany. The awareness of the individual, of the characteristic, in communities as well as in human beings, was quickened. Now that the limitations of human reason, both as the motive force and as the instrument for the unraveling of the process of history were realized and the conceptions of an organic cohesion and of continuity had entered the mind of that generation, the past acquired a reality of its own, irreplaceable and equal to the present in value. In the teaching of Savigny, the great founder of what the Germans call the Historical School of Law—and Savigny was a friend of Ranke's, although some ten years older than he—the antithesis between positive law and hypothetically desirable law, between the actual and the ideal, was not admitted. What had developed by the historical process had to be accepted not only as real but as valuable.

One can see implied in this view that same reluctance to pass judgments in conformity with either rational or moral standards which is so characteristic of Ranke. And, indeed, this is the school of thought to which he belongs. But it will be clear at the same time that this attitude of mind cannot be described as merely neutral, nor is the resulting view of the past in the full sense of the word "objective." The attitude has its positive implications, and these are of a trend decidedly conservative. Whereas the radicals felt themselves completely free with respect to the past and criticized it to their hearts' content in order to make men's minds ripe for the reform of actual conditions, those who, moved by the reaction to the French Revolution, embraced this new historical doctrine felt themselves firmly wedded to the past, accepting it as the basis of existing conditions which they also accepted. Abstention from criticism, therefore, was no sign of a lack of conviction. It was the expression of a conviction.

Indeed, Ranke was far from indifferent to the great problems of state and society; he was more than a registering memory. This appears strikingly from the fact that in the thirties he edited—or, rather, wrote—a little review called the *Historical-Political Review,* which was a Prussian Government organ. Ranke was born as a subject of the King of

Saxony, but in 1815 his native region had been annexed to Prussia, and it was there, in that larger state that afforded infinitely greater possibilities, that he sought a career. He was not much past thirty when he obtained a chair in the University of Berlin; soon afterwards he was sent by the Prussian Government on that famous tour of research in Austria and Italy, where he feasted on the then completely unexplored riches of the archives; and after his return he was made editor of that little sheet the *Historisch-Politische Zeitschrift* in order to defend Prussian Government policy against the Liberals and their theories of Constitution and Parliament. Two essays, of some thirty or forty pages each, have survived of what he wrote in those few years of his editorship, and they are indeed little masterpieces.

In one, *The Great Powers*, Ranke gives a historical survey of the rivalry among the five European powers which were acknowledged *great* at that moment and whose leading position he seemed to regard as something for all time. What he brings out is that they seem to be kept mysteriously (and again he implies, eternally) in balance. There is a meaning, too, in this unending movement. Each state strives by its very nature after power and thereby helps, in rivalry and conflict with the others, to keep the European community and civilization in being. Did not the Greek philosopher say that war is the father of all things?

The other essay, *A Political Conversation*, is concerned with the nature of the State, and the relationship between it and its citizens. A leading motif is that each state possesses, as against all others, a spiritual individuality. That is why reforms cannot, by logical argument in the abstract, be applied to all or be imitated by one from another. The States are "ideas of God." The individual can live his life in its fulness only through the state to which he belongs. Active participation such as prevails in countries where there are elected representative assemblies is by no means necessary. Even without this the Prussian citizen can find his liberty in a spontaneous devotion of his forces, in a voluntary subjection of his will, to the State.

With these ideas Ranke took his place in the reaction against the French Revolution which not only in Germany but in France and England as well inspired a number of powerful thinkers. I need hardly point out the dangerous tendencies in these ideas. Some of you must have been struck by the invitation to a pure power policy, and even to totalitarianism, that they contain. But let me remind you that, in spite of this, Ranke's belief in a European community was perfectly sincere, as was his belief in the necessity of a diversity of national civilizations, the only guarantee, as he saw it, of a sound and rich European civilization. Equally sincerely, and I might say equally naively—for is not *naive* the only fitting word to characterize his belief in the salutariness of the struggle between the States and in the durability of that equilibrium which was to control all conflicts?—equally sincerely, and equally naively, he believed in the good intentions of the autocratic Prussian Government; and indeed he had personally experienced nothing but benefits at its hands; he believed in its wish and its ability to promote the interests of the whole nation.

We see, then, Ranke in the grip of a great contemporary intellectual movement. We observe, moreover, that his career under the protection of the Prussian Government could not but confirm him in the conservative temper that went naturally with this new view of human society and of history. Was there not more? something rooted more deeply in the personality? something strictly individual? Von Sybel, his disciple and later his critic, said: the aesthetic sense. And one can indeed imagine the pure pleasure in the spectacle and in its picturing imparting a satisfaction that leaves little attention for the question of good or bad, beneficent or pernicious. I am inclined to believe that in the case of Ranke this factor should be taken into account. But it cannot sufficiently explain the figure he made as a historian; it fades into insignificance compared with another trait of his mental make-up. I mean the mystical religious faith which he drew from his Lutheran family tradition. It is there that his acquiescent view of man's fortunes and misfortunes had its foundation. He acquiesced, because in the rise and fall of historical forces, of the "ideas" striving to realize themselves and doomed to lose their purity before their complete triumph and be pushed aside by others, he discerned "God's vicissitudes in the world." *There* lay for him the never-fading enjoyment of his study; it was not merely his aesthetic enjoyment of the ever-varying scene, but the sense that it afforded a view of God's government.

As early as 1820 he wrote in a letter to his brother: "God lives and is observable in the whole of history. Every deed bears witness of him, every moment proclaims his name, but especially do we find it in the connecting line that runs through history." This last remark is worth noting. Even at that early stage the colorful spectacle did not satisfy him. We see him looking for the context, for the significance. And, moreover, then and always—for I could quote dozens of passages—he gives expression to the notion that the historian works on God's tracks. "The unutterable sweetness," so he says, "of sharing in the divine knowledge." Does it not become clear that one gives a mere caricature of Ranke if one represents his "only what really happened" as indicating the true object of his indefatigable labours? It was no more than the key to the mystery—not that it opened complete access to it, only a glance, a respectful, an awed guessing. In that holy service Ranke was eager, if he could, to renounce his personality. "Oh highest bliss!" he writes in his diary, and this is the true language of mysticism. Even toward the very end, in the preface to the *World History*: "I wish I could as it were extinguish myself."

Was Acton right after all when he said that Ranke wanted to vanish from his books? No, *this* blotting out of the personality is something quite different from what *he* imputed to Ranke, and we can now see that the abstention from moral judgments is no sign of a cold heart. Ranke's soul is flooded with reverence at the spectacle afforded by history, for it is all God. Evil and destruction have their places in God's plan. Shall the human being who is permitted to cast a glance into the mystery presume to find fault? We are there beyond good and evil. God's triumph is assured, but it springs from the conflict of opposing principles.

It is impossible to build on such views as these a hard and fast system. That is what Hegel did, the philosopher, who was some twenty-five years older than Ranke and whose ideas up to a certain point—on the State, and on power, for instance—ran parallel with his, but who proceeded infinitely more rationalistically. Hegel subjected history ruthlessly to his general conceptions, to his evolutionary scheme. Ranke, on the contrary, always took care that his general conceptions or his scheme (if even the *word* is applicable to his thought) should remain elastic, or vague. He realized that he could only lift a tip of the veil. Even on the relative significance of the impersonal forces compared with the individual factor as embodied in the great leaders of nations—even on that problem, which poses itself in the very center of his work, you will not find him making any very positive pronouncements; you will have to set statements pointing in one direction over against others of an opposite tendency.

It was this indefinite, supple character of his general vision which enabled him to give to the particular his unshackled attention and to interpret it in its own context. All the appearances of history equally belonged to God's plan. He expressed this in a phrase of profound meaning: that every epoch is "immediate to God"—that is to say, that it is due to every epoch that we should consider it for its own sake. The exact opposite, this, let me remind you once more, of Macaulay's doctrine, or at least practice, in which the past is always related to the present, in which it is judged on what it seems to him to have contributed to progress, or more exactly to the outcome of that process, his own glorious mid-nineteenth-century moment. It is here that we touch Ranke's inspiring value to the study of history: his gift of looking at the ideas, the great historic currents, and their individual exponents, each in its own right, one might say from the inside. There lies the novelty of his treatment of history; and how novel it was we cannot now realize without in our turn transporting ourselves by an effort of the historical imagination, for this very capacity has ever since been cultivated by historians and has come to be one of the essential features of our civilization.

The whole of that enormous production is governed by this attitude of mind. How shall I select an example to make you see it? Quite arbitrarily then—take, in the *History of France*, his chapters on the Gallican Declaration of 1682 and the Revocation of the Edict of Nantes in 1685. The first thing that has struck Ranke in that ecclesiastical assembly which sided with the King, with Louis XIV, against the Pope, is the grand air; he admires the style, the form. Was he for or against? It is difficult to say. He finds in the proceedings evidence of the sense of power animating that French community, of its inclination to regard itself as a world apart, sufficient unto itself and able to take independent decisions. The treatment of the Revocation in the next chapter corresponds with admirable aptitude. Ranke does not extenuate the horrors of the persecution, but it is to him, he admits, "a painful business" to expatiate on them. This is what, for instance, Michelet does with a certain eagerness. It is as if Michelet wants to make you feel that the great crimes of history were worse even than you thought before, and the perpetrators more cruel, more brutal, more detestable. From Ranke, on the contrary, you will realize that more can be said than ever you knew to excuse, not the deed, but the doers—men, after all, like their victims and like ourselves, imprisoned within the illusions of their time, of their country, of their kind, and driven. . . . All that Ranke asks himself at the close of his account of the Revocation is which *idea* must be held responsible. Was it the universal Roman Church? No, it was the urge toward unity dominating French history, and the Revocation was as it were the counterpart, the complement, to the Gallican Declaration of three years before, when the French clergy had stuck to the King, who now granted them their long-cherished wish.—A vision as if from a great height, where the tragedy of those happenings can hardly make itself heard. But a great and fascinating vision, for which I for one am glad to dispense with any amount of moral exclamations.

Let me stress again the fact that in Ranke's mind these currents or tendencies, these ideas for which he searched in history were not material or mechanical forces ruled by the law of nature. It is instructive to note the violence (most unusual for him) with which, in his old age, he protested against the thesis of Gervinus (Schlosser's pupil) that the historic process is in the main subjected to laws; it is only in the outward appearance (according to Gervinus) that a certain latitude is left to man's choice. This view is typical of the influence exercised by Positivism and by the imposing development of science in the later nineteenth century. And now Ranke, in 1871, after Gervinus's death, inveighs against this subjection of human will and human gifts to a dry, prosaic, unescapable law of nature. Can, he exclaims, a more desolate philosophy of life be imagined? and, as regards the effect on the historic comprehension, it must be paralyzing and humiliating. It is clear that he regards his own large historic movements, even though they, too, generally drag the individual along or overshadow it, as something essentially different. Indeed, they had a human as well as a divine quality. In them (I think that I may thus render his conception, which is hardly capable of any very precise definition)—in them a mysterious synthesis was realized between human striving and the divine will. In the contemplation of this mystery, he felt, individual morality was not denied but transcended.

Yet after all this, Acton's saying that Ranke sometimes talks of "transactions and occurrences" when he would have done better to speak of "turpitude and crime" does evoke a response somewhere within me. This view of history which aims at *understanding,* and to which *understanding* means: the discerning (or guessing) of the leading features of God's plan and the assigning to the great historic figures their place therein—this view of history undeniably contains the risk of weakening the responsibility of the individual in the historic drama; and especially of the powerful individual, of the leader, of anyone who in any way, be it by birth or by intellectual eminence, catches the eye of history.

Indeed, these historic personages, these rulers or founders of religions, have it all their own way with Ranke. When contrasting Charles XII of Sweden and Peter the Great as the representatives, in a great historical moment, of the Germanic and of the Slav world respectively, he feels that he is in the presence of "an exalted spectacle." To tell the truth, in the characters and behavior of each of those two there was much that does not seem particularly *exalting.* Only, from that Ranke averts his eyes.—When telling the story of Frederick the Great's attack on Maria Theresa and the conquest of Silesia in 1740, he remarks: "Fortunately it is not the historian's task to pronounce upon the justice of the King's claims." Not the historian's task? What, then, *is* the historian's task? To describe (it seems) the growth of power; and is not that to say: to serve power?—There is not, in the history of the Reformation period in Germany, a more painful incident than that of Philip of Hesse's bigamy. The virtuous young lady would not surrender to the Grand Duke without a marriage. Unfortunately the Grand Duke was married already. But did not the Old Testament, which was now regarded so highly, tell of lawful marriage with more than one wife? When Luther and Melanchthon were faced by a demand from their powerful ally, one of the indispensable supporters of their movement, to have their approval for this way out, they were thrown into a severe struggle with their souls. They did in the end give their approval, on condition, be it noted, of the strictest secrecy —in spite of which the whole of Germany was soon talking of the scandal, the Catholics with righteous disgust not un-mixed with amusement. Is it possible to tell this story other-wise than sarcastically or with indignation? Ranke tells it without any accent whatsoever. The Grand Duke is given a good mark for his conscientiousness; and as regards the conduct of the two new prophets and masters of men's morals, he abstains from all comment.

It is only during the last period of his long life that Ranke's influence swept all before it. At one moment there had been a good deal of opposition among German his-torians, even those who, like von Sybel, had been his pupils. That serene acquiescence, that insistence on supernational values, acknowledging a European community and enclosing national power politics within an equilibrium—all that was little to the taste of the generation that in the fifties and sixties wanted to use Prussia in order to get German unity forced through against Austria—on a little-German basis, as was the current phrase. These men chafed at Ranke's objectivity, and his universalism, and called it moral flabbi-ness and lack of national sentiment. This so-called Political

School, or Prussian School, of historians—Droysen, von Sybel, Treitschke—resolutely placed history in the service of the great cause.

One has only to look a little closely at the latest and most brilliant representative of this school, at Treitschke, who did his best work between 1870 and 1895, and one will notice that for this man *moral* had no independent value, that for him (and he was fond of using the word) it was identical with national, with Protestant, with Germanic, and that he wanted to clear away the last restrictions from the path of the power State. And suddenly you feel in Ranke's mind a breadth, a balance, a humanity, a distinction, and you realize what a precious gift was this self-restraint, this striving to understand and to enter into the past and its own sphere, different as it might be. And, indeed, even before the succeeding generation of historians had in their turn gone, that unruffled figure gradually rose over their heads and began to dominate the scene. Particularly the academic scene. The universities came to swear by Ranke.

Historicism, this was the term that came into use for the approach to history that was derived from his example. Minus the mystical urge, no doubt; but the abstaining from judgment, the accepting, the acknowledging of no other standards than those supplied by the historical process itself—these came to constitute the spirit in which history was studied. The great personages were seen as the exponents of impersonal forces, driven. *Fert unda nec regitur.*

Although the title of this essay is "Ranke in the Light of the Catastrophe," thus far I have been discussing Ranke and have kept you waiting for the catastrophe. To introduce a discussion of *Ranke today*, of the struggle with or against his influence, of the revision of the figure with the help of wisdom gleaned from recent experiences, I want to quote a passage from an article that appeared in the *Times Literary Supplement* in 1950—anonymously, as is unfortunately the custom of that excellent paper. In this case it is not difficult to guess who was the writer.

The German interest in Ranke is one attempt among many to evade the responsibilities of the day, as Ranke evaded them, by a sort of political quietism—finding God in history in the hope that He will take the blame for anything that goes wrong. . . . Ranke spoke of historians as priests; he regarded kings as the most sacred of priests. The State could never sin, and if it did, this was not his affair. This was the spirit of the learned classes in Germany which brought Hitler to power and which still dominates academic circles.

You will recognize in this brilliant and bitter tirade the Ranke I have sketched; and you will recognize in it the Germans as well. Nevertheless, it is unfair, both to Ranke and to the Germans.

Ranke a pioneer of National Socialism?—for that is what is implied. When one remembers the man and his mental and moral habit, doesn't it seem absurd? Yet is it possible to deny that some of his ideas must have tended to weaken the powers of resistance? All that the *Political Conversation* admits as the citizen's contribution to the public cause is: private activity, and loyalty toward the State. And not only that propagandist publication but the whole of Ranke's impressive production led away from that active participation in political life which occupies a central position in the political thought of Western Europe. The subordination of everything to the State, and to the contest of power between the States, summed up in his famous phrase of the Primacy of Foreign Policy—is not this, which belongs to the essence of his view of history, full of dangerous consequences, made more dangerous perhaps by the idealizing touch with which he presented it?

Also, if toward the end of his life and after his influence was so enormous, in what sense did it make itself felt? Did objectivity and universalism drive out nationalism? Or did not, rather, the doctrine absorb it, cloak it with its authority? The rule of forces and tendencies, which leaves to the individual no other part than of an exponent, was proclaimed and applied by German historians. Take, for instance, Max Lenz's biography of Napoleon, which appeared in 1908. Here Napoleon is the man driven by irresistible necessities and thus is exonerated from all guilt or responsibility. No doubt French historians had already given that reading of the career, especially Albert Sorel, in his *L'Europe et la Révolution française*. But, indeed, historicism was by no means confined to Germany, and the influence of Ranke had helped to spread it over the world. Lenz, at any rate, in his preface, mentions not only Sorel but also, and emphatically, Ranke. "Our interpretation," he says, "has been inspired by ideas derived from Ranke."

And yet the question may be asked, was Lenz justified in saying so? According to Meinecke, he was not; according to Meinecke, Lenz, and others such as Rachfahl and Oncken, while adopting Ranke's ideas, unconsciously did them violence by systematizing them; in their method the master's subtlety became crude, his feeling for the finer shades of reality was lost.

Meinecke, who was born in 1862 and is still among the living,[1] is one of the finest minds among the German historians of this age. His work is mainly concerned with the history of ideas. It will be interesting to trace the development of his own ideas—as exemplified by what he has had to say on Ranke at various times—under the impact of the terrific changes which he was fated to witness in his lifetime. In his first great work, of 1906, *Cosmopolitanism and the National State*, he describes the rise of nationalism in Germany, the transition from the cultural cosmopolitanism of the eighteenth century to pride in nationality and the conception of the State as the natural expression of it, which came to be characteristic of the nineteenth century. Here he still shows himself serenely pleased with a development that seemed to him one toward the ideal international society. Ranke was indeed his master, and after his early protest against the adulteration of Ranke's ideas committed by all too zealous pupils such as Lenz and Rachfahl, he was only gradually driven to admit that the ideas themselves did contain unsound elements.

As late as 1916, during the First World War, he wrote an introduction for a new edition of Ranke's *Great Powers*, in which he unhesitatingly applied the leading idea of that famous essay to the new circumstances. Only the sphere within which those powerful States gave way to their rivalry had expanded—so much he realized. Germany and England meeting and clashing on the high seas, that was a development of which Ranke had never dreamt. But that the aim of the war must be to end England's maritime supremacy, not in order to replace it by a new German supremacy, but in order to create an equilibrium analogous to the continental one which had been the last truth to Ranke, an equilibrium needed not only for Germany's interest as a world power but for universal civilization, which should rest on equality, competition and exchange—that was still, in 1916, Meinecke's belief, entirely in the spirit of the great predecessor.

After the defeat of 1918, however, Meinecke began to consider the familiar conceptions more critically and more sceptically. Already in an essay of 1919 he showed a flash of insight that, as far as international affairs were concerned, Ranke's historical system had lost all applicability. Instead of an equilibrium between a given number of historic States, he now foresaw a world-embracing hegemony of the Anglo-Saxon peoples, while for Germany there remained only the part played by the Greek city states within the *Pax Romana*. A striking suggestion, but one that was never followed up either by Meinecke or other German historians—a point to which I shall return.

In a book of 1924, *Die Idee der Staatsräson*, Meinecke is concerned to point out how different from Hegel's was Ranke's attitude of mind toward Machiavellism. Hegel was by the logic of his thought inevitably led to the legitimation (as he puts it) of a system of statecraft which had always been regarded as a bastard among the family of European political thought. Ranke, on the contrary, stuck to a dualism of labile historical and immutable moral standards. He goes on to reflect that Ranke can hardly have been profoundly conscious of this dualism, for would he not in that case have fallen a prey to the tragic pessimism characteristic of Burckhardt, the great Swiss historian, who reacted sharply against the master and the unclouded optimism in which he proceeded on his long life's journey? It was, says Meinecke, his reverence for God's action in history, his happiness in being allowed to contemplate it, that enabled Ranke to preserve that serenity.

One can see Meinecke struggling with the problem without attaining a solution. He goes a little further in criticism in an introduction he wrote in that same year, 1924, for a reprint of Ranke's other essay from the *Historical-Political Review*, the *Political Conversation*. He now speaks of an excessive spiritualization of German thought in the age of Ranke. In that grandiose optimistic view of the world, expressed in Goethe's and Ranke's objective idealism, so he says, "the night side of life receded to the background. And as a consequence the power policy of States, which has a crude and elemental aspect, is presented by Ranke as a spiritual rather than as a natural force."

It was hard for German historians to free themselves from the influence of the "Rankean" view of history. The intellectual atmosphere of Germany was indeed impregnated with it. Even in the Germany of the Weimar Republic, when one wants to hear an utterance of real independence one has to search for somebody exceptional, for a man who for some reason or other took a solitary, an oppositional course in the academic world. I might quote one or two cases of that kind [2] but, more interesting because more significant, seems to me the spectacle Meinecke presents of a man who, formed in the heyday of the Wilhelminian period, continued a mental struggle with the ever more depressing actual developments. It is this that gives a poignant interest to his writings after the second defeat—after the catastrophe, that is, which befell not only the position of power but the civilization of his people—and how proud had he been, with his people, of both, only a short time before. Earnestly he tries to account for the errors committed, for the wrong turnings taken (*Irrwege der deutschen Geschichte* is the title of a brief but pregnant article written only a few years ago). But at the same time, and I think it does him credit, he is out to preserve contact with what was valuable in the national past.

You may have been struck by the, I should almost say, tenderness with which in 1924 he explained Ranke's blindness to the dangers of power by his noble confidence in the strength of spiritual forces. Even now he does not repudiate Ranke. It is indeed significant that he rarely mentions him any more. The symbol of the heritage which the German people has jeopardized is now to him Goethe rather than Ranke. And, indeed, when he admits that Germany has to choose between acquiescing in the thankless role of "depressed area" and "becoming a living member of a European federation," what use then are the theories of *The Great Powers* and of *The Political Conversation*? Well may he speak of "a completely novel historical situation." The love of our national past, he says, which cannot die in the hearts of our grandchildren or of theirs, will become "in a sense less egocentric." And now, in this noble essay of his extreme old age, he refers to Ranke. After *his* example, history must teach us to see historic periods and phenomena *sub specie aeterni,* each related directly, or immediately, to God. Their value, their connection with the divine, springs from the secret root of the ephemeral individuality of each. In tracing that, the question of success or failure, of effect on subsequent developments, will almost vanish from sight.

Do not let us grudge the Germans that loving contemplation of their history—provided that they will not at the same time shrink from noting the wrong turnings. But, indeed, many German historians of the present day—most of them, of course, a full generation younger than Meinecke—are at grips with this problem of the re-orientation with respect to their past. It is indeed unfair to speak, as did the writer in the *Times Literary Supplement,* as if the spirit of Ranke were still dominant over the academic world of Germany. It is true that all those writers try, like Meinecke, both to revise and to retain. With some the first tendency is more pronounced; with others, the latter prevails. The discussion ranges over a multitude of aspects. It is perhaps Bismarck who claims the largest part of the attention, but Ranke too is being studied and revalued.

From innumerable instances I shall mention two, both articles in the *Historische Zeitschrift:* one by the editor, Dehio, on "Ranke and German Imperialism"; the other by Fritz Fischer on "German Protestantism and Nineteenth-Century Politics." I shall not go into any detail about either: it would only lead me into repetition, for the writers cover the same ground that I have already gone over. The interest of their contributions from my point of view is that one finds these remarks made by academic Germans in the leading historical review of the country. One point in Dehio's article I will touch upon. He explains why Meinecke's suggestion, in his prophetic essay of 1919, about the role left to Germany in a world henceforth dominated by the Anglo-Saxons fell flat: because (he says) the United States' repudiation of the League of Nations and withdrawal from European affairs veiled to the perception of German historians a change that was nevertheless to be permanent. As for today (Dehio wrote in 1950), *Periculum in mora*—Fischer's theme is the tendency of Lutheranism to abdicate in the face of the secular power, and when he distinguishes between the German ethos of Obedience and the Western ethos of Liberty and calls upon the German Protestant Church to act, in unison with the Reformed Churches of the West and with Roman Catholicism, as the world's public conscience, this, too, amounts to an assertion of the need of an emancipation from Ranke's outlook of acquiescence—which in fact the writer expressly rejects.

Let me now try to formulate a conclusion. It will not be an easy task. There always remains a *for* and an *against*, and perhaps to bring the two into a stable equilibrium is not even possible.

I would state that first of all (and I am still thinking of the vehement one-sidedness of the *Times Literary Supplement*) that this looking for the pioneers of National Socialism among generations which had not the remotest notion of that evil thing is a dangerous game. Ranke assembled certain tendencies of his age into a mighty system, which then proved to be possessed of a dynamic of its own. No doubt in it there were evil potentialities mixed with the good. But is not that inherent in our human insufficiency? Is the beneficent effect of any great system of thought imaginable without evil potentialities, and is not the measure in which either the one or the other will be realized determined by circumstances over which the thinker has no control and which he could not possibly foresee?

If we are tempted by our horror at the culmination of evil that we have just experienced or witnessed to pick out in the past of Germany all the evil potentialities, we may construct an impressively cogent concatenation of causes and effects leading straight up to that crisis. But the impressiveness and the straightness will be of our own constructing.[3] What we are really doing is to interpret the past in the terms of our own fleeting moment. We can learn a truer wisdom from Ranke's phrase that it should be viewed as "immediate to God;" and he himself, too, has a right so to be considered.

This does not mean that I want you to take him without criticism. That is not how I, myself, take him. Historicism, in the sense of an interpretation of history which acknowledges no standards outside the object, is abhorrent to me. I can see that Ranke, although not a historicist in that sense, has by his influence contributed to the development of that attitude of mind. Indeed, there is in his own presentation of the past enough of amoralism and of passivism to give one frequent cause for impatience; and the illusionism, the spiritualizing of the brutish forces, leaves one with a feeling of dissatisfaction. Yet how admirable, nevertheless, is that serene matter-of-factness, that striving after comprehension, that openmindedness for historic phenomena other than those with which the writer himself felt in agreement—as a Protestant for the Papacy, as a German for the French absolute monarchy and for the English parliamentary monarchy, as a conservative sometimes for the French Revolution—qualities which have had a broadening effect on nineteenth-century civilization and which (need I remind you?) are the complete opposite of the revolutionary fanaticism and doctrinairism of the men who half a century after his death threw Germany and the world into the catastrophe.

Comprehension, a disinterested understanding of what is alien to you—this is not the function of the mind which will supply the most trenchant weapons for the political rough-and-tumble. The man who has made up his mind for all contingencies will often be too quick for one who tries to understand. We live in a time when it is important to know your side and there are dangers involved in keep-

ing an open mind. Yet if we all of us devote all our efforts
to the struggle, what shall we in the end have struggled
for? To understand is a function of the mind that not only
enriches the life of the individual but is the very breath
of the civilization we are called to defend.

II MACAULAY IN HIS ESSAYS

It is impossible that Macaulay's *Essays* should still be as widely read as they used to be. They are too much imbued with the spirit of the age in which they were written, an active, self-confident spirit which easily grates on our susceptibilities. They are too much attuned to the expectations and prejudices of the contemporary public, expectations and prejudices that we no longer share; some of these, indeed, we could never have shared, because they were so exclusively and intolerantly English. Nonetheless, the *Essays* will never be quite forgotten, because in spite of all they are masterpieces through which there speaks to us, directly and insistently, a mind of rare clarity and immense vigor. The very fact of this work being so eminently representative of its period, which once enhanced its appeal and now impedes it, ensures to it an enduring quality of historic interest. I shall try to indicate some of its motive ideas and characteristics.

The first essay Macaulay ever published was the one on Milton. He was only twenty-four years old (he was born with the century, in 1800), but when it appeared in the *Edinburgh Review*, the leading organ of the Whigs, it at once established his name. It was not only what he had to say about Milton the poet that attracted attention; it was especially his apology for Milton the politician, Milton the supporter of the revolution against the Stuart monarchy.

Against the background of the situation around the year 1825 this was a striking confession of political faith. The Tories were still continuing their long period of power. It was the war against France, against the France of the Revolution and Napoleon, which had enabled them to entrench themselves. Since the peace, public opinion had been swept by a strong countercurrent, but this could have no practical effect, as the ruling class managed to protect itself by means of the completely antiquated electoral system. Rarely had there been so complete a lack of harmony between the people and the government; between the structure of society, in which there had grown up an active, prosperous, ambitious middle class, and the machinery of power, which had for generations been artificially kept unchanged. Reform was the battle cry of the Whigs, behind them the Radicals threatened revolution; while the Tories stubbornly maintained that salvation lay only in the maintenance of traditional forms, in authority and subjection. In that contest, appeals to history were constantly being made. Each of the parties had its own reading of the English revolutions of the seventeenth century. The Whigs used them as a warning, to the Radicals they were an example, and to the Tories a deterrent. Now along came young Macaulay and raised his voice in no uncertain manner. It is the voice the world was to hear throughout his lifetime.

Listen to the sarcasm which he pours on the advocates of Charles I because they avoid the great constitutional issues, preferring to praise the King on account of his blameless personal life. "A good father!" mocks Macaulay. "A good husband! Ample apologies indeed for fifteen years of persecution, tyranny, and falsehood!" Hume, whose *History of England* was a standby for the Tories, had argued that Charles's authoritarian acts were in the tradition of the English monarchy and for each of them had pointed a parallel from Tudor days. "The answer," says Macaulay, "is short, clear, and decisive. Charles had assented (in 1628) to the Petition of Right. He had renounced the oppressive powers said to have been exercised by his predecessors, and he had renounced them for money."

"The answer is short, clear, and decisive." That is how Macaulay settled the great problems of history when he was twenty-four years of age. And that is how he continued to do it all through his life. It is what gave to his presentation of the facts that unsurpassable lucidity and to his argument that unimpeded movement. It is what readers of not too critical a turn of mind find irresistible, but what rouses distrust and annoyance in those who are less amenable.

Just as the Tories are used to divert attention from the public transgressions of Charles I by holding forth on his private virtues, so, Macaulay continues, in their attacks on the Long Parliament they generally avoid the great points at issue and "content themselves with arguing some of the crimes and follies to which public commotions necessarily give birth." The passage which now follows is typical of innumerable ones that were to appear in the writings of Macaulay. He will never leave his reader with a mere general statement; he will always drive it home by giving particulars. He does this with such breathless conviction, seeming to draw effortlessly upon an inexhaustible knowledge, that the rush of his eloquence is not embarrassed by what in most writers would produce an impression of showing off or of laboring the point. It is astonishing that already, in this earliest of his essays, he should be the master of both his matter and his style.

"They bewail," he says, speaking of these evasive "enemies of the Parliament," "the unmerited fate of Strafford. They execrate the lawless violence of the army." And for a page or more he goes on particularizing the excesses and the deeds of violence.

But now he repeats the assertion that public commotions, for all that they cannot but be attended by crimes and follies, are not on that account necessarily less salutary. And he illustrates his thesis by telling, after Ariosto, "the story of a fairy, who, by some mysterious law of her nature, was condemned to appear at certain seasons in the form of a foul and poisonous snake." Those who injured her during those periods were forever excluded from her blessings. Those who, in spite of her loathsome aspect, pitied and protected her, were afterwards granted a view of her true beauty and all imaginable benefits besides. "Such a spirit is Liberty. At times she takes the form of a hateful reptile. She grovels, she hisses, she stings. But woe to those who in disgust shall venture to crush her. Happy are those . . ." who on the contrary—et cetera.

The events of the seventeenth century, although belonging to their own national history, were perhaps less present
to the minds of that generation of Englishmen than was the
French Revolution. That Macaulay meant the passage which
you have just read to apply to it as well cannot be doubted.
There are in later essays several direct references to the
French Revolution, and, always, while deploring the excesses, he insists that on the whole its effect was beneficent.
This readiness to take the excesses into the bargain is not
without dangerous implications. In practice, of course,
Macaulay was very far from being inclined to revolution-
making. He stood firmly by the middle position of the Whig.
He wanted reforms in order to ward off revolution and the
deplorable excesses to which revolution gives rise.

One thing will at any rate have become clear: Macaulay
came to the contemplation of the past with a mind brimming
over with ideas and sentiments about the present. Indeed,
in the early part of his career he was first and foremost a
politician and an administrator. In 1830 he entered the
House of Commons, nominated (as was still possible in the
"unreformed" days before 1832) by a Whig nobleman, who
saw in him a promising recruit for the party; and he threw
himself into the struggle with ardor—and of course on the
side of Reform. In 1834 he obtained a very lucrative ap-
pointment as member of the Supreme Council of India.
In the four or five years he spent out there he did work
of really historic importance, helping to reform the judicial
system and to introduce the English language as the medium
for all higher education in India. After his return, with an
independent fortune, he entered Parliament again and twice
held office as a Cabinet Minister.

Many historians, and some of the greatest, have had similar
careers, and it is obvious that the contact with the reality
of politics and of affairs can be of inestimable value in the
writing of history. At the same time the immersion in impassioned controversies, such as were raging in Macaulay's
youth, brings with it the temptation to judge men and
events of earlier ages as present-day preoccupations may
dictate. Macaulay was not wholly unaware of that pitfall.

In an essay written ten years after the one on Milton he deals expressly with it, and it will be worth our while to analyze that passage.

The essay in question was occasioned by a posthumous edition of the writings of Sir James Mackintosh, a Whig historian of an older generation, toward whom Macaulay felt both gratitude and respect. He thought that the editor, a Mr. Wallace, had done less than justice to the work of his venerated friend, and the review he wrote of the book is a remarkable instance of the unmerciful vehemence with which he could trounce a man from whom he differed in opinion. *Trounce* is the word. The weapon he employs in controversy is not the rapier, it is the bludgeon.

With what a contemptuous pity, says Macaulay, does this editor, whose intellectual order is not remarkably high, think fit to speak of all things that were done before the coming in of the very last fashion in politics. "The men to whom we owe it that we have a House of Commons" (the parliamentary leaders at the time of the Great Rebellion) "are sneered at because they did not allow the debates of the House to be published. The authors of the Toleration Act are treated as bigots, because they did not go the whole length of Catholic Emancipation. Just so we have heard a baby, mounted on the shoulders of its father, cry out: 'How much taller am I than Papa!' "

Follows a long tirade, written with all the usual brio, a dazzling enumeration of one concrete instance after another such as Macaulay's overflowing and ever-ready memory enabled him to reel off, all tending to prove what an easy trick it is to pride ourselves on the advances in knowledge and insight for which we are indebted to the unceasing efforts of the generations. Sir James Mackintosh himself, he concludes, sets a very different example. "His doctrines are the liberal and benevolent doctrines of the nineteenth century. But he never forgets that the men he is describing were men of the seventeenth century." You will note that he is careful to mention that Mackintosh's "doctrines" are as modern as they should be. And, indeed, he has also, in the course of this very long disquisition from which I am quoting little bits, a reflection of a quite different tendency:

"Undoubtedly we ought to look at ancient transactions by the light of modern knowledge." What are we to make of all this?

We are facing here one of the central problems of historiography. To look at the past from within, so to speak; to think in the terms of earlier generations—that is what historians have been trying to do ever since Ranke inspired us with his example. At the same time we know well enough that this is more than even the most powerful or best trained historical imagination can wholly achieve, and, also, that the historian's entire personality, including his modern knowledge and outlook, will inevitably, and rightly, enter into the final representation and valuation. Here is a statement composed, like Macaulay's, of two more or less contradictory parts, each pointing in the same direction as the corresponding one of his statement. How comes it, then, that Macaulay's writing of history strikes us as decidedly old-fashioned precisely on this point? The seventeenth century as he sets it before us seems to us distorted through nineteenth-century spectacles; the author and his period seem every moment obtruding themselves between the reader and the events described or personages pictured.

Let us observe, first of all, that he reveals himself, even when insisting that the difference of the times should be remembered, as a man in whom the intellect was far more developed than the imagination, a man who seemed, in spite of his being bred in an emotionally religious home, to issue straight from the eighteenth century, completely untouched by the Romantic Movement. He never expresses, as Ranke so frequently did, a feeling of awe before the mystery of the past, nor a desire to enter into a bond of sympathy with it, to get closer to it by *feeling with it.* He merely wants to *know,* in order to *judge.* He wants to distribute praise and blame, even though in doing so he is anxious to be just and "to make allowance for the state of political science and political morality in former ages." In other passages he mentions various branches of knowledge, but it is clear that he had a very narrow conception of the domain in which the difference of the times should be taken into account.

He drops an extraordinary utterance in another essay,

written in 1840, on Ranke's *Popes* (in which, by the way, he has much more to say about the Popes and the Roman Church than on Ranke or his book). The increase of knowledge and the progress of science, so he remarks, is not reflected in any greater rationality of man's religious opinions. "A Christian of the fifth century with a Bible is neither better nor worse situated than a Christian of the nineteenth century with a Bible. . . . The absurdity of the literal interpretation [of certain texts] was as great and as obvious in the sixteenth century as it is now." An extraordinary statement indeed! How can a man who expects the early Christians and the Protestants in the first flush of their fervor to read in the Bible what he himself, son of the Enlightenment and of Utilitarianism, finds there—how can such a man penetrate into the spirit of the past?

But, indeed, the essay on Mackintosh itself contains other passages which are sufficiently revealing as to the limits of Macaulay's capacity to transfer himself by means of the imagination to older or different civilizations. He cites not only Mackintosh himself, but also Mr. Mill, for their indulgence in judging the men of a less enlightened age. Mr. Mill, the father of John Stuart Mill the philosopher, was the author of a *History of British India*. The "indulgence" of which Macaulay speaks is not apparent in the author's attitude toward Indian civilization. The influence exercised by his book has often been deplored on the very ground that Mill judged the Indians strictly from the British and rationalistic point of view, without taking any notice of their own particular traditions. But then this is exactly what Macaulay did himself when he was in Calcutta, where, as I said, he did very excellent work; but as for penetrating into Indian ways of thought, he left India as impenitently British and devoted to his Greek and Latin classics as he had gone there. Mill's *History* is indeed much more concerned with British administration in India than with the Indians, and Macaulay, too, when he praises it, thinks of nothing else.

We know no writer who takes so much pleasure in the truly useful, noble, and philosophical employment of tracing the progress of sound opinions from their embryo state to their full maturity. He eagerly culls from old despatches and minutes every expression in which he can discern the imperfect germ of any great truth which has since been fully developed. He never fails to bestow praise on those who, though far from coming up to his standard of perfection, yet rose in a small degree above the common level of their contemporaries. *It is thus that the annals of past times ought to be written.*

It is now very plain that Macaulay means something quite different from what *we* have in mind when we speak of envisaging historical personages in their own surroundings of time and civilization. His desire to remember that they are not (poor fellows!) nineteenth-century people is completely subordinated to his ruling conception of progress—a progress which, for the time being, culminates in *his* time. So it is *his* time, after all, which supplies the standard.

And he now works out that idea in a rapid survey of the history of England, which is like a canvas for the great work to which he was to turn a few years later and to devote the rest of his life.

"The history of England," he says, "is emphatically the history of progress." He touches upon the successive stages, beginning with the subjection to foreign invaders and a rigid caste distinction, from debasing and cruel superstition, from brutal ignorance, to the glorious present of:

The greatest and most highly civilized people that ever the world saw . . . , which have spread their dominion over every quarter of the globe . . . which have carried the science of healing, the means of locomotion and correspondence, every mechanical art, every manufacture, everything that promotes the convenience of life, to a perfection which our ancestors would have thought magical; have produced a literature which may boast of works not inferior to the noblest which Greece has bequeathed to us; have discovered the laws which regulate the motions of the heavenly bodies, have speculated with exquisite subtlety on the operations of the human mind, have been the acknowledged leaders of the human race in the career of political improvement.

The paean continues with mention of the significant moments in that splendid and unceasing development, and I will quote the concluding passage. (But let me, before doing so, remind you that Manchester obtained representation in the House of Commons only through the Reform Act of 1832, when Old Sarum, typical of "rotten boroughs" generally, lost hers.)

Each of those great and ever-memorable struggles, Saxon against Norman, Villein against Lord, Protestant against Papist, Roundhead against Cavalier, Dissenter against Churchman, Manchester against Old Sarum, was, in its own order and season, a struggle, on the result of which were staked the dearest interests of the human race; and every man who, in the contest which, in his time, divided our country, distinguished himself on the right side, is entitled to our gratitude and respect.

One is reminded of the argument that Macaulay set out in his very first essay, on Milton, and illustrated with the fable told by Ariosto. Whatever is done in the cause of Liberty is right; whatever is done in the cause of Progress is right.

Liberty and Progress are noble battle cries. I shall certainly not depreciate them. But is it not clear from these quotations that Macaulay used them for conceptions that are bound up with national or time-tied delusions? Especially dangerous was the fact that he himself was so blandly unconscious of the mix-up. He assumed as a matter admitting of no discussion that his England was "the greatest and most highly civilized people" not only of the world of his day but of the world of all times. He assumed that in each of the struggles marking the history of England there had been a side, "the right side," by which, to the exclusion of the others, the cause of Progress had been served; and that he knew, in every case, which it was. The Saxons had been right against the Normans, the Villeins against the Lords, the Protestants against the Papists, the Roundheads against the Cavaliers, the Dissenters against the Churchmen, and the supporters of the Reform Bill against the adversaries. In each of those antitheses one side represented the sons of Darkness, the other those of Light. No doubt he admitted that the latter, too, were men and imperfect. But their shortcomings should be treated leniently by the historian, for they have a claim on our gratitude and respect. As for the others, I could quote formidable denunciations and withering sarcasms, often very good reading too—which would make you wonder whether the word "bludgeon" which I used earlier was sufficiently evocative of the ferocity of the treatment Macaulay was used to meting out to *them*.

I have already mentioned Ranke. In the middle of the nineteenth century Ranke and Macaulay were often mentioned in one breath as the two greatest historians of the civilized world. I do not want to question the greatness of Macaulay, but I do want to suggest that it was of a very different quality from the greatness of Ranke. In fact, the two men offer a striking contrast. I shall not expatiate on the characteristics of Ranke, his desire to comprehend rather than to judge, his search for the "ideas" or "tendencies" ruling a period. But I shall quote one of his general statements on history. "Every period," he said in 1854, "is immediate to God, and its value does not in the least consist in what springs from it, but in its own existence, in its own self."

Ranke was able to view the past in this tolerant and affirmative spirit because he was a conservative in the present. He accepted things as they were, confident that they were in some mysterious way in consonance with God's will. Similarly he accepted things and the leading men of history as they had been, because always and everywhere he was convinced that they were evidence of God's plan. I am far from suggesting that the historian, in order to get into contact with the past and to write about it with understanding and sympathy, must be, like Ranke, a conservative and a mystic. But so much is certain, that the religion of Progress, such as Macaulay held it, predisposed a man to look at the generations that had gone before with self-righteous condescension, with an impatience tempered, as Macaulay himself put it, by "indulgence." That feeling of absolute certainty about the superiority of the present and about the unqualified beneficence of the gradual increase of the technical and scientific knowledge at the disposal of mankind—

the feeling, rather, that this process is the pre-eminently important and significant one in human history—must lead the historian to view the past in terms which may be entirely irrelevant and result in a picture lacking in the truth of intimacy. It is the mental attitude against which Ranke's *dictum* was obviously directed, and, however stimulating and instructive and powerfully intelligent I may find Macaulay's work, I consider this mental attitude toward the past in the deepest sense unhistoric.

It was, no doubt, in Macaulay's case, largely a matter of temperament as well. "I wish I were as sure about anything as Macaulay is about everything," is what Lord Melbourne is reported to have said about this brilliant member of his Cabinet.

It has often been observed that Macaulay's style and method of conducting an argument were those of the orator. The early essays show that he did not need the House of Commons to teach him the trick. It is, however, true that Macaulay the parliamentary speaker and Macaulay the essayist were much alike. How he enjoyed the clash and the thrust of debate! When reading the proofs of a collection of his parliamentary speeches he remembered with a thrill of pleasure (as we know from a note in his diary) how pale Peel looked when in 1845 he had charged him with the inconsistency of his conduct. "There you sit," so he had addressed the ex-Prime Minister, "there you sit, doing penance for the disingenuousness of years. If it be not so, stand up manfully, and clear your fame before the House and country. Show us how, if you are honest in 1845, you can have been honest in 1841."

This is exactly the tone of some of the more vituperative essays. An example of Macaulay at his deadliest is his essay of 1844 on Barère. Why this passionate onslaught against a not so very interesting member of the Committee of Public Safety during the French Terror half a century ago? Because the present generation of French radicals, in trying to whitewash this man and, generally speaking, in reviving the glories of the Revolution, were appealing to the inveterate French resentment against England. So Macaulay demolished Barère—and his recent biographer into the bargain—and trampled on the remains, in eighty pages of unflagging contempt and scorn—a denunciation abundantly fed with facts and tight reasoning, which he managed to swell to a climax at the close where another writer would have been limp with exhaustion.

One can hardly call this history any more. One feels instinctively that the real Barère must have been less completely wicked, less completely vile. And, indeed, the modern historian (I am thinking of Palmer's *Twelve Who Ruled*) draws a very different portrait. In the heat of battle, while remaining coldly master of his argumentative powers, Macaulay was apt to lose all sense of measure and, it must be said, all respect for his antagonist's personality.

It was not only political passion or antagonism by which he was sometimes swept along; often it is as if it were the style itself, that style which was a projection of certain features of his mind, or perhaps of his temperament—of his passion for straight, unhesitating phrasing, for surprising effect, for sharp, dramatic contrasts. There was in him no sympathy with his fellow men, no instinctive understanding of them, to hold this passion in check. He was a loving brother; his nephews and nieces cherished the memory of their unmarried uncle. One of them, Otto Trevelyan, the father of the George Macaulay Trevelyan of our day, has in his biography of Macaulay told a charming story of his unfailing high spirits and thoughtful kindliness. But Macaulay viewed the world outside that small circle with the eye of the zealot for public virtues and for progress and for the cause of liberty. He could approve, he could admire, as well as detest and denounce. But he was incapable, so it seems, of establishing what I may perhaps call "disinterested" contact with the human being in historic or even literary personages. To complicated and tormented personalities especially—one can cite Samuel Johnson and Lord Byron —he could never do justice. He generally constructed his character sketches in accordance with a formula, a striking, a daring one, preferably one indicating a paradoxical contrast. Some of his portraits have as a result become not only unlike the originals, but unlike anything that can be imagined in human nature. Take, for instance, Boswell.

Boswell's biography of Johnson is, according to Macaulay, the greatest of all biographies. But there is not "in the whole history of the human intellect so strange a phenomenon as this book." Superlative piled on superlative—will not the reader's attention be roused? The strangeness lies in the fact that Boswell the man was so petty and pitiable a creature. There have been foolish men besides Boswell who managed to write great books. But they attained literary eminence in *spite of* their weaknesses. As for Boswell (notice how paradox is called in to reinforce superlative):

He attained it *by reason of* his weaknesses. If he had not been a great fool, he would never have been a great writer. Without all the qualities which made him the jest and the torment of those among whom he lived, without the officiousness, the inquisitiveness, the effrontery, the toad-eating, the insensibility to all reproof, he could never have produced so excellent a book.

It is as if the pleasure in elaborating so striking a picture intoxicated Macaulay, blinding him to the most evident psychological truth. If Boswell's *Johnson* is indeed so great a book (and I agree wholeheartedly that it is), Boswell must have had qualities other than the base and ridiculous ones that Macaulay takes such delight in noting. And indeed Carlyle was soon to describe Boswell—unmistakably polemizing with Macaulay, although he does not mention him—as a *reverent man*.

The maltreatment of Boswell is characteristic. Bacon, whose philosophy Macaulay lauds to the skies, he reviles as a public character. He does so, moreover, as was shown not long after his death,[1] by garbling and distorting the evidence. For Macaulay frequently went to that extreme. Even essays that are not primarily argumentative can be considered early samples of his later, graver manner in the great *History*—so, to mention only one, in the essay on Warren Hastings, in which Mr. Justice Imply is most unfairly treated. Even that *History* itself is not free from bad instances of this reckless giving way to the passion of persecution and of paradox—I mention only the well-known cases of William Penn and of Marlborough.[2]

But let me look a little more closely at the foundations of that doctrine of progress which Macaulay professed with almost strident confidence. He reveals them very plainly in an essay of 1830, in which he attacks the Tory views of Southey, and in the essay (to which I have already alluded) on Bacon, written, curiously enough, in India, in 1837.

Not everyone was prepared to agree that England was in so flourishing a condition and a so much pleasanter land in which to live than used to be the case. In 1829 the Poet Laureate, Mr. Southey, published his *Colloquies on the Progress and Prospects of Society*, in which he put forward a very different view. Macaulay accepted the challenge, and what he had to say in the *Edinburgh Review* about the state of England at that moment is interesting.

Southey was deeply concerned about the wretched conditions in which the new industrial proletariat had to live in that prosperous England. In contrast he draws an idyllic picture of the unspoilt countryside, where the good old times survived. Macaulay is very scornful about this, and not without good grounds. Mr. Southey, he says, judges by appearances. Those old villages are more picturesque, no doubt, than the naked, rectangular dwellings of the cotton-spinners. But look at the statistics, and you will find that in the West Riding of Yorkshire and in Lancashire, the industrial districts *par excellence*, the poor rate is considerably lower than in the agricultural counties, and mortality figures in the towns have immensely improved. Southey sees the country hastening to destruction. The Government, he thinks should carry out its paternal duties and protect the poor from the capitalists, who will else swallow up all. He dreams of a state of affairs in which the Government, representing the community, would manage industry. What pitiful errors! "History," says Macaulay, "is full of signs of a natural progress of society." England will be wealthier in 1930 than she is now in 1830. She will dispose of machines constructed on principles yet undiscovered. Compare the England of 1830 with that of a century ago—and for a full page the comparison is elaborated: larger towns, faster stage-coaches, a higher yield of taxation; in short, a glorification of the present and disparagement of the past altogether on the lines on which he will, nearly twenty years later, construct the famous Third Chapter of his *History*, containing the description of the state of England in 1685.

But the particular scorn of Macaulay is moved by Southey's call for government interference. Governments, he exclaims, are not so wise that we should wish for that.

Our rulers will best promote the improvement of the nation by strictly confining themselves to their own legitimate duties, by leaving capital to find its most lucrative course, commodities their fair price, industry and intelligence their natural reward, idleness and folly their natural punishment.

How cocksure, indeed, was Macaulay. When we consider his vision from the point of vantage afforded us by more than a century of further development, it appears thickly sown with blind spots. Wealthy, wealthy, and wealthier—this is the burden of his hymn of praise; and bigger, and faster, and more ingenious, and more powerful. He may occasionally slip in such words as intellectual or moral, yet the most marked feature of his view of history is its materialism. He was right in thinking that the material development would have progressed further in 1930; and probably it had, as he suggested, been progressing through the centuries. In his own country, at any rate, he was witnessing a moment of furious expansion. But how is it possible, one feels inclined to ask, that he did not observe the social tension that accompanied the economic development? He merely repeated the lesson of liberal economics (of the science of economics, as he said; the Dismal Science, as Carlyle was soon to label it), according to which everything would come right of its own accord and the division of the new wealth between capitalist and proletarian was ruled by a law of nature, which kept society in being and with which therefore it was wrong to tamper. He knew nothing, or he did not care to know anything, of the horrible conditions prevailing in those new factories, of the long hours of labor, of the exploitation of women and children, of the housing conditions destructive of all human dignity—in short, of all the wretchedness of what a modern book calls the Bleak Age.[3] All his statistics cannot disprove those terrible facts. And has not the intervention of the State in the end been found to be indispensable in order to deal with those evils? The delight which the despised Tory Southey took in the thatched roofs and the rose bushes of insanitary cottages, and his belief in the eternal call to leadership of the wise and benevolent aristocracy of landowners, may have been naive; yet he did see certain things more clearly than did his critic.

The exclusive cerebral nature of Macaulay's mental make-up, as well as the frankly materialistic strain in it, come out very strikingly in his essay on Bacon. Not only Indian thought, not only the Christian religion—Greek philosophy, too, he tested on its conformity to practical everyday rationality, on its usefulness, and found it wanting. What profitable truth has it taught us which we should not equally have known without it? Whereas, on the other hand, if the follower of Bacon is asked what the philosophy of empiricism and of usefulness has effected for mankind, his answer is ready: "It has lengthened life; it has mitigated pain; it has extinguished diseases; it has increased the fertility of the soil; it has given new securities to the mariner; it has furnished new arms to the warrior" (note that the statement causes him no qualms!); "it has spanned great rivers . . . it has lighted up the night . . . it has . . ." (you will forgive me if I skip; the flow of Macaulay's eloquence is as overwhelming as is his knowledge); it has facilitated intercourse, correspondence, et cetera, et cetera. All this we owe to the inductive method, to the careful establishing of facts and the unprejudiced advancing to a conclusion, to the philosophy of Progress and of Utility.

It is a view of the world and of history that makes one shudder. And yet it is impossible (I at least have found it impossible) not to be impressed by the brilliance of the argument and the daring of it; but more than that, by the fervent belief by which it is inspired. And so it is with the whole of Macaulay's work.

Nothing could be more wilfully one-sided. The indifference to unfamiliar or uncongenial aspects of life is at times horrifying, and the unshakable self-satisfied certainty almost unbearably irritating. It should not be thought that contemporaries completely overlooked these unlovely characteristics. Macaulay did, in his literary life, go from triumph to triumph. Yet there were those who dissented. Not only the Tories such as Southey and Croker, but Forster, who on behalf of the Quakers criticized the treatment meted out to Penn; Paget, who published a very able pamphlet containing searching criticism of a number of passages in the *History;* Carlyle, whose heart was oppressed by "the condition of England" which seemed to Macaulay so wonderful and who muttered imprecations in his letters and in his journal. ("Eloquent commonplace talk," said Carlyle when he had met Macaulay at a dinner party.) And hardly was Macaulay dead when a reaction set in. The mood of the intellectual public in the sixties and seventies was certainly not yet dominated by doubt, but doubt was now at least admitted. A tendency made itself felt to make subtler distinctions, to reach out toward a more comprehensive understanding, to try the bridging of all too schematic antitheses. The finest spirits of that generation—Matthew Arnold and Cotter Morison and Leslie Stephen and John Morley—all pointed out the lack of profundity, the philistinism, the over-confidence, of the most popular writer of history the world had ever seen.[4]

Our generation is not so enamored of the religion of progress that we are likely to question that verdict. And yet, this cannot be the last word. Macaulay is entitled to the benefit of the historic appreciation which he himself was by temperament and outlook so little fitted to extend to others. This does not mean that we need retreat on to the last entrenchment and plead that he was a child of his age and could not help it if that age happened to be one so closely wrapped in illusion. We must first of all recognize that the age, for all that at first sight it will perhaps impress us disagreeably and even comically, had a greatness of its own. And not only in its material aspects. It seems to me undeniable that this sudden technical and economic expansion opened to that generation new horizons and lent to its life a mighty dynamism. The material was not necessarily a drag on the spiritual; it acted in many ways as a spur. The breach opened by the Reform Act in the aristocratic oligarchy, the emancipation of Catholics, of Dissenters, later on of Jews, the questioning of all established conventions, the soaring upward of science—this rejuvenated England does, with all its blemishes, present an impressive spectacle. And in that metallic voice, arrogant but convinced, impassioned but powerful, proclaiming the holiness of facts and the imprescriptible rights of criticism and of liberty, we can recognize the authentic spokesman of a great period of our common civilization.[5]

III CARLYLE: HIS SIGNIFICANCE
   AND REPUTATION

When Ranke some time ago was made to appear as a pioneer
of National Socialism, I felt bound to demur.[1] At the same
time I admitted that his affirmative attitude, his respect for
the manifestations of power, was bound to weaken resistance
in circumstances that he could not foresee but that unfortunately came to pass. Carlyle's contribution—like Nietzsche's,
whose message was in so many ways similar to his—was
much more direct.

Why was this? No doubt there existed between the out-
looks of Ranke and Carlyle a close affinity. Their thought
was fed by the same German current. Both accepted the
reality of the historic process as showing the imprint of the
Divine will and declined to judge it by the standards of
human reason or even of morality. Carlyle mentions Ranke
once or twice in *Frederick the Great,* and not without a
certain respect; yet the *Herr Professor* was to him probably
no more than an unusually clever Dryasdust. His veneration
went to another representative of that great romantic reaction against mechanical rationalism, to Goethe.

Each of these three men presents an appearance markedly
different from that of the others. So much so that the assertion of a common basis, or origin, of their thinking may at
first sight cause surprise. Indeed, so different was the temperament in each, so widely divergent in aims did their messages
tend to be, that Carlyle's coolness toward Ranke is more
readily understandable than the enthusiasm with which,
even when his own development had reached its full
maturity, and still in his old age, he appealed to Goethe;
the impression created has a touch of paradox. There was

48

nothing of the Greek in Carlyle; not for him the acceptance of our human nature and of human life in their entirety, nor the effort to comprehend them in harmony—for this was how Goethe tried to give form to the new revelation. In Carlyle, on the contrary, it is the spirit of the Old Testament that seems to be present, coupling anathematisation with adoration. And picture to yourself Ranke beside Carlyle: you will see the common starting point leading to a no less striking contrast. In history, instead of testing it by the abstractions of philosophy, both looked for God. But in how markedly different spots did Carlyle find him. Not in currents or tendencies, not in the States. Kings and rulers did not necessarily fill him with awe. Nor did he discern in history an uninterrupted development, and if he knew the phrase about every epoch having its immediate relation to God (although I do not think he had ever sufficiently penetrated into Ranke's views), he must certainly have rejected it with scorn. Whole generations, according to him, lived without inspiration, like plants or animals. It was by fits that God revealed himself, in crises and catastrophes, in thunder and lightning. The Eternal Truth tends to appear in great personalities; not "ideas" but heroes and creative minds are what Carlyle looks out for.

And, yet, in the final reckoning, the sign of that Truth is to him power, by which Ranke too traces the action of God.

If for the third time we compare Carlyle with a thinker belonging to that same sphere of thought, we shall once more hit upon a contrast, and for all the indubitable kinship Carlyle's peculiar quality will come out more clearly. I am thinking of Coleridge—his senior by twenty years, the friend of Wordsworth and Southey, and, like them, at one time under the spell of the French Revolution. Coleridge, like Carlyle, had laid a new foundation for himself with the help of German philosophy pursued those fundamental ideas with a depth never attained by Carlyle. One of the two great "seminal minds" of the England of his time— Bentham was the other—was what John Stuart Mill called him in 1838, indicating with rare discrimination the scission in English thought. In spite of the close relations that Carlyle had in his youth entertained with Bentham's circle, fundamentally he belonged without a doubt to the school of Coleridge. Yet what he noticed before all was the subtilizing or rarefying in which the other took delight, whereas to him, Carlyle, the mystery could be approached only in action or in the relating of action; and he scoffed at Coleridge's inclination to make the new ideas in practice serve forces which he, Scotsman of peasant and nonconformist origins, looked upon as dead beyond reprieve: the traditional forces of English society, especially the Church of England.

As late as 1851, when he had already broken definitely with the Radicals, Carlyle turned on Coleridge and his influence, if not with his customary vehemence, yet with corroding sarcasm. He did so in a chapter in that charming *Life of John Sterling*, among all his books an oasis of friendship and understanding, devoted to a younger man taken away by death. The chapter on Coleridge is a gem of English prose. In it is described, years afterward, Coleridge's conversation as it was listened to by a group of disciples sitting at the master's feet in his quiet retreat at Highgate. By his conversation more than by his writings Coleridge had impressed contemporaries. Carlyle now makes it appear as a dizzy rambling through a befogged labyrinth. For one moment—in his remark that Coleridge passed for the only man who understood the German philosophy—one seems to be aware of a feeling of jealousy toward that other prophet (and one remembers the envious detraction noticeable in certain of his diary notes on the occasion of the death of Mill). But, in truth, Carlyle loathed both the journeys into metaphysics and the acquiescence in what was handed down by the past, the act of imputing significance to institutions which were regarded as deserving of respect because they were old—and for that reason only. Even in 1851 that was not his kind of conservatism.

But once again: Coleridge, too, believed that in his way he was tracing God's revelation in history. Compared with Ranke's, his way was lacking in dynamics; but when Carlyle is placed side by side with those two, their mutual differences will almost sink to nothing, so violent and passionate and sharply drawn is *his* reaction to the heroes, and the catastrophes, in which alone he can see the Eternal or the Divine taking form.

Violent, passionate—such words as these can put us on the track of what distinguishes Carlyle: it is the personality. It is his impatience with baseness and cowardice, his feeling of being out of place in a world of superficial sentiment and mediocre living, his pride, his ambition, his disappointment. It is the tragedy of a man who is at loggerheads with his time and with his world and who, with unbridled subjectivity (for he derided reason and had lost the directive of a historic faith), made of that conflict the center of a view of life. The Hero was a compensation for personal impotence and an escape from the democratic sphere; power was a protest against what seemed to him the babbling of lifeless religiosity or the sham assurance of modern idealism. Instinct, intuition, the myth, these were his challenge to the rationalists and glorifiers of science who (unappeasable grievance) had made the Christian certitude of his childhood untenable for him.

Merely a personal case, then? Yet at the same time typical. There is an unbroken line, reaching into our day, of those protesters against the middle-class society that came to dominate the nineteenth-century scene, with its slogans of liberty and equality and reasonableness, with its peculiar mixture of idealism and materialism. They all of them started from the concepts of organic growth as against mechanical reform, and of realism as against the adoration of abstract thinking; but at the same time they were moved by a savage hatred, or by fear, feeling out of tune with their age and with their class, calling for daring and for entirety, despising alike deliberating scholarship and the thoughtless multitude and intoxicating themselves with imaginings of great men, great, decisive, hard deeds, the fruit of passion rather than of reflection. Under the collective appellation of Heroic Vitalists, Eric Bentley brought together with Carlyle Nietzsche, Wagner, Shaw, Spengler, Stefan George, and D. H. Lawrence.[2] The similarities are striking.

It is true that Nietzsche disposed of Carlyle in a few scornful sentences:

Eternally tortured by the longing for some strong faith, which is no evidence of a strong faith but rather the reverse. . . . An English atheist, who made it a point of honor not to be one. . . . A painful craving for noise. An attitude of constant and impassioned dishonesty toward himself. Such is his proprium.

But the utterance might easily mislead as to the real relationship between these two. I see in it primarily the passion for independence, characteristic of the *genus*, converting itself into unmeasured virulence against a possible rival or patron. At the same time, no doubt, one is struck by the supreme clear-sightedness with which Nietzsche brings to light the hidden malady of Carlyle's inner life, unconscious though he remains—by wilful suppression or through genuine inability (the venomousness suggests the first)—that, if not exactly the same, something very similar might be said about himself.

And, finally—the filiation could not be clearer—these moods of aristocratic radicalism, or of aristocratic revolutionism, caught up and strengthened by social currents in which there was certainly nothing that might be termed aristocratic, flowed out into the twentieth-century movements which were to strike at the heart not only of the middle-class society but of Western civilization; and this time not only in some intellectual's inflamed fancy but in stark reality. Neither Carlyle nor Nietzsche would have hit it off with Lenin or Stalin, with Mussolini or with Hitler; propaganda with their work was only possible because they themselves were safely dead. But by recognizing this obvious fact, we have not solved the problem of the connection existing between the teachings of these two and the twentieth-century antiliberal revolutions.

How well—so it is possible to exclaim—did Carlyle foresee it all: the crisis of democracy, the crisis of capitalism, the crisis of liberty, law, stability, assaulted by passion and by power. His reputation as a prophet, which had never thriven very greatly during his lifetime and which in the early decades of this century was badly on the wane, seems lately here and there to have revived. It is, however, also

possible to say: how much ammunition—against reason,
against science, against the parliamentary method, against
gradualness and compromise, humanity and peace—was
supplied by his philosophy to the powers of destruction!
A prophet? An abettor of the upheaval rather! But, nevertheless, while recognizing in his appearance the elements
at war with the positive traditions of Western civilization,
one can point to much that is different. In the end (always
remembering Ranke's *dictum*) one will admit that he may
claim to be judged apart from the evil that came after him,
which, perhaps, in a certain sense, he helped to prepare
but which, poor prophet, as hermetically shut off from the
future as we are ourselves, he could not foresee.

For there is indeed much that is different. There is not
only the imposing figure, imposing through its burning
passion and that amazing power over the language which,
in spite of the sometimes disconcerting eccentricity, grips
the attention and is so intimately connected with the writer's
personality. There is in the historical works a wealth of
imperishable truth and beauty, which by itself is proof that
all has not been said about his philosophy when the objectionable conclusions to which it led him (or which he
wantonly drew from it?) have been criticized. And, indeed,
a further proof is the bracing effect of the protest sounded
by Carlyle in his early period against soulless and heartless
capitalism. More than anyone he roused attention for the
terrible social conditions resulting from the Industrial Revolution. Dickens, Frederick Maurice, Kingsley, and others
owed much to him.

With that philosophy from which sprang such curiously
conflicting utterances about the human race and about
society, Carlyle belongs to a kind of men who from generation to generation play a role of indispensable significance
in the life of civilization. Those who are conscious of belonging there will immediately recognize him as their kin,
will be aware of having something in common with him.
When viewing him in historic perspective, they will delight
in watching him in conflict with an age given over to the
most superficial and crude mammonism, mechanism, Progress
optimism. Their hearts will respond to the appearance of

that truthful herald of man's spiritual calling and of a world governed by eternal, mysterious, nonmaterial forces! They will applaud that courage of a desperate conviction from which he shed over the infatuation of middle-class self-sufficiency and over foolish human presumption a flood of biting ridicule and of deadly hatred. However, as soon as they want to argue that it was to his fundamental principles that he owed this profound insight and this noble indignation, the problem presents itself of his later derailment into ever more vehement glorification of power, racial pride, cult of instinct, and revilement of reason—a problem that clearly has taken on a more compelling aspect since Western civilization has seen Fascism, National Socialism and Communism rise against itself. Particularly the Germanomania and the specific authoritarian sentiments and preachings of power policy—these cannot now be brushed aside so lightly as purely personal eccentricities, innocent or at least innocuous. Not that there are no attempts being made any more—as we shall see.

In 1895 Frederick Harrison still made an attempt, but in a way which must irremediably destroy the unity of the figure. As a positivist, and one to whom positivism was a religion (as it had been to Comte himself), as, moreover, an idealist and self-sacrificing social reformer, Harrison felt allied to Carlyle in his first period. Not only *The French Revolution* but even *Cromwell* were to him great liberating works.

The whole weight of Church, monarchy, aristocracy, fashion, literature, and wit, had for two centuries combined to distort the character of the noblest of English statesmen. And a simple man of letters, by one book, at once and for ever reversed this sentence . . . and placed Oliver for all future time as the greatest hero of the Protestant movement. There are few examples in the history of literature of so great and so sudden a triumph of truth and justice.

But in *Frederick the Great* Harrison sees the Hero submerged in "a welter of dull garbage." Indeed, the prophet's voice had before that become "shrieky and monotonous." *The Latter Day Pamphlets* had revealed his sad decline to the

world and, so Harrison thinks, "his true friends will hasten
to throw such a decent covering as Japhet and Shem threw
around Noah over the latest melancholy outbursts about
Negroes, Reformers, Jamaica massacres,[3] and the anticipated
conflagration of Paris by the Germans."—His true friends?
Maybe. But can he who wants to know Carlyle avert his
attention from one half of his life? Does it not cast back
light on the other half?

In the same (not overprofound) fashion, G. M. Trevelyan,
in his well-known paper *Clio a Muse* (1905), distinguished
between the earlier and the later Carlyle. *The French
Revolution* was a masterpiece of understanding: "it was
not till later in his life that Carlyle went mad with hero-
worship and ceased to understand his fellow-men with that
all-embracing tolerance and sympathy which is the spiritual
hall-mark of his *French Revolution*." As if this development
had happened by accident. The intuitive understanding in
The French Revolution is indeed striking and has a perennial
fascination. But must one therefore keep silent on the dom-
ineering one-sidedness and arbitrariness by which that work,
too, is marked and which announce the later Carlyle? I
have the highest regard for the truth that can spring from
fantasy, intuitive feeling for human psychology, and an
artist's style. To assert, however, that scientific historians
are capable only of "a cold analysis of events and conventional summings up of persons" and are therefore "less
true" is, it seems to me, to introduce a false and an exceedingly dangerous contrast.

The real weakness in Trevelyan's argument (and it comes
out even more clearly in an article[4] which he devoted to
Carlyle many years later) is that he fails to link up either
the wisdom or the blindness of the work with the author's
philosophy of life. It is as if Trevelyan regards imagination
and a fascinating style as isolated and absolute values.

Very differently again, but also without coming to grips
with the problem I am considering, does Cazamian, the great
French *connoisseur* of English literature, approach the subject. Cazamian admires in Carlyle "the man who with his
disciples changed the intellectual atmosphere of England;"
and speaks of "the indomitable courage with which he set

out to conquer the world and to change the tone of his age." When Cazamian praises Carlyle for having placed over against "the rationalism of Gibbon and Macaulay and their cold and clear analysis of a past completely knowable and divested of all wonder his sense of mystery, his religious idealism, his imaginative intuition of life," I can sympathize. In what I quoted first, however, I am struck by the exaggeration both of the completeness of that transformation and of Carlyle's contribution toward it.

It may have seemed for a moment as if his spirit triumphed —in the triumph of imperialism. When Carlyle, in *Past and Present* (1844), denounced the basely materialistic mentality which valued the white colonies only in so far as they were immediately useful for the mother country, he gave utterance to a profound truth and, if the further development is noted, a prophetic truth. But also, when Seeley and, especially, toward the end of the century, Kipling and Cecil Rhodes trumpet and apply his slogans in their own fashion, it appears only too clearly that this superiority of the British race, this claim to special rights for it on account of its gift for rule and its love of work, led in practice to materialism no less base and to dangerous adventures into the bargain.

Yet Cazamian, a conservative Frenchman, did not seem to have an inkling of this, nor of the fact that the current which the prophet had wished to stem, Liberalism, had continued underground in forms that were by no means purely materialistic. In fact, even while Cazamian was writing (in 1913), the vaunted imperialism was already succumbing of its own excesses.[5]

Even more remarkable are the observations with which, in 1937, Professor Neff, of Columbia University, concluded his book on Carlyle; especially as thirteen years earlier he had given so well balanced an account of the relations between Mill and Carlyle.

He reflects thus:

[At the present moment] unemployment seems to threaten a worldwide breakdown of capitalism. Thoughtful men question the wisdom of seeking further command over nature until means have been devised to prevent fools and knaves from misusing in war and peace the terrifying power already unloosed by science. The cry is for strong government. Growing doubt of the capacity of the average man to rule himself through his representatives is driving a desperate world to the experiments of Fascism and Communism. In the crisis he foresaw, Carlyle is being remembered. Editions of translated excerpts from his writings in 1920, 1921, and 1922 accompanied the rise of Fascism in Italy. Shaw's *Apple Cart* has preached to England, in the manner of *Frederick the Great*, the parable of a patriot king striving to protect the people from their elected rulers . . . Germany, under the frightful strain of war ruin, reparation payments, and economic and political instability, is imbibing courage from selections from Carlyle . . .

And Neff deplores that the preceding generations did not take heed of Carlyle's warnings. May new titans rise, possessed of his wisdom and cogency of utterance! . . .

Here, then, we find Carlyle placed where undoubtedly he belongs, in a line of which the present-day totalitarian movements constitute, if not the straight prolongation, yet a normal branch. But the American critic only admires him the more fervently on that account. Not only the economic and social crisis, of which it can reasonably be maintained that it had been anticipated in Carlyle's admonishments and warnings, but the phenomenon of these revolutionary movements themselves is unhesitatingly adduced as proof of his prophetic greatness.

The Second World War drew suddenly sharper lines of demarcation. In December 1940 Professor Grierson read a paper for the British Academy in which Carlyle appears as the preacher of a doctrine from which the natural outcome was to be what really is a revolt against the true trend of Western civilization. A prophet? Yes; but not because he tried to foretell the future (there were many such) nor because what he foretold came true; but because his approach to the questions of the day is that of the Hebrew Prophets; because he spoke as if inspired.

"Yea friends," said Carlyle himself, in as early a work as *Sartor Resartus,* "not our Logical, Commensurative faculty, but our Imagination is King over us." Hence his aversion to the rule by discussion of a democracy, of a constitutional, parliamentary community. The Hero was to fill "the vacancy left by the decay of his early faith." Milton, too, who, "as his early confidence in the Long Parliament and the English people failed him," rallied to Cromwell and the Army, had said that "the less should yield to the greater," the less and the greater to be measured "not in numbers but in wisdom and virtue." Professor Grierson might have mentioned Plato in this context. Carlyle did not read *The Republic* until late in life: his comment was: "Mere *Latter Day Pamphlets*, refined into empyrean radiance and the lightning of the gods." And then there is always Nietzsche, in whom we find Carlyle's vehemence and passionate interest in actual problems transposed in a different key again (far from heavenly), but whose contempt for reason and the multitude, and whose proclaiming of instinct and deeds and the *Ubermensch*, shows his fundamental kinship. They celebrate the Hero, Carlyle and his like? In order to see themselves projected in him. Or, as Bagehot put it sarcastically: "a despot who will work out *their* ideas." "What failed them," says Grierson—and in 1837 the Dutch Liberal thinker and statesman Thorbecke had leveled exactly the same reproach at Groen van Prinsterer, the "Anti-revolutionary" Calvinist[6]— "was faith, faith in God and in their fellow-men."

Grierson was rooted in the liberal-rationalist tradition. This it was that made him see so clearly that Carlyle's derailment was the direct consequence of the glorification of inspiration, another word for subjectivism or egotism, and of the rejection of discussion and investigation.

That Grierson's analysis was far from being entirely novel will appear in a moment when we go back to older critics. But he pointed out, as we saw, the connection with the contemporary phenomenon of the revolt against reason, democracy, humanity. It was this which drew attention to his paper, although of course it did not put an end to the diversity in the appreciation.

This appears very striking in a review devoted by the *Times Literary Supplement* on February 15, 1952, to a new biography, *Thomas Carlyle*, by Julian Symons. The book— the first to appear about Carlyle for a number of years—

makes excellent reading. The eccentric, the son and the husband, the struggling and the celebrated writer, the man in his vehemence and his tenderness, all have been sketched vividly and with understanding. The thinker at odds with his age, too, has been presented strikingly enough, yet here the book lacks depth. What the reviewer in the *Supplement* criticizes in Mr. Symons is that he is inclined to make excuses for Carlyle. Mr. Symons, indeed, suspects that Carlyle "is likely to appear uncongenial to most contemporary readers." And why? "Apparently," the *Supplement* critic remarks sarcastically, "because, though he started off on the moving stairway leading up to the Century of the Common Man" (his radical youth), "he lost heart or was seduced away, and started furiously trying to step downwards" (the *Latter Day Pamphlets* and afterward), "an undignified and enraging enterprise." In the *Supplement* writer's judgment, however, Carlyle was perfectly right.

More clearly than any of his contemporaries, he saw through, and exposed with devastating force and humour, the whole Victorian doctrine of progress . . . It showed remarkable prescience thus to detect in the march of progress the Gadarene rush it was to become, and to reduce its shallow, sanctimonious materialism to a series of "Pig Propositions":

1. The Universe, so far as sane conjecture can go, is an immeasurable swine's trough, consisting of solid and liquid, and of other contrasts and kinds: especially consisting of attainable and unattainable, the latter in immensely greater quantities for most pigs.

2. Moral evil is unattainability of pigs' wash; moral good attainability of ditto.

To Mr. Symons this famous passage out of the *Latter Day Pamphlets* was only one more instance of the savageness with which Carlyle, when his initial sympathy with the miseries of the masses had given way to conservatism and admiration for the aristocracy, had turned on his one-time allies, "the intellectual Radicals, the rationalists and the overpious Christians." But the *Supplement* reviewer thinks it splendid.

How right he was, the Welfare State, the American Way of Life and the Russian Classless, Socialist Society alike testify, in all of these "attainability of Pigs' wash" constituting the basic issue. There is really no need to apologize for such views. Apologize for Godwin, for Walt Whitman, for William Morris, for Marx himself, for all the fearful progeny begotten by steam-power out of Rousseau, but for Carlyle who saw where they were going, no.

So Carlyle, who raised his accusing voice against *laissez-faire* and a selfish aristocracy, who revealed the degrading conditions in which the new industries were worked, has become a great prophet in the eyes of a man to whom there is no difference between the Welfare State or the American Way of Life and Soviet Society. Farther on in the article his going astray into an adoration of power is regretted, but as if it were something quite accidental.

As for Mr. Symons, even he, on the contrary, after having blamed Carlyle's vituperation of the social reform movement as a Pigwash Doctrine, expresses his admiration for a note in the diary in which "rights of Negroes" are said not to be "worth much discussing, nor the rights of men in any form; the grand point . . . is the *mights* of men." How much more wisdom, he suggests, does this view contain than the definitions of liberty attempted by J. S. Mill and H. G. Wells. "Wholly impractical" Carlyle might be, yet how much better did he understand that it all turned on "the power of the State, direction of labour, the use of coercion to obtain the better organization of society." And his catastrophic view seems nearer the truth of the world we live in than the liberal and Fabian doctrine of gradual social evolution.

A prophet, then, in the eyes of Mr. Symons as well! Only, according to his biographer (himself, it would seem, a man of somewhat leftist socialist views) he foresaw something completely different from what he did according to the *Supplement* reviewer (whose political views impress me as almost improbably running to the other extreme; for can one see in his anti-materialism anything but a cloak for arch-conservatism?). It is curious to note from how many different points of view Carlyle can be "excused." For that is, on close inspection, what the *Supplement* does no less than Mr. Symons; but the reviewer excuses the adoration of power with the aversion to systematic social reform, whereas the biographer excuses it on the ground of the services it can render thereto.

But there is, in addition to all this, Carlyle's philosophical or religious premise, his sense of the mystery of the Eternal and of the Personality, and the allied conviction of the insufficiency of human reason. This is the impressive keynote of his thought and feeling, and in many it evokes too strong a response of awareness of kinship (and this of a purer quality than I can detect in the *Supplement* writer) for them to have heart for really unsparing criticism.

I find an example in Professor Basil Willey's chapter about Carlyle in his *Nineteenth Century Studies* (1949). This Cambridge professor is a critic of delicate perception as well as broadmindedness, who has lovingly traced the religious and philosophic tendencies in the great figures of the last three centuries. His treatment of Carlyle can certainly not be called uncritical; yet, when toward the end he discusses the political implications, the tone of extenuation and evasion seems to me unmistakable. He remarks that the Heroes in *Heroes and Hero Worship* are not all of them "Führers," but also prophets and poets. True, he continues, the warriors and rulers are in the majority: Caesar, Cromwell, Frederick, Napoleon; "but Cromwell was the chief of Heroes, because he was the soldier of God. I do not think that Carlyle would have mistaken Hitler for a Cromwell, any more than Plato would have mistaken him for a Philosopher-King."

Is Carlyle's uncritical glorification of the destroyer of the papistical Irish thereby justified? I am not suggesting that there is nothing to choose between Cromwell and Hitler, but might not Professor Willey have asked himself whether the great Protector really *was* "the soldier of God"? Cromwell imagined he was, but was not there his danger? And what was Carlyle's glorification but purely human presumption and self-deception?

Willey next tries to dispose of the accusation that Carlyle taught that Might is Right by quoting Carlyle's own rejoinder to Lecky. The apologists like to quote that state-ment.[7] "Quite the converse or reverse is [my] real opinion —namely, that right is the eternal symbol of might."

The reply leaves me completely unconvinced. In both phrases the emphasis falls on the indispensable connection between the two concepts. And when Willey goes on to render Carlyle's explanations (that "Might is Right *in the long run*," that "Might and Right do differ frightfully from hour to hour, but give them centuries to try it in, they are found to be identical"), he fails to say more than a passing word about the hopeless embarrassments into which the prophet landed himself by these distinctions. The prac-tical application, too, is passed over almost completely. Not a word, for instance, on Carlyle's attitude toward slavery or the Jamaica business, or on his treatment of the history of the "Berserker" (a word of praise in Carlyle's vocabulary) Frederick William of Prussia, or of the Hero Frederick.

What we can learn from Carlyle is that "democracy," in order to survive, must be born again; it must unlearn its economic idolatries, cease to be self-seeking and mechanical, and recapture its soul by returning to its own inmost ideas, which will turn out, on reflection, to be those of Chris-tianity.

Is that indeed what we must learn from Carlyle? Either that, Professor Willey adds in conclusion, or we shall be sent "seeking after strange gods." Are stranger gods thinkable, and less Christian, then those adored by the embittered old man in his study in Chelsea? And the "liberal" principles which, if understood in the Christian sense, constitute this "inmost" being (for this, too, Willey assures us)—did any-body reject them more resolutely than did Carlyle, who was indeed definitely not a Christian, however respectfully he used to speak about the Christian faith, or at least about the Old Testament?

And, yet, how many times had all these objections been set out before Grierson (with whom Willey obviously polemizes, although he does not mention his name) ex-pressed them in the terms of our contemporary ideological contest. There is an unbroken line of mainly disapproving Carlyle criticism side by side with the mainly admiring tradition cultivated by his disciples and kindred spirits. There was, for instance, Matthew Arnold, himself a penetrating and discriminating critic of contemporary thought, who had at first been not insensible to the impression of that extraordinary figure. Later, in 1849, he called him "a moral desperado," and in 1859 he spoke of "that regular Carlylean strain which we all know by heart and which the clearheaded among us have so utter a contempt for." [8]

These were expressions of impatience in private letters. But there was also John Morley, who wrote, in an essay published in Carlyle's lifetime:

We need light more than heat [the fundamentally different mental attitude manifests itself at once], intellectual alertness, faith in the reasoning faculty, accessibility to new ideas. To refuse to use the intellect patiently and with system, to decline to seek scientific truth, to prefer effusive indulgence in emotion to the laborious and disciplined and candid exploration of new ideas, is not this, too, a torpid unveracity?

(Carlyle had written that the poison of our sins "is not intellectual dimness chiefly, but torpid unveracity of the heart.") In an earlier passage Morley had compared Carlyle to Rousseau on the score of the "triumphant and dangerous sophistry of the emotions." He had recalled the fact that Robespierre, the dictator of terrorism, was a disciple of Rousseau's.

We in our days have seen the same result of sentimental doctrine in the barbarous love of the battle-field, the retrograde passion of methods of repression, the contempt for human life, the impatience of orderly and peaceful solution. We begin with introspection and the eternities, and end in blood and iron.

Morley was thinking of Bismarck, as Grierson was to think of Hitler.

It is not as if Morley in that very fine essay does not

find anything to admire in Carlyle. He observes, for instance, that Carlyle's preoccupation with the Mysterious, his stoical acceptance of man's dependence upon a Power against which he cannot advance a single claim, elevated him above all too easy and precise moralizing. In that way he, as against Macaulay (always that contrast!), introduced into history and into literary criticism a deeper truthfulness.

Even more generously is appreciation voiced in a no less excellent essay by Leslie Stephen. The wish to understand, the looking upon criticism as a loving approach, helped a mind of so different a structure and attitude toward life to discover the beautiful and the constructive. The Dutch reader is reminded of Allard Pierson's essay on Bilderdijk, the great poet of the reaction on the turn of the eighteenth and nineteenth centuries. Pierson, though, drew of an even more refractory and in a literary sense much less convincing subject an even more idyllic sketch. For after all Stephen does bring out how Carlyle, impelled by his despairing view of man and of society, misrepresented history: the multitude pressed down in order to make the Hero rise the higher, history a succession of troubles, of revolts against "shams," and, in between, times without significance, such as he had to live through himself, with no other comfort but the prospect of another great Prophet and another upheaval.

I will mention one more appreciation by a younger contemporary of Carlyle. Julia Wedgwood, in an article that appeared in the *Contemporary Review*[9] on the occasion of Carlyle's death, went more deeply than most into the central problem of his struggle with life, the relationship of might and right. Carlyle, she says, had remained fundamentally a Calvinist.

The Calvinist idea of virtue is adherence to divine law; that law itself, therefore, must be something deeper than virtue. If goodness consists in obedience to the will of God, we cannot say that God himself is good; there is no superior will in conformity to which we may trace goodness in Him.

When Erasmus reproached Luther with ascribing to God conduct which would be hateful in man, Luther answered boldly that this was just what he had a full right to do. God was not bound by His own laws and He might deal with His creatures as He pleased. Carlyle, likewise, held that:

. . . enthroned above all that man can discern of the laws that guide his fate, sits an awful Power . . . for whom he never ceased to claim an absolute, unfaltering submission . . . . And though he often used language that implied justice in the Divine Ruler, yet often also—and more and more— he seems to have felt, as the Calvinists did, as if God were rather the fountain of justice than just. The impression left by his allusions seems to be that all that we *can* know of God is power. And if the rulers of men were powerful, it was because they were at one with the designs of the Ruler of man. Thus his worship of Force was in fact always a part of his worship of God. His reverence for power—even when it took such forms, for instance, as that glorification of Frederick William of Prussia[10] which seems to us the most repulsive thing he ever wrote—should never be regarded apart from his profound sense that all strength was divine.

In those last sentences one seems to detect a turn toward apology after all. For is the adoration of power really made more acceptable by that sense? Or should we not rather remember the saying: By their fruits ye shall know them?

That the most recent English criticism has not attained a synthesis of the divergent judgments I have already shown. To me, the most comprehensive and satisfactory view is to be found in the American book which I mentioned before, but which is not even included in Mr. Symons's bibliography: Bentley's *Century of Hero Worship*. It will be remembered that Carlyle there appears as the first of the Heroic Vitalists of the hundred years which culminate in Hitler. Mr. Bentley does not fail to caution his readers that they should not, in spite of similarity and connection, assume identity, no identity in particular with the destructive mass movements the rise of which is properly a contemporary phenomenon. He is consistently alive to the positive features in Carlyle. One side of Carlyle, he says, prefigures the best in democratic thought. But he also sees the elements of amoralism and of abdication in the face of power, "so subversive of civilized values," and thus "another side prefigures the high-brow fascism of our time, the fascism of Knut Hamsun, Léon Daudet, Lawrence Dennis, and the professors of Hitler's Germany."

Through his protest (so I should like to sum up) against the prevailing mechanical-rationalistic view of life, against the smug *bourgeois* and *laissez-faire* code, against the neglect of the misery of the people; through the powerful historic imagination of the *French Revolution,* of *Past and Present,* even of *Cromwell* (the critic of his age and the historian cannot be separated), Carlyle in mid-life remains a great and in many ways an attractive figure. Already apparent, however, are the signs of an attitude of mind to which keeping within bounds was irksome and attempting a syn-thesis impossible. I mentioned the scission running through English intellectual life at the time. Owing to his character, to his origin, and to his own inner split—the sentimental tie to a spiritual heritage which his intellect rejected, the painful reaction against the false teachers who gave him nothing in exchange for what they had robbed him of— Carlyle could not overcome that contrast, he could only choose, and blindly and obstinately advocate, one side. And without his noticing it, or condescending to notice it, those feelings, and especially pride irritated by disappointment and resistance, drove him off his course. Fact, Power, Force, Instinct in its rawest manifestations became his gods, and to them he sold his soul.

That spiritual career impresses me as profoundly tragic. How rousing had been the clarion sound with which the warrior against Cant, against False and Hollow, had entered upon the great struggle! And how lonely do we see him in the end, carried past his aim, seated with his hatred and his contempt and his bitterness. How uncertain a stand-ard did Veracity marked out by Power turn out to be, Power interpreted in that wilfully one-sided manner and, in spite of all the glowing phrases about the Eternal and the Divine, materialistically. Not always, it is true, but as it suited him. It is this arbitrariness which made him lose the way, and it resulted from the self-willed passion with which he re-jected the control of reason. It is not the reasoning faculty,

I know it very well (and Carlyle has helped us to see it more clearly, his surpassing merit); it is not the reasoning faculty, but conviction, invention, intuition springing from the depths of the heart or of the personality, which constitute in great minds the most precious creative force. Nevertheless, how can that force lead astray, how dangerous does it become, if the bridle of reason is let slip and if (we heard Carlyle do it) the Imagination is proclaimed as Sole Ruler?

Without that contempt for reason, without his reaction against Bentham's dry rationalism having turned awry into a presumptuous anti-intellectualism, his idolatry of Power and Violence and Race and Instinct remains inexplicable. And in the influence which he exerted, that anti-intellectualism is one of the most treacherous features. It is that which makes him an important figure in the disturbing and destructive tendencies that appear, beside the main current, in the development of European civilization during his lifetime and after.

His influence? In England it may be said to have shown itself mainly, after that wholesome shaking administered to liberal and middle-class self-satisfaction, in the imperialism which, toward the end of Carlyle's life and for a generation after his death, was to be so unpleasant a phenomenon. This new sentiment extended its ramifications through the whole of the political thinking of that period, although the English people were by their traditions rendered practically immune against the last consequences of dictatorship and anti-parliamentarism. So it had been possible for Disraeli, in 1874, when he was Prime Minister, to offer to Carlyle the Grand Cross of the Bath with an annuity. The gesture really meant that politically the old man was not taken seriously. There was another reason why it embarrassed Carlyle. He had always as wholeheartedly poured his scorn over Disraeli as he had over Disraeli's antagonist Gladstone. He replied with a refusal, not without an unrestricted acknowledgment of the generosity of the offer—but in those last gloomy years of the eternal grumbler the incident strikes a somewhat comical note.

To trace the effect of his thought abroad is practically

impossible. Speaking generally, it can be said that, owing to its form, Carlyle's work was difficult to transplant, even though translations did appear not only in German but in all languages. But the form was not all. An unmistakably provincial flavor permeated his work. He was ever the Anglo-Saxon, if not the Scotsman. Mr. Bentley remarks very truly, while comparing Carlyle and Nietzsche, that the civilization to which each of these two belonged partly determined the value of his work, and that the German-Italian-Swiss cultural region within which Nietzsche worked was infinitely richer and more varied than was the English in Carlyle's day. Yet, in spite of the limitations of his intellectual vision and his self-chosen aloofness from immense cultural spheres, Carlyle, through his vehemence, his deadly earnestness, and the originality of his mode of utterance,[11] has without any doubt been a factor in the European life of the mind. And this with the two-sided potentiality which we know.

It was especially *The French Revolution* and *Heroes and Hero Worship* which penetrated. The later works remained largely confined to England, except for the suitable admiration and awe with which *Frederick the Great* was greeted in Germany.[12] He was rewarded for it with the order *Pour le mérite,* which he did accept, and with a letter from Bismarck, which gave him a moment of happiness, for this was a Man. In the tide of anti-democracy and anti-reason, of glorification of Power and of the right of Great Men, all this certainly supplied some impetus.

As a writer of history Carlyle could hardly be expected to create a school. For that, his work was too peculiar, too extreme, too personal. What he could do was to stimulate the historic imagination, and this he did not only in special cases where minds similarly attuned used his influence creatively (I am thinking particularly of Nietzsche and of Spengler) but in the widest circle of his readers. Who ever before had thus, with the whole of his inner being, participated in the past? Who had re-created it so full of life, so palpitating and throbbing with life? Who had managed so to evoke the mystery, the connection with dark backgrounds? He opened up unsuspected possibilities, if not for the historic understanding, yet for the organs of historic feeling.

At last he lost himself in the comfortless and inhuman philosophy which I have sketched, and in the history of Western civilization his name will remain marked with a query. However, the word *tragic*, which I used above, contains the deepest truth about Carlyle, and it adds to our reflections a conciliatory touch. It implies that he succumbed to what was his strength; that he fell into evil because he resented the imperfect so keenly and searched for the good with so unsparing a passion, unsparing especially also with respect to himself. What affects tragically is that this man, shrinking at the spectacle of the world such as it was, struggling and imposing tasks upon himself in order to get at the pure core of things, ended up in a dream world, empty, it might be, of all modern illusions, but mocking his earnest with grinning shadows, true gods in his imagination only. And the perception of that tragic quality makes it possible to accept gratefully that which is vivifying in his work and serenely to enjoy its beauties.

IV MICHELET AND HIS HISTORY OF THE FRENCH REVOLUTION

Michelet before 1847

Jules Michelet was born in 1798—in the same year as Carlyle, three years after Ranke, two years before Macaulay, three years before the Dutch historian Groen van Prinsterer. He is not the least of the five. Outside his own country his influence has made itself felt less than that of Ranke and of Macaulay, but in France it was enormous, and even today he is still regarded by many as the great national historian.

Jules Michelet was born in Paris of a lower middle-class couple originating from two widely distant parts of France. His father had, as a very young man, done his bit in the Revolution. After Thermidor, he had set up a printing establishment in a nationalized church building. It was there that Jules grew up and worked as a boy at the printing press. Owing to the censorship under Napoleon, the business declined. The memory of the Revolution was thus, in that poverty-stricken family, allied to detestation of the Corsican despot. Jules soon came to be regarded as a prodigy. His father managed to get him accepted at a college. The life was a hard one for the penniless boy, but with iron will power he pulled through and finally—shortly after the Restoration—qualified with supreme distinction. He was noticed by the grandees of the new regime, by the Duke of Richelieu and the Duke Decazes.

There was indeed nothing revolutionary about him then. In those formative years of his life that tradition seemed to have been lost. No contact with it was to be obtained at school, nor in the press or in the open contest of politics. It was not until the twenties that it was, so to speak, rediscovered under the impact of the excesses committed by nobility and clergy. His experience was that of the whole of his generation, of Quinet (later his bosom friend,) of Victor Hugo, of Louis Blanc, all men who, after having in their youth accepted Catholicism and royalism, before long came to hail the Revolution as the rebirth of France, as the beginning of a new, fertile, or rather of *the* fertile, era in the world's history. Young Michelet, who had not even been baptized, found Catholicism in the very first years of the Restoration. A needful acquisition for a university career, too; and that was the career he entered upon; in 1826 he was even selected to give lessons to a little Bourbon Princess.

Then occurs the Revolution of July (1830), and this was to him as a flash of lightning (so he expresses it himself) in which was suddenly revealed to him the mission of France, and his own calling to announce it. He abandoned his Roman studies and planned a great *History of France*. Insatiable reader, gifted with a demonic power for work and concentration, he did not shrink from the new self-imposed task.

Still nothing of the revolutionary. The delight with which he greeted the return of the tricolor was entirely proper under the new regime. His career prospered. Again a Princess to teach, an Orleans Princess this time; and, in addition to his courses at the *Ecole Normale* and soon at the *Collège de France,* he became director of the Historical Section at the National Archives. In his great work, too, he began by allying his new faith with the old. With enthusiasm he described the Middle Ages, the period of Catholicism and of the Monarchy. The co-operation of those two forces in the building up of French unity culminated in the grandiose episode of Joan of Arc, and the chapters in his fifth volume in which he dealt with it still constitute a peak in the *History* as a whole. "Yes," he exclaims, "both by Religion and by the Fatherland, Joan of Arc was a saint."

The discriminating reader will be in no doubt that it was *la patrie* that mattered to Michelet. Perhaps he did not clearly realize it, but his exalted nationalism responded to the deepest craving of his heart. It was at any rate its most constant passion, for, although in other respects, as we shall see, he swung about in the most startling fashion, there he was to remain true to himself. In the second volume of his *History* he gave that famous *tableau* of the various provinces of France in which he sought to bring out the particular quality and character of each. The colorful picture is irresistibly charming and suggestive, yet sober criticism will find a good deal to question. That intimate connection between the soil and the inhabitants' character, those sharply drawn features of the latter presumed to be constant in each region—I, for one, remain sceptical. This France, however, so full of diversity, was at the same time growing to be a unit; rather, it *was* a unit, made not really by Church or King but by her own efforts. The people shaping its own history, this was a fundamental conception which Michelet, believer in will and in liberty, had found in Vico and eagerly made his own. "For there *was* a people, there *was* a France!" he exclaims in his characteristic, emphatically assertive manner, and: "France was herself a woman (like Joan), she had the feminine mobility, but also a woman's charming sweetness."

This in spite of the horrors and turpitudes which in that same volume he has to relate of these same French. The observation and even the faithful recording of these do not prevent him from denigration of the English—not, of course, that the English were a whit better, but why worse? On account of their pride and conceit, of their hypocrisy, according to Michelet. But his aversion was hardly based on objective observation. Was it perhaps his subjective reaction to the spectacle offered by the fifteenth-century struggle, when this French unity, the object of his worship, had to be wrested from these very English, who moreover (although with the collaboration of a good many Frenchmen!) sent Joan to her death? Rather it was that, after the initial acquiescence in the tame Bourbon kingship, Michelet, like countless other Frenchmen, had been awakened by the shock of 1830 to the humiliation of the defeat of Waterloo. When in 1834 he spent a month in England as a tourist, it was the memory of Waterloo that had darkened the view he took of men and of conditions. Since then he had shared the annoyance caused by England's blocking of French ambitions in Syria; the crisis of 1840, soon the Pritchard case, irritated his oversensitive chauvinism. So he came to see "the English soul," Germanic, oppressor of Celtic elements, as being in everlasting opposition to "the Celtic soul" of France; yet he combined with this an idealization of "the Germanic soul" of Germany, which did not at that time seem dangerous.

Michelet had at the outset of his historical studies undergone the influence of German Romanticism, but very particularly that of the until then little-known work of the solitary Neapolitan thinker Vico, the daring precursor of the anti-rationalistic philosophy of history (died 1744). It was in Vico that he had found proclaimed the triumph of imagination over analysis and the feeling for the fulness that is true to life. Also, a lasting impression was made on him, not so much by that eternal recurrence in which Vico believed, but by his search for what is common in the multiplicity of phenomena and, above all, by his realization of historic life being a whole and being in motion. But for Vico, his *Introduction à l'histoire universelle* (which appeared in 1831 in preparation for his big undertaking, the *Histoire de France*) could never have been written. The vision presented there of a world history moving from East to West as a triumph of liberty, the progressive triumph of the individual in the ancient struggle of man's liberation from the God-Nature of enslavement to Fate, may not be Vico's eternal recurrence of successive stages, but it is Vico none the less. And in fact he had to adapt Vico in yet another way, for he indicated that France was the particular agent of that process.

France the country of action. Love of conquest? No, proselytism. What France wants above all is to impose her personality upon the vanquished, not because it is hers, but because she holds the naive conviction that it represents the type of the good and beautiful. She believes that she can render to the world no greater benefit than by presenting it with her ideas, her manners and her fashions . . . The universal assimilation promoted by France is not that of which England and Rome have dreamt in their egoistic and materialistic policies. It is the assimilation of intellects, the conquest of wills,—and who, so far, has succeeded better than we? Each of our armies has in withdrawing left a France behind it. Our language rules supreme in Europe. . . .

In 1835, Michelet, between his other activities, composed an anthology from the writings of Luther. He was reproached with partiality for Luther. In his reply can be heard the echo of the view of history characteristic of German Romanticism at least as much as of Vico.

I might with equal justice be reproached with partiality for the Vaudois, and later on for St. Theresa and St. Ignatius of Loyola. To penetrate into all doctrines, to understand all causes, to plunge with one's soul into all sentiments, these are the ineluctable demands of history. . . . The historian shall sympathize with the whole of man, with his reason, his imagination and his heart; with liberty and grace, with dogma and with morality. Let him pick up the members scattered everywhere in order to compose the whole, and let him honor and cherish them all; for in all is to be discerned that sacred image of Himself deposed by God in man only.

It is worth our while to listen well to this, for it was not long before the upholder of sympathy with the for and with the against came to regard history in a very different mood.

Emphatically as he expressed himself, and in spite of the tireless perseverance with which he devoted himself to his labors (five o'clock every morning saw him at his desk), Michelet was a troubled spirit, restlessly seeking, exceedingly open for impressions and for influences. Hardly had he, in his fifth volume, celebrated Joan of Arc, when he was swept along in the fight that arose about the monopolistic position of the University (that is, of the all-embracing organization of education established by Napoleon). The attack on the monopoly was started by liberal Catholics raising the cry of freedom. The defenders replied with the taunt that behind this transparent veil were assembled the forces of intolerance and of spiritual tyranny. At that moment the great Polish refugee Mickiewicz made an overwhelming impression on audiences in the *Collège de France* by the prophetic tone of the lectures in which he proclaimed a new gospel of liberty and fraternity between the nations. Michelet, too, shed tears while listening to him. The monopoly controversy was here touched upon only in passing, yet it was Mickiewicz's example which inspired both Quinet and Michelet (both now held chairs in the *Collège de France*) to courses in which they reacted vehemently to the Catholic attempt on the University. In 1843 Michelet exploded against "The Jesuits"; the next year he held forth about *Woman, the Priest, and the Family*.

A new Michelet. To work upon the public at large, to swell the wave of excitement and expectation passing over France, this he now felt to be his task. He, too, donned the prophet's mantle. He spoke desultorily, throwing ideas about rather than working them out. Ideas about man, and life, and religion, about France and the world; noble ideas and ideas less noble, striking, practical ideas, and vague, cloudy, wild and sentimental, democratic and chauvinistic ideas. And meanwhile anti-ultramontanism had become downright anti-Catholicism. All this before turbulent audiences, out for sensation, demonstrating for and against.

Sainte-Beuve, who attended one of these lectures, thought the performance merely ridiculous. Heine, too, mocked at "the man who really felt at home only in the blue forests of Romanticism," and who now as a polemist was driven to deal in logic; "M. Symbole," he says, was the nickname by which people referred to him.[1] Obviously there were many who preserved their critical faculties with respect to the romantic bearing to which Michelet, in his new role, remained addicted. Many, indeed, felt directly threatened, for the debate soon swept far beyond the question of education. The government, although far from ultra-Catholic (rather, typically middle-class conservative in temper), suspended the three professors one after the other.

But now the revolutionary spirit which had already stirred

in 1830, the spirit appealing to the example of the great Revolution, rose ever more menacingly. Louis Philippe, the great profiteer of 1830, imagining that he could, with the assistance of Guizot, allay that spirit, kept his equanimity down to February, 1848, when, first, he was forced to drop his prime minister, and then was swept away all the same. It is true that this time, too, under the Republic, there occurred a speedy and even much more severe reaction—as early as June of the same year—nevertheless, that spirit has never been exorcized from the political and intellectual life of France.

Michelet's important contribution was to be his *History of the French Revolution*. In 1847 he had the first volume ready. For, although after Joan of Arc he had only described Louis XI's reign, he felt unable in his new mood, which was in consonance with the tense atmosphere around him, to plod on through the darkness of the three subsequent centuries when the rule of priests and kings put man's higher nature to shame (that is how he now saw it). His heart longed for the epic of liberation, the liberation of the French people, nay, of the human mind. This, to him, is the true greatness of that mighty episode, the Revolution, that France fought and suffered for mankind and, after the long gloom of Christendom and monarchy, kindled the light of Justice and Liberty. But the diffusion of that light was now threatened at its very source. In a course published in 1846 under the title *Le Peuple*, he drew a gloomy picture of the state of affairs in France.

The times in which we live, he reflects, are far from being a period of fulfillment. France, in her heroic struggle assailed from all sides, had, in the face of treason and aggression, allowed her generous undertaking to be sidetracked into the Terror. And now there she lies, pale and exhausted. The Terror made her detested in Europe; the Terror, which was unnecessary, which did not save France; rather was France saved in spite of the Terror. But the Terror stopped the great movement of education which was an essential part of the Revolution. A moving picture of the terrible conditions existing under the liberalist class rule, a bitter admission of the prevalence of mean passions and the shortage of ideas, serve as an introduction for an exhortation to turn to a new faith, a new religion, as the indispensable animating force behind the great task of educating the people that has to be resumed. Catholicism is a spent force. The humanitarian cosmopolitanism recommended by some does not appeal to him. *France* is what he preaches, the fatherland, the country blessed above all because it has vowed itself to the truths of the Revolution and has been called to teach them to Europe for its happiness. This is the faith that the schools must inculcate into the minds of the coming generations.

The fatherland, first as dogma and principle; next as legend. Let the child be told, before all, that God has vouchsafed him the mercy of possessing this fatherland, which announced and wrote with its blood the law of divine equity and of fraternity, and that the God of the nations has spoken through France.

In that sense, believing that France thinks for the world at large, Michelet is an internationalist. But, for the practical politics of the moment, he teaches that England is the enemy, that every Frenchman must be warned not to count upon Europe since he has no friend in the world but France. Also, that war is sure to come, and that France has no need to fear it, provided she firmly hold this faith.

This, then, is the theme upon which Michelet was going to embroider the history of the Revolution. Yet, as we shall see, the change in his mind was not, in 1846, completed. The subject itself was to impel him onward beyond this programmatic declaration of faith.

His *History* was not the only one which was devoted to the Revolution in those years when the struggle between old and new burst forth once more. Almost simultaneously appeared one by Lamartine and one by Louis Blanc. To Lamartine, the Girondins were the true representatives of the principles of the Revolution, and of the three his hymn of praise to those victims of the Terror was the most immediate popular success. Louis Blanc, whose work, like Michelet's, was to be continued in volume after volume in the succeeding years of new and disconcerting upheavals, glorified the

Jacobins and Robespierre; Rousseau and the social revolution supplied him with the acid test, and Thermidor meant the end of the truly significant phase. With this Michelet agreed, but he differed in that he refused to choose between Jacobins and Girondins. The hero of his story (in accordance with the philosophy of history which he had learned from Vico and the Germans) was to be the French people.

2.

The HISTORY. The Happy Years of the Revolution

In the long run it was his of the three *Histories* that was to exercise the most profound influence; and it is still making its influence felt. The view of the Revolution as it is taught in the schools bears its mark, and it still finds numerous readers. And indeed it does still impart an impression of life. It is not only its impassioned and striking address—when borne along on that vivid tale one feels in immediate contact with the concrete reality of the events. Michelet's imagination did not work in a void; he had a sense of the fact, his imagination throve on the truth and genuineness of archive documents. His vehement comments, his moans and his cries of joy, were often wrung from him by the actual matter, and if at other times they spring from his hopes and dreams and fears for the present, he has managed to build out of all that—the combination of the palpable and colorful data and the exclamations—a powerful structure which must fill even his severest critic with awe.

Nothing, however, has contributed more to the survival of the work in France—I believe that its popularity is largely confined to the French reading public—than the fact that the ideas (or, should I say the sentiments and aspirations) which it proclaims still evoke a response there. This makes it a phenomenon in French cultural and political life, and so much the more rewarding will be the attempt to enter into and to understand its spirit.

Let us observe first of all that the *History of the Revolution* was Michelet's definitive farewell to the philosophy of history which, as we saw, he espoused in 1835, and which,

two years earlier, in the preface to the first volume of the
Histoire de France, he had expressed as follows:

You gentlemen the dead [*Messieurs les morts*; for he saw them
stir in the documents at the Archives], all of you have a
claim on History. The individual is beautiful in its individuality, the general in its generality. The Fief is right, the
Monarchy more so, still more the Empire. Your turn, Geoffrey [of Bouillon, Commander of the First Crusade], come
on, Richelieu, now then, Bonaparte. . . .

But in his new mood he only recognizes the Revolution.
His "all-powerful interpreter," whom he consults for his
teaching and for his book, he says in the preface of 1847,
is "the spirit of the Revolution." "*It* knows, and the others do
not know. *It* possesses the secret of all preceding ages."

And he opens with an Introduction in which those preceding ages are painted black indeed. The Revolution is
Justice; Christianity arbitrariness, original sin, sacrificial
death, grace. To attempt a reconciliation between those
two is feeble compromise: the Revolution must conquer.
The great principles of human society and of the human
mind—*le crédo de la lumière*—were discovered by the
eighteenth-century philosophers once and for all. It follows
that the medieval church was the organization of a plot
to make mankind miserable with damnation and persecution, and royalty a mistake. Why were they not any longer
given credit for having assisted in the evolution of French
unity? Unity remains the greatest good, but not without
liberty, and true unity was only created in the Revolution
by the people itself. With so many words he now repudiates
his earlier volumes:

What is the Revolution? The reaction of equity, the tardy
arrival of eternal justice.—Justice, my mother, Law, my
father, who are one with God. . . .—Forgive me, oh
Justice, for having thought you severe and hard-hearted,
and for not having realized before now that you are identical with Love and Grace. And this is why I have been weak
towards the Middle Ages, which repeated this word of Love
without doing Love's works.

The question rises unbidden: What about the Revolution? Did *it* accomplish the works of Love? The Terror. . . . But Michelet will at once interrupt: The Terror is not the Revolution. The Revolution is beneficent. The Revolution is the achievement of the French people in its entirety; and the people is good. All that is bad, therefore, was done against the Revolution and against the French people.—But then, by whom?

When describing the early happy days of the Revolution, Michelet takes an inexhaustible delight in the entrancing spectacle of unanimity in the new revelation. The taking of the Bastille, for example. That great deed (by which, our author affirms, all the nations, down to the barbaric Russians, felt themselves liberated, shedding tears of joy) was not thought of by anyone in particular, nobody arranged it. How then did it happen? "Who possessed the devotion and the strength to act in accordance with their faith? Who? The people! Everyman."

So that passionate, confused, miraculously successful venture becomes a dramatic struggle between "the people" and the Bastille—for this old castle, too, Michelet's imagination transforms into a person, symbolizing arbitrary power and so obsessed by a bad conscience that she cannot, at the critical moment, show fight. No wonder that the killing of the governor De Launay is not taken too tragically, although the barbarous way in which it was done comes as a surprise from that good people. One need not consult any other book, either, to learn that the old town government under Flesselles, with its well-meant attempts at mediation, roused the suspicions of the besiegers to such a pitch that the lives of its members were seriously endangered, and indeed the unfortunate Flesselles lost his life. Did not he and his friends belong to "the people," were not they "everyman"? Unanimity does not seem to have been so complete after all.

But, seriously, can an attack undertaken by the entire Paris population even be imagined? Is it even thinkable that there were no cross-currents in that commotion? But to Michelet those who kept aloof or were hostile are alien elements. "The people" is in his vocabulary the term to indicate those who were active on the side of the Revolution.

No episode gives him an opportunity for so whole-hearted a paean to the national unanimity as does that of the movement of regional federations, crowned by the national celebration on the Champ de Mars, on the occasion of the first anniversary of the taking of the Bastille (July 14, 1790). In the preceding chapter he had spoken at length about resistance to the Revolution and its countrywide effects. Royalist plots; opposition from the privileged, menaced in their positions; from provincial States, Parliaments, nobility; religious strife in the South; Nîmes in open rebellion. But everywhere the new ideas triumph, the new religion, the religion of the unity of the French fatherland. "*There* is History, reality, positive and durable. The rest is nought." Is nought? That is a strong expression to apply to a resistance and to sentiments which within a few years were, under the cry of Federalism, to cause civil war in the South and to turn the Vendée into a running sore for the Republic. Michelet again does tell his readers about "the rest," even, according to his own estimation, "at length"; but he does it without sympathy, without the slightest attempt at understanding. "Evil is nothing but an exception, an irregularity." That is the one side; and as for the other: "The good, the natural, which flows of its own accord."

Is it necessary to insist that what really happened cannot in this fashion be made clear? No doubt the new organization springing up over the length and breadth of France, new local administrations entering into regional federations which in their turn reported to the National Assembly and sent delegations to that famous festival where the French nation came to know itself as such—no doubt all this presents an important and an imposing spectacle, and nothing is more natural than that Michelet felt deeply moved, and was at the same time proud, when he discovered the documents enabling him to give the first full account of this great event. But one cannot help feeling that his delight is somewhat excessive and remarkably naive.

Ainsi finit le meilleur jour de notre vie. With these words the federationists[2] of a certain village on the evening of their local celebration concluded the account they sent to the Assembly, their mother. I was tempted to use them for the conclusion of this chapter. It is done, and I can expect nothing like it as I go on. In it I leave behind me an unrepeatable moment of my life, a part of myself which, I feel it in my bones, will stay behind and won't accompany me on my journey. Impoverished and diminished, I take my leave.

And, in fact, after those charming feasts, with the grey-beard in the place of honor, the virgins in white garments surrounding him, the oaths, the dancing, there comes "the bitter book" in which Michelet has to relate the beginnings of a reaction, of quarrels, of strife. If he had not taken those touching reports so literally, if he had examined the counter-forces with a little less contempt, he need not have been so disappointed now, or so embarrassed. For how to explain that miscarriage?

He admits that there were "internal obstacles." The middle class, however much imbued with Voltaire and Rousseau, and more humane and less moved by interest than their present-day successors who are shaped by the new industrialism, were timid. This, intelligibly enough, since "that wretched *ancien régime* could form only weak characters." Note that the *ancien régime* is made responsible. That middle class, then, was sufficiently feebleminded to be frightened of the popular excitement. Thus there was fear, attended by hatred.

But with much greater emphasis he sets out "the external obstacles," which indeed promoted, or even caused, the other.

An inimical fatality interfered from outside, hindering the childbirth in which France was engaged. (*Who was guilty of that unnatural crime, more unnatural than if someone were to stop Newton from giving to the world a new thought, or a woman from giving birth to a child?*) Thrice, nay a thousand times accursed he who, witnessing that wonderful spectacle of a people in this state of heroism, magnanimous and disinterested, attempts to hinder, to stifle, that miracle from which a world was ready to spring. How did the nations come to agree upon arming against the nations' interest? Tragic and dark mystery.

Michelet then recalls how the Wars of Religion were, by the efforts of the diabolic Jesuits, stoked up into that hellish night of massacre called the Thirty Years War. Fifty years had been required for that fell work; how is it that this time the effect was attained so much more quickly? Two explanations: first, the press, that great modern machinery; second, that the lies this time issued from two very different laboratories and could thus be better adapted to varying stupidities. In addition to the old Catholic and despotic one, there was now the new English—the so-called constitutional—laboratory of lies.

The Middle Ages knew but one hypocrisy, we are cursed with two: hypocrisy of authority, hypocrisy of freedom; that is to say, the *Priest,* and the *Englishman,* the two shapes of Tartuffe. The priest influences the women mainly, the Englishman the middle class.

There follows a rabid attack upon the slanderous pamphlets distributed on the part of the Catholics; next, on the English side, upon Burke and his *Reflections.* The worst traitors are the Frenchmen having a hand in these dealings, but Burke, too, is in Michelet's eyes no more than a miserable muddlehead and paid scribe of Pitt's. That he dares to invoke *pity,* pity for the royal family, for the noblemen and prelates anxious for their safety, pity "against the only nation which aimed at the happiness of mankind"—it fills him with fury. How did they dare, these English, enslaved by their aristocracy, to boast of their freedom in comparison with that of the French! How can there have been Frenchmen —and there are still such, *anglomanes!*—who secretly or openly admire the English constitution, holding it up as an example! Can greater stupidity be, he exclaims, or greater arrogance!

The exhibition of prejudice and national self-conceit in passages like these is startling. International relations or conditions in foreign countries are not examined; on no point is Michelet's historical writing technically weaker.

The innocence of revolutionary France, the wicked intent of the European powers, especially of England, are simply taken for granted.

But there is method in that madness. For here, in relating the events of 1790, Michelet prepares for the apology of the Terror. The guilt of it is from now on to be imputed to these foreign evil-doers and their tools. They, by means of the Vendée uprising, have caused "that frightful contraction of France which is called the Terror." It is the crusade of the Kings which created for France that desperate situation "and threw her into the murderous necessity of the Terror." Observe that in this last quotation the advocate of the Revolution goes one step further than in the first. The Terror was a necessity. It will be remembered that in *Le Peuple* he had still maintained that France had been saved *in spite of* the Terror. Now the Terror is accepted as a weapon that had to be employed. But even so it was the outside world, it was the English and the traitors, who were responsible. The French people and the Revolution were guiltless.

3.

The HISTORY. *The Terrible Years of the Revolution*

We come to those terrible years; 1792—the attack on the Tuileries (the 10th of August), the Convention, the proclamation of the Republic, the September massacres; 1793—the execution of Louis XVI, the arrest of the Girondins in spite of their inviolability as members of the Convention, their execution, the reign of Terror; 1794—the execution of the Hébertists, of the Dantonists, finally Thermidor and the execution of Robespierre. Simultaneously the war. Spring of 1792—rupture with Austria; September—Valmy; November—Jemappes and occupation of the Southern Netherlands. Spring of 1793—loss of the Netherlands, the French frontiers threatened on all sides. Spring and summer of 1794—turn for the better.

To such a man as Michelet, torn between his sincere desire for a humane and happy national and international way of living and his deification of the Revolution and of the French people, to have to describe all this was a heavy trial. It was worse because at the same time his belief in the present, in that French Republic of February 1848 which was at long last to realize the ideals of 1789, suffered such heavy shocks. The working class rising of June 1848 and its pitiless suppression; an adventurer such as Louis Napoleon posing as the "savior of society" and all "decent citizens" longing for the moment when he would establish "firm government"; finally, when this came to pass in December 1851, Michelet immediately dismissed from his chair—it was a sad demonstration of a very different reality. But it could not discourage the lonely, indefatigable worker in his outlook upon history. The Revolution remained the announcement of all the bliss for which mankind can ever hope, the French people remained the chosen people, that message of salvation the true expression of the national soul.

In describing the September massacres Michelet employed a method exactly the reverse of that which had served him for the taking of the Bastille. It is not now "the people"; it is "three or four hundred drunks." But from where did these spring if not from the crowd organized for revolutionary action or, to use Michelet's own terminology for other occasions, from "the people," from the good and unanimous people? And how was it that they were left to do their fell work for days at a stretch? Afterwards the leaders and smaller men were all eager to assert that they had taken no part. But what had they done to prevent the crime?

The crime? Michelet does not repudiate the word. ("Heaven forbid!") Yet he cannot refrain from remarking that among the thousand victims there were only too many who had caused great harm to the Revolution and to France. And massacres are common enough in the histories of other nations, whereas none records so imposing an explosion of heroism as occurred at that very moment among the French people! He much resents those superior foreigners (for example, Goethe) who, in order to vilify the Revolution and France, will see nothing but that deplorable incident.

From the menace of the Austro-Russian invasion, "a flame shot up, a burning jet of heroism." Brilliant pages are those in which Michelet describes the resistance offered to the intruders. Among the motive forces, he does mention fear for the revenge and persecution to be expected from an occupying army bringing the returning *émigrés* in its train. But this does not prevent him from affirming that "our fathers did and willed those great deeds for the liberation of the world. . . . So many things which will eternally do honour to human nature." And Europe remained blind to them, seeing only "that mud stain."

The worst, however, was that the event had demonstrated the impotence of the Convention. To me, the way in which that assembly allowed itself to be tyrannized over by the Paris *Commune* (in which the lowest elements now had the upper hand, as Michelet admits) seems an undeniable proof of moral cowardice, dishonoring the Revolution. And, indeed, Vergniaud, the Girondin orator, himself, addressing the Convention, spoke of a "stain" which should be wiped off the French name and exhorted the assembly to show "in spite of calumny, that all respect for humanity and all civic virtue have not vanished from among us." He did so in the melodramatic tone belonging to the period. "Let the assembly perish if only it saves liberty. Let all of us perish, and let our successors, more fortunate than we, assure the happiness of France and Liberty . . ."

And Michelet is more than satisfied.

The entire House rose, and so did the public in the tribunes. That heroic generation, in that moment, sacrificed itself for those who were to come. All repeated, in one shout: "Yes, yes, let us perish if it must be, and let our memory be effaced."—The people that uttered these words did not deserve to perish. And in that very moment it was saved. Three days later France won the battle of Valmy.

Had the stain, then, been wiped off? Had Liberty been established? Nothing like it; it was all words. What was established, before a year had passed, was a much stricter tyranny. In June 1793 the Convention which had cheered so bravely allowed itself to be coerced, by the Paris Sections led by Hanriot, to deliver up thirty-four of its own members, the Girondins, suspected of "federalism" (Vergniaud among them!). Here is Michelet's description of the scene.

The President [Hérault], nobly: "What does the people desire? . . . The Convention's attention is engaged on nothing but the people and its happiness."—The General [the drunken chief of the armed section bands, Hanriot]: "Hérault, the people has not risen to listen to phrases, but to give orders. . . . It claims thirty-four victims."—"Victims?" cry the deputies: "We shall all share the same fate!" —"To your pieces, artillerists!" cries the General.

This settled the matter. The Girondins were dragged off and months later were guillotined. For a year the Convention crawled under Robespierre, suffering other expulsions (Hébert, Danton) without daring even to murmur.

Always this ambivalence with Michelet. He not only describes the events, he describes them with horror and deep-felt sorrow. But in the final reckoning he does not allow the radiant beauty of his dream to be darkened by what he has so keenly observed.

Was the Convention, then, an assembly of cowards? Let us be fair. Gripped in the tongs of necessity . . . it has, for good and evil, given the full measure of human nature . . . No, whatever may be said, no assembly ever contained so many live forces, so many men prepared to die for their duty. [Examples of brave *"représentants en mission."*] Great assembly, ever fruitful, even when most beset by shortcomings, not to be conquered by events! [Hymn of praise to the institutions bequeathed by it to France and which succeeding regimes, while cursing it, maintained.]

In this passage one still detects an apologetic note. But what shall we say of the following, as a comment on the incident of which we have just read his description? "The records of that epoch, however barbarically violent or rude in form, all testify to an exalted character, worthy of that great century: the cult of the Idea, the living belief in the Law."

The Law!

Michelet did not like Robespierre or the Jacobins. He deplores their lack of "that kindness which befits heroes." Their political orthodoxy and intolerance strike him as akin to those of their hosts (it will be remembered that the club took its name from the monastery of the Jacobins in which it met; Michelet, by the way, ever sensitive to surroundings and atmosphere, gives a splendid description of the place). But the Girondins, much as they appealed to his sympathy, he considers deficient in "that relentless severity which it seemed that the hour required." "The situation demanded a force which, without exactly dragging the assembly along, strode before it, inexorably thrusting aside whatever might impede its course."

This is how he had put it in an earlier chapter, thereby clearing the way for what was to come in dread reality, the Jacobin dictatorship, the Terror. It had to be, so it was right. Truth to tell, the methods employed by Robespierre were not to Michelet's taste.

In the memory of men so slanderous a piece was not produced. Never have the rage of *esprit de corps,* monkish fanaticism, the intoxication of a devout brotherhood working itself up behind closed doors and step by step, without meeting contradiction, proceeding to the very limits of absurdity, thought of anything like it.

The document thus scathingly denounced was a circular sent by Robespierre, in October 1792, to the Jacobin clubs all over France in order to throw suspicion on Brissot, the other Girondin leader. But for all that, we find our author writing a little later with no less of the usual bombast (and doubtless profound conviction) on Justice as the great aim of the Revolution. "Justice blind to interest, Justice deaf to politics, Justice ignorant, divinely ignorant, of the reasons of the man of state."

If humanity was suspended, it was in order to insure the safety of this Justice. Nor was this done only on account of the danger of France, but also because France was the apostle and the keeper of the common rights of the entire human race, because in the death of France the death of mankind was comprehended.

Thus are justified not only the horrors to come but also the deceit and the calumny; and, last but not least, thus was French vanity flattered.

The Girondins were talkers, Robespierre a fanatic who, for the sake of Virtue, trampled under foot both honor and life. But—they were all patriots. It was untrue, Michelet insists, that the Girondins wanted to disrupt the sacred unity of the fatherland. There was not in the Convention one traitor.

In the last chapters (for his book ends with Thermidor) he gives a gruesome description of the tyrant shut up in his dream which Robespierre had come to be; his dream, in which he himself, the Servant of the Supreme Being, helped to establish the eternal reign of Virtue by exterminating the unvirtuous.[3] Two half-witted persons had made ineffectual attempts on his life. On that account fifty-four human beings, dressed in the red shirt of the parricide, were guillotined in one *fournée*, several women among them, one ignorant girl of eighteen. "No children!"—that cry was heard when she mounted the scaffold. Michelet does not spare his readers the particulars, and shudders with them. He tells of the veneration vowed to Robespierre in those very days, after the festival of the Supreme Being, at which he, one would almost say, had officiated, and of a devout baroness who addressed him with folded hands: "Yes, Robespierre! thou art God." In Paris! Michelet exclaims, after Voltaire! in the heighday of the *Contrat social!* Yet in an earlier passage he had written:

What a spectacle! those men of immeasurable talents and of still greater hearts [Vergniaud, Brissot, Danton, Desmoulins, Robespierre, St. Just and the rest], in full agreement as to all questions of public welfare, and who are about to throw themselves into that embittered struggle, in which soon not one will survive.

Their internecine feuds sadden Michelet inexpressibly. One comforting thought he cannot deny himself, namely:

That these great citizens, who died so young, and who, *whatever they may have done* [my italics—P.G.], died in preparing for us this France, may have had time, on the other side of death, to get to know and, entering the light of justice and of truth, to embrace each other.

There is in that sentimentality about the bloody maniacs of 1793-94, moved by the new revelation of eternal truths but also by hatred and fear, something positively repulsive. But they were all patriots, they were all faithful servants of the Revolution; it is *that* which, in Michelet's estimation, is decisive, *there* he takes his ultimate standard. So even Robespierre remained a servant of Justice, and not of France only but of mankind.

The Revolution—the standard of all things. As in the eyes of Robespierre, so to Michelet, all those who tried to obstruct the Revolution were unvirtuous. That is why, in so far as they were Frenchmen, he did not take them into account. A light punishment, one might say, compared to that demanded by the orthodoxy of the Incorruptible; from the consequence of the guillotine Michelet did indeed shrink back. But the adversaries, in his estimation, did not count, and that is why he could always speak so confidently of the unanimity of the French people.

Nobility and clergy? The slaves of King and Church, the two powers of Hell. Don't count. . . . The poor, from whom the National Assembly, in October 1789, had taken away the suffrage? Dependents of those two first-named groups, their tame voting cattle; a danger to the Revolution, away with them! Don't count. . . . The *bourgeois,* moderately reformist, but anxious that what was rooted in history should be dealt with gingerly? An opposition group, the victims of English opium, Frenchmen only by half, *anglomanes.* Don't count. . . . The peasants and the women? Simple-minded folk, who allow their gentry, or (and especially) the priests, to lead them by the nose. Don't count. . . . The remainder: the well-intentioned: these equal the nation, they are, to speak with Rousseau, the bearers of "the General Will."

Rousseau's influence on Michelet is glaringly apparent. Popular sovereignty in Rousseau's system does not mean that the will of the majority is to be acted upon. The majority can err. The General Will, on the contrary, cannot err, for it is the people's purified will directed toward its

own well-being. That will is sure to result from all delibera-
tions, *provided that* the people is well informed; and *provided that* it is not thrown into confusion by group interests.
(Thus Rousseau in Book II, ch. III, of the *Contrat social*.)
Sovereignty must be indivisible, every particular organization
detracts from it, and only by submitting to the true sovereignty of the General Will (no bargaining can be allowed)
does one find one's rights, true freedom and safety (chs. II
and IV).

It was these ideas, since invoked by every minority dictatorship for its justification, that wrought such havoc in
the French Revolution and gave to Robespierre and the
Jacobins that crushing self-confidence with which, no doubt
against the large majority of the French people, they upheld
the General Will. In their own eyes they were not, of
course, minority as they might be, a group spelling confusion in the State, but rather the true faithful, serving no
particular interest but the Revolution and consequently the
interest of the entire fatherland. Such ideas as these inspire
the work of Michelet as well.

The chapters in which he sobs out his ecstasy about the
federations movement of 1789-90 are entitled: *De la religion
nouvelle*. Unity, unity! Away from the old temples to nature
and unity, that eternal dream of mankind. *Patrie* was what
the Frenchmen of that period called it, but the whole of
humanity was present in the soul and in the aspirations of
France. Michelet knew all along that the dream was to be
disturbed, yet, faced with the events of 1792, when the
cry of federalism is raised and civil war threatens, his fury
is boundless. Unity, unity, he cries again. "The unity of the
fatherland, the indivisibility of the Republic, there you have
the sacred, the holy word of '93. *No life outside unity*. There
is no surer axiom."

Those wretched Vendéeans said: "There is no authority
any longer, no priests and no king. Well, then, we shall
do battle with the Nation." "They never realized," exclaims
Michelet with commiseration rather than with reproof, "that
they themselves were the Nation." That, in other words,
they would find their freedom in submission to the General
Will as proclaimed, if not by, at least in, Paris.

Practically speaking, however, the ascendancy of Paris over the Convention was hardly the best way to inspire confidence in the purity of the General Will as it was there manufactured. Michelet, however, sees unity necessarily concentrated in his own beloved Paris, and, although he has described the tyranny of the Commune and of the Sections with a clearness that leaves nothing to be desired, he passionately rejects the charge that Paris wanted to rule the country. That charge is as false as the other one that the Girondins did not believe in "the religion of the fatherland." Paris, he admits, has committed grave errors; but, in spite of that, "when I reflect on what it has done for the liberties of our human race, I feel impelled to kiss the stones of its monuments and the pavements of its streets."

How sad a spectacle, nevertheless, did the Christmas of 1792 present in this same Paris! St. Stephen's Church, where a wonder-working relic was preserved, was filled to overflowing—mostly, it is true, with country people. But everywhere the churches were more crowded than before '89, "filled with a people praying against the Revolution, against the victory of the people." Can the use of that term *the people* in the interests of a minority dictatorship more patently betray itself for the juggling trick it is?

And yet Michelet never was clear in his own mind with respect to that fundamental point. His vehemence sometimes gives the impression that it is an attempt to shout down his inner uncertainty. Immediately following upon the passage quoted, there is the chapter in which he discusses the moods manifesting themselves in the Convention concerning the sentence of Louis XVI. The democratic principle of deference toward the wish of the majority of the nation (which was undeniably against a sentence of death) was there upheld by the Girondin speakers; the principle of the minority's right, or duty, to force through a measure which in their opinion the people *ought to* wish, by the Jacobins. "Sincere, patriotic, heroic," says Michelet—yet, how dangerous! If *the best* must prevail despite *the number*, would it not be possible to defend the rule of the Ten in Venice—nay, the rule of One, of a Pope or of a King?

Exactly! and one prepares curiously to watch our eloquent

author freeing himself from the horns of that dilemma. But it is very difficult to follow his argument. He wanders off into pathetic exclamations about the Girondins being also patriots and heroes, and especially about Danton, who in the end caused the decision to fall out in favor of the sentence of death. Without facing the problem squarely any more, he winds up by explaining, in a somewhat involved argument in which unedifying tactics seem to have the better of principle, that (as usual) it had to be and therefore was right. No lack of high-sounding phrases, but as for justification no more than what every tyrant can advance. ("Necessity, the tyrant's plea.")

Michelet, apparently without being in the least disturbed by these unsolved contradictions, wishes, with unshaken confidence, to gather the other nations within the perfect unity of the Revolution. We saw how he imagined the nations looking on in breathless expectation at the drama of liberation in France. It is of course a fact that in many countries there were parties that eagerly drank in the message of 1789. But everywhere it was parties only, and when the possibility of French interference presented itself in real earnest, in 1792, the zeal of many neighbors soon began to cool.

Michelet, however, knows no doubt. When the battle of Jemappes has been won, in November 1792, he tells us that the victory song of the French soldiers: *"Allons, enfants de la patrie!"*

. . . was answered with: *"Allons, enfants de la France"* by all peoples, who threw themselves into our arms . . . Great and fruitful day for them! Through us they gained in one day the conquest of centuries. That heritage of reason and liberty for which so many human beings had sighed in vain, that promised land of which they longed to have a glimpse if at the price of their lives, France gave it to anyone for the asking. [It should be remembered that at this moment the blood of the September massacres was hardly dry and that the Convention, in spite of all brave words, had to do the bidding of the armed roughs from the *Commune.*] For three years already she had been laying down that wisdom in laws won with her blood and with her tears. Those laws, that blood, and those tears she gave to all, saying: Here is my blood, drink.

He sketches the delegations of refugees from various countries imploring the Convention that they may be annexed. What these men represented he does not inquire. They are "the peoples," they are "the world giving itself to France." And when the decree of the 19th of November promises "assistance and fraternity" to all peoples wishing to be free, "the flag of France has become that of mankind, that of universal liberation." There is but one people wilfully blind, alas! the Vendée. . . .

It appeared soon enough that at least one of the peoples which had actually been occupied by the French troops, the Belgians, was also badly stricken with that infirmity. The Belgian revolution of 1789 had been a conservative revolution—at least, that was what it had become. The Vonckists, who wanted reforms, had been expelled from the new Belgian Republic, and the Statists, Van der Noot's party, who swore by the old constitution, wishing only to safeguard it from being tampered with by the enlightened despot, Austrian Joseph II, had remained masters of the situation, with the approval, indubitably, of the large majority of the population. Dumouriez, the French general who had now wrested the country from the restored Austrian regime, wanted to work with the authorities such as they were rooted in the population. In Paris it was Cambon who forced through a different policy: a complete revolutionizing of Belgium, all the possessions of church and nobility and, in fact, all the public funds and institutions, to be seized. A ruling motive was clearly the wish to acquire a new basis for the *assignats*, which had already collapsed in France, and to have the French occupying army maintained by the conquered country. This policy of extortion, introduced by a decree dated December 15th, 1792, caused a complete reversal of feeling in Belgium with respect to the French, and the Dutch "Patriots" too, who had been ready to welcome the French, began seriously to reflect. Michelet has seen nothing of all this.

In the struggle which Cambon, on behalf of his hard

and realistic policy, had to wage with Dumouriez and his friends, the Girondins, Michelet resolutely sides with Cambon. He does not seem to realize that Cambon's policy *was* a hard and realistic one and that it must call forth resistances among "the peoples" and bereave the war of its ideological character. How many times had he assured his readers that "the Revolution was disinterested"! Axiom. What can the facts do against a primary truth! Cambon is to him "this man of violent genius, who was the Revolution itself, in its palpable shape of the *assignat* and of the landed interest." And he goes on to relate how, to Dumouriez's objection that his policy was bound to reduce the Belgians to poverty, Cambon replied, crudely: "So much the better! We, too, are poor. They will be compelled to cling to us and together we shall march on and the entire globe will, after our example, become the Revolution." Dumouriez shrank back: "The man is mad!"

The lunacy of the Revolution [comments Michelet] was here wisdom. The Revolution could not accomplish anything unless it made its attempt everywhere. The first condition of its durability was to become universal. The second was, everywhere to seize the land and to dig itself in.

He blames Robespierre for his shortsightedness in being averse to the war. Robespierre (at that moment!) recommended that "the war should be prudently kept within limits." "Did he not understand that to try to dam in such a Revolution was impossible, ridiculous, and unfair? Unfair, for we owed it to the world."

As regards the Belgians, Michelet has nothing but scorn for the party of Van der Noot and of the monks.

The scoundrels, leading the blind population for no other purpose than to fasten the yoke upon it once more, did not scruple, in their pamphlets, to talk about popular sovereignty: "Is not the Belgian people a free and independent sovereign as well as the French?" The freedom to commit suicide. And indeed, a people? How could a people be known as long as it remained scattered over that confused multitude of towns, which did not even attempt to unite?

No General Will except through unity, free from the confusing influence of separate groups: Rousseau. But in any case those scoundrels and misleaders, those men of the past and of darkness, went for nothing in the scales of revolutionary morality. They were not "the true Belgians," Michelet assures us in so many words. And as for France's right to dispose of their possessions:

Was it not for Belgium and for the world that France undertook the war, which between 1792 and 1815 cost her ten millions of her children? In view of that frightful quantity of French blood, it did not become the Belgians very well to grudge us a little money. They ought to have wholeheartedly accepted the union, to have stood with France to the last man, and to have thrown themselves blindfold into that path of sacrifice at the end of which stood the inestimable aim, the conquest of the liberties of mankind.

An out and out revolutionary imperialist was Michelet. Even for his own day he coolly asserts that Belgium, "an English invention," cannot exist, and that the Belgians, like the Alsatians, can become complete human beings only "by joining us."

Let it be noted, in the previous passage quoted, that Michelet credits the account of France with the wars of Napoleon, in whom he saw a despot but who is nevertheless supposed to have fought for the liberties of mankind. Indeed, he cannot at any time mention Waterloo without the bitterest resentment. That attitude of mind was common enough among his compatriots—then and even much later. The small frontier correction of 1815, which was the price France had to pay for the reckless and criminal adventure of the Hundred Days, seemed to them insufferably high; indeed, few Frenchmen would ever be brought to admit that any action of France might with justice be regarded as blameworthy. Michelet sheds bitter tears when recalling the invasion of France in 1814. But how many countries had been invaded by France since 1792? They were invaded disinterestedly, in order to bring them freedom, Michelet would say. In that case, what of those invaded before 1792?

To that his reply would be: That was not France, that was
her kings. . . .

4.
The Cult of the Revolutionary Tradition

Dr. Gooch, in his *History and Historians in the Nineteenth Century*, concludes his paragraph on Michelet by
saying: "No historian has loved France so tenderly. To
him that loved much may be forgiven."

I cannot rise to that degree of kindness. Michelet over-
flowed with noble and generous thoughts. He meant them.
Injustice and oppression, the living conditions of the working class and the unfeeling attitude of the employers—he
could not look at the world and not be saddened. I alluded
to the bitter experiences he had to swallow while writing
about the Revolution: the June uprising of 1848, the coming to the fore of Louis Napoleon, that idol of the egoists
and the materialists. It was not until 1869 that he completed
his volumes on the period between Louis XI and the Revolution, which he had in 1844 decided to skip. There is no
lack of brilliant passages, but in no portion of the great
work are whole periods more arbitrarily reduced to one
single motif. After an astonishing identification of the Renaissance with the Reformation, and of both with Joy, the
seventeenth century is called the century of sterility. The
Kings are lampooned in a pettish and often almost childish
style. But indeed we know already that Michelet does not
seek any longer for the principle that may actually have animated any of the past centuries: he judges them all by the
spirit of the Revolution. Yet the epilogue which he now wrote
is among the most impressive of his many self-revelations.

My life was in this book. It has gone into it. This book is
all that has happened to me. . . . When one penetrates into
the subject ever more deeply, one begins to love it. . . .
The heart, when moved, has a second sight, it sees innumerable things which remain invisible to the indifferent crowd.

The history and the historian get mixed up. Is this good? is it evil? A process takes place, never before described, and which I will reveal.

It is that in the course of time the history makes the historian, much more than the reverse. . . .

So forty years have passed by . . . I have lost myself in this work. . . . For it I have given the world a miss, and history to me has become life.

My life at all events has run its course. I rue nothing. I ask for nothing. Oh what should I ask for, beloved France, with whom I have lived, from whom I part with so much sorrow. In how close a companionship with you have I passed forty years (ten centuries). The many moving, and noble, and sober hours that we have had together, even in winter time before daybreak! The days of labour and of study in the archives! I worked for you, going and coming, searching, writing. Every day I gave myself entire, perhaps more than entire. The next morning, finding you at my desk, it seemed to me that I was the same, strong through your mighty life and eternal youth.

But how is it, after the extraordinary happiness of that intercourse, that I did not within myself gain from it more? Alas, it is because, in order to recreate all this for you, I had to trace again that long course of misfortunes, of cruel vicissitudes, of a hundred maladies and disasters. I have drunk too deep of that bitter cup. Too much pain, too much ignominy, too many kings have I suffered.

Well, then, my France, my great one, if to recover the story of your life someone had to give himself and had to cross and recross the river of the dead so many times, he is comforted, he thanks you in spite of everything. And his greatest sorrow is that here we part company.

This is genuine; this has a touch of greatness; this is moving. We shall gladly, because of it, forgive the man his shortcomings. Which of us will dare to affirm that, against his own smaller perhaps or at least different shortcomings, he would be able to point to anything of equal value? But in judging the writer of history we do not efface the one with the other. There, if anywhere, the road to hell is paved with noble sentiments. The good intentions and the generosity of the absolutist thinker who, for all his inimitable gift for the recreation of the facts, puts them aside in order to argue in accordance with his system; of the illusionist and self-deceiver,[4] of the man living on his emotions, who can disconnect his reason (or his common sense) whenever it might disturb him in his enjoyment of them—what use are the good intentions and the generosity of such a one? They have not prevented him from powerfully contributing by his work to the dominance of that cult of the Revolutionary tradition, which has had such disastrous consequences for his beloved France.

This is not to say that I want everybody absolutely to reject the Revolution. Far from it! I only expect of the historian that he shall explain it, making distinctions and appreciating the consequences in their relative aspects. Nothing is less historical than to identify the struggle between men with the contest between good and evil, as Michelet does, or it must be his working with bold generalizations and static conceptions in which the human beings masquerade in the guise of symbolic figures or exponents of ideas: the Revolution, the beginning of Justice; the people, the master of goodness and maker of its own history; France, or the French people, blessed among the nations; materialist and hypocritical England; the Church, wily seducer of the stupid crowd. Often he succeeded in making the blood run warm once more through the multiple, contradictory and struggling mass of human reality—only in Europe, however, was he unable to see anything but that fantastic spectral dance of wicked oppressors and helpless oppressed round his idol, France. But when it came to expressing a judgment, he always subjected reality, even where he had properly discerned it, to the abstractions of the doctrine. Dictatorship, violence, deceit, were never praised; in his heart Michelet abhorred them all; only, at the dictate of his fixed ideas the distasteful phenomena were condoned. When he writes, "unity, outside which there is no life," it is as if he, who has the word liberty constantly in his mouth, passed a sentence of death on all variety, all individualism, all resistance.

A cult such as this is a misfortune for a people. Already, in 1848, it helped to make the commotion result in confusion and mutual hatreds, unappeasable and sterile. A mood had been nurtured in which a feeling for relative values and for reality could hardly thrive, and another outburst occurred in 1870-71. The cult obtained a permanent hold on the imagination of a large portion of the French people, and under the Third Republic, somewhat adapted to the less excitable temper of the time, it became, so to speak, official. The University, that powerful teaching machine, instilled it into the minds of the young; "Secularism" (*laicité*) became the pass word.

The operation was assisted by the anaesthetizing capacities of one integral part of the cult, the flattering of national self-conceit. We have observed how easily Michelet's love for France changed into idolatry. "The French, the first nation of Europe; what France does today, the world will do to-morrow; immeasurable obligation of the world to France; whatever is modern and enlightened, liberty and justice, discovered in France, bound up with France's well-being or the reverse; the sacred mission of France to spread those spiritual treasures." On all sides such phrases are heard in the France of '48, and again after '70 and indeed down to the present day. And of this philosophy—Revolution, Secularism, and the unique French Fatherland intimately and indissolubly connected—Michelet was the prophet.

We saw that in 1843 he had to make way, with his doctrine, against a powerful current. That current has known ebbtide and flood. Under Napoleon III the power of the Catholics in the University was again considerable. After 1870 Secularism was part of the popular national temper, and its allied interpretation of the Revolution established a firm foothold in public instruction.

The violent exchange of the twenties between Professors Aulard and Mathiez[5]—master and disciple in Revolution study at the Sorbonne—should not make us overlook the fact that in reality both pursued the tradition of Michelet. To Aulard, the hero of the critical years was Danton, because he *was* a hero, and because he embodied the idea of anti-clericalism. To Mathiez it was the priest-like Robespierre, because he foresaw, or forefelt, and began, the social revolution. Of the two scholars Aulard, no doubt, stood closer to Michelet, but both he and Mathiez, by singling out one chief personage in the Revolutionary drama, neglected the master's

leading idea that the Revolution was *the people's* doing.
Michelet had insisted that the Revolution should not be "shut
up in a club," the people itself has been the promoter of its
liberation, it has been "its own Prometheus." Aulard and Mathiez certainly never directly disputed this view, and, in any
case, like the great romantic visionary from whom they differed so markedly by their academic style and accurate research, they both built their work on the fundamental revolutionary assumptions without including these in the debate.
Their work, too, was offered as a contribution not only to
scholarship but to the Revolution. Seignobos, Pariset, even
Lefebvre[6]—to a greater or a lesser extent the same could be
said of them and of many others. The University, where Napoleon had so bad a press,[7] remained devoted to the tradition
of the Revolution.

Naturally, the tradition can be traced in the work of many
others who were, or are, less immediately connected with
the great institution than the scholars I mentioned. First of
all there is Jaurès.[8] Although his presentation of events is
consciously differentiated from Michelet's by the strong
emphasis laid on the social motives of the commotion and
by the prominence given to all that resembles a positive
striving after social reform—this was soon to be carried
still further by Mathiez—the spiritual affinity with Michelet
shows itself nowhere more plainly than here. The same belief that the Revolution had to fulfill a mission with respect to
a backward Europe, the same sorrow in relating the horrors
of the Terror and yet unwillingness to drop the great Ter-
rorists as patriots and apostles of freedom. Even the tone
is at times reminiscent of Michelet.

Not many years ago Gérard Walter edited a new edition
of Michelet's *Histoire de la Révolution française*. Walter
is a University man, and, though hardly a scholar of any
originality, he is a first-rate expert. This is evident not only
from the precious annotation with which he has enriched
the edition but also from a number of monographs he has
written about personalities or aspects of the Revolution.[9]
And nobody can use more resolutely the Revolution as the
standard of all things. When Mathiez, to the greater honor
of the incorruptible Robespierre, revels in uncovering Dan-

ton's worse than questionable financial practices, Walter reproaches him for having supplied the enemies of the Revolution with ammunition. As an editor, Walter sets Michelet right on a large number of points of fact; occasionally he indicates a difference of opinion on larger issues. The evidence of absolutistic thinking and of national self-conceit, however, which I have stressed in this essay, Walter passes by in silence. The edition, in the beautiful Bibliothèque de la Pléiade, is in itself significant: it is not the earlier volumes on the Middle Ages, or Joan of Arc, which used traditionally to be considered Michelet's masterpiece,[10] but the *History of the Revolution* which is thus honored.

Then there is Lucien Febvre, a much more interesting mind than Walter, leading personality in an important new historiographical school in France. In 1946 a little book appeared under his name, which is extraordinarily instructive for the better knowledge of the line of thought which I am tracing in contemporary France.[11] It is a eulogy of Michelet, and at the same time an homage to the spirit of the Revolution as he interpreted it. And more than that, it is an attempt to recall him and his message to the respectful attention of French youth, unsettled by the humiliations of the German occupation and a prey to scepticism. Professor Febvre himself found strength for his soul, during the occupation, in the enthusiasm of those who in 1830 hoped "to wipe France clean of the mud stain of 1815!" The patriots of 1830 were deceived in their expectations, but Michelet spoke for them in 1846 (*Le Peuple*) and tried, in the tragic debate raging since 1789, or since 1793, between Revolution and Contra-Revolution, to infuse the right side with his fighting spirit. The debate, as Febvre defines it, "rages between the spirit of fear and the spirit which we have no choice but to call the spirit of revolution. That is to say, the creative spirit." The middle class of today, he explains, is still governed by fear; two Medusa heads stare at them frighteningly—the Terror, and Communism. What a tonic he found it (between 1940 and 1944) to read how Michelet describes the nations (the passage from *Le Peuple* will be remembered) pressing round the sickbed of France, France pale since she had given them her blood, poor since she had poured out her treasure for them, and finally given her soul, from which they are still drawing life.

Delightful reading indeed for a patriot feeling crushed by his impotence, but will it impart strength or merely intoxicate? "The breakdowns of France are the agonies of Europe," Febvre says, and is it not as if we heard Michelet? And when faced with the question whether the *liberty* of the Revolution was not after all mainly *equality*, he calls this a typically English objection and, again wholly in the spirit of Michelet, feels that he has disposed of it. "Let the English enjoy freedom in their fashion, what we need is a freedom in the French fashion." He has every sympathy with Michelet's anti-English feelings, sprung from the humiliation of Waterloo: "Is it not the same with our generation with respect to the Germans?"

But what, then, is this French freedom? To Febvre what Michelet's teaching aims at is "moral freedom"; as against the aristocratic tendency of the English, the equalitarian; as against their materialism, the insistence on the moral aspect. I feel impelled to ask whether in order to enjoy "moral freedom" one should not be on one's guard against making a fetish of unity; ought not conceited chauvinism to be regarded as a snare; and, taking a more general view, should not one disdain to spare one's illusions the touch of rational criticism? A pernicious mixture, after all, this drink that Febvre in his little book on Michelet recommends to the youth of France as a strengthening tonic.

However, in a recently issued Sorbonne textbook on historiography,[12] Professor Georges Lefebvre, the respected veteran of *connoisseurs* of the Revolution period, rates no other French author so high as Michelet (he gives him three times as much space as is available for Tocqueville, or Fustel de Coulanges, or Taine), and no other part of his work, in his estimation, equals the *History of the French Revolution*. On the strength of that book he describes Michelet as *"notre plus grand historien national."* Note well: not *the greatest French historian,* but *our greatest national historian.* That means that he accepts the contents of Michelet's national conception, in the center of which there stands his glorification of the Revolution. And, although he permits himself a smile at the personifications and symbolisms, not a word of warning escapes him against the illusions, the excitable chauvinism, or the confused thinking.

Illusions and confusions, nevertheless, which lend themselves only too well for use in support of the absolutist conceptions of modern world revolution propaganda.

But I said—indeed, it goes without saying—that other tendencies manifested themselves in French thought. I leave on one side the positively Catholic opposition to the Revolution. Michelet had declared war on Catholicism so vehemently that the Catholics could not but be critical of his presentation of the Revolution. Those Catholics who understood the implications of their faith—which was far from being the case of all—must reject above all the paganistic idolization of France. "Eternal France?" said Simone Weil, to quote only her, a late figure in a company scattered over generations. "The words amount to blasphemy."

But from the first there were the sceptics: I mentioned Sainte-Beuve[13] and Heine. At a later stage of Michelet's lifetime there was Edmond de Goncourt, who confessed (in his not overbenevolent *Journal*) that he, with all respect, could not refrain from a movement of irony (he had just paid a visit to the old historian) when listening to "this mystical jargon" of men like Michelet and Victor Hugo, "so hollow and sonorous," in which they "uttered their oracles, trying to impose themselves on their circle as prophets having commerce with the gods." [14]

But scepticism is no answer. More had to be opposed to the earnestness and fire with which Michelet appealed to the instincts of youth. Was what was needed supplied by Tocqueville in the great book he published in 1856? *L'Ancien régime et la Révolution* set out to show that the centralization and other reforms of the Revolution were not really a reaction against, that they were rather a carrying to its logical conclusion of, the policy of the monarchy.[15] We find here none of these flashes of insight and intuition, but not that rigid commitment to a system or a party either, the combination of which in Michelet results in the striking and the fantastic standing so often side by side. Rather, a book of acumen and of wisdom that might have served to bridge the all-too-simple antithesis. Liberty, which had not come into its own in the years following upon 1789, was what Tocqueville wished for his country. He was a liberal in the true sense of the word. But the entirely unromantic tone and spirit proved unavailing against either the passionate cult or the passionate rejection.

Not that Tocqueville's influence was not immediate and considerable. It can be noticed in Lanfrey and in Quinet, both of whom wrote on the Revolution in the fifties. Even Quinet, so closely allied to Michelet by a life-long friendship, his comrade in arms in 1843, gave expression to fundamental criticism. Disillusion, natural enough under Napoleon III, speaks very plainly. Freedom? It is not to be found in the Revolution. "Do not let us look for it behind us." [16] In his view nothing remains, either of the doctrine of Salvation through the revolutionary tradition alone or of the identification of that tradition with France and of France's sacred mission with respect to the world. But what had Quinet to offer? It was his opinion that Liberalism could not flourish where Protestantism had failed to break the dominance of the Catholic Church—was it likely that the French at that time of day should turn Protestant?

The truest disciple of Tocqueville was perhaps Albert Sorel, who belonged to the next generation. He analyzed the foreign policy of the Revolution without any respect for the slogans and the fine-sounding phrases with which it had disguised itself.[17] What he brought out more particularly, just as Tocqueville had done for the policy of internal reform, is that the Revolution, in that sphere too, had soon adopted the tradition of the Monarchy and worked with the *raison d'état* as if to outdo Richelieu and Mazarin. He was very far from being a prophet if revolutionary idealism, but working as he did with the conception of determinism his work had more of an apology than of a denunciation.

But in the meantime the feeling of malaise engendered by the Second Empire, but especially the disasters of 1870-71, the defeat by Germany and the uprising of the Paris proletariat in the *Commune,* had led others into ways of complete negation, not without purifying effect, but largely barren. I am thinking of Renan and of Taine.

Once the leaders of positivist thought and denounced as dangerous influences by Archbishop Dupanloup, they turned against the revolutionary legend which at first they had accepted as belonging to their general political philosophy. Already in 1859, however, Renan asked, with obvious concern, whether the everlasting crisis in which France was wasting her strength did not prove the revolutionary principle to which she had pledged herself to contain serious flaws.[18] But after the events of 1870-71 these doubts gave way to unmeasured detestation.[19] He now saw France suffering the fate of the Jews whose Messianism had lured them into ruin. He preached a return to the military virtues exemplified by victorious Prussia, to the principles of subordination and of birth; he still called himself a Liberal and wanted the intellectual *élite* to which he himself belonged to remain emancipated from the Church, but he sought the alliance of that Church to keep the lower classes in their proper place.

The great attack, however, now came from Taine.[20] It is only too true that one of the factors working on his mind was "fear." The fear of the *bourgeois;* fear, giving rise to hatred. Hatred runs through his book like a poison, hatred for the proletariat, the monster, which had shown its true face once more in 1871. But was not a reaction against the over-simple *"Le peuple est bon"* a healthy move? And, in addition to that, Taine's work will always remain significant on account of the onslaught on the phrases and conventions dear to the other side, as, for example: that the revolutionary leaders were in any way the representatives of "the nation"; that the Terror was an answer, and an effective one, to the invasions; or that France, when she "rushed to the assistance of the peoples," was moved by nothing but disinterested enthusiasm. Nevertheless, the bitter *bourgeois* prejudice of these Daniels come to judgment weakened the Liberalism which they imagined they were supporting.

The positions were taken. But the fight moved wildly beyond them. Deep calls unto deep. Absolutism engenders absolutism. The counter-revolutionary tradition has proved to be not less disastrous than the revolutionary tradition in France. Augustin Cochin, who replied to Aulard's attack on Taine's *History*,[21] Daniel Halévy who, a generation later, wrote his *Histoire d'une histoire*,[22] a brief *History of the Historiography of the Revolution*, still keep within certain bounds. I have learned much from both these little books. Cochin illuminates very strikingly the confusion resulting from the plentiful use of the hollow phrase "the people," in which Aulard, for all his enthusiasm for Danton, still indulges. Halévy, with searching criticism, pursues more particularly the Messianism to which the writers of the other side are given, their overstrung sentiment of France's mission to save the world, and, if the world won't listen, of her duty to save it in spite of itself.

I hinted above that the revolutionary tradition, when handled by a certain type of modern propagandists of absolutist politics, presents a danger even today, but, during the transition of the nineteenth into the twentieth century, the ideas of its critics were taken hold of by men of a no less objectionable stamp. It began with the detestable league against Justice entered into by army and church in the Dreyfus affair.[23]

Barrès and Maurras, and their spiritual progeny, the Bainvilles and the Gaxottes, placed the struggle against revolutionary phraseology in the service of the most uncompromising, and in its turn superpatriotic, reaction. In Péguy, whose mind was as much inclined to absolutism as Michelet's (and one might say the same of Maurras), a curious contamination between the two tendencies can be observed. For, although in reading him one has, every now and then, the impression that here is a spiritual son of Michelet's (equally proud of his being *peuple;* and, like Michelet, combining veneration of Joan of Arc with enthusiasm for the Revolution), he vies with Pierre Lasserre,[24] at that time still a full-blooded supporter of the *Action française,* in frenzy against the University, against Seignobos, and Lavisse, and Lanson. Lasserre's book is cruelly unfair; yet, more than do most writings from that side, it compels one to admit that its author had got hold of a reality, to wit, that at the

University, under the guise of objective scholarship, an un-historic, politically dangerous cult was celebrated—the cult of the Revolution.

The worst evil resulting to France is the unswerving vehemence with which the two sides drive to extremes their opposing views. I read the essay of Daniel Halévy which I mentioned with genuine admiration and felt myself largely in agreement. It was a shock when afterwards I came across a book of his, published in 1941, and found that at that time he was a fervent supporter of Marshall Pétain and the Vichy regime. But that is how things are in France. And here Michelet and his influence must be accounted partly responsible.

For that, too—no, I cannot forgive the historian his short-comings. Not the least of the five, I said, when I began by mentioning him side by side with four other great writers of history born within the same few years. And great he remains, great by the passion of his devotion, by his life-creating imagination, by his love—I won't rule out the word—but a love which suffered conspicuously from the defect with which the popular saying charges love: that it is blind. Blind, although at other times astonishingly clear-sighted. But, really, is not the one side by side with the other? The worst, and what I personally find very hard to bear, is that impotence of the judgment in the face of emo-tion and sentiment, that muddled mixture of the two, that sentimentality, these specious pleadings in order to talk wrong into right.

He remains great. Far be it from me to make it a con-dition that great historians, or other great persons, shall never have been in the wrong; or that we shall be allowed to enjoy their fare only so long as it does not contain harmful ingredients. In that case our intellectual diet would indeed lose flavor. I will take Michelet (and the others whom I mentioned as well; for they all present us with this problem, each in his own particular way), I will in the end take Michelet, and I must take him, as he was. But with my eyes open.

V TOYNBEE'S SYSTEM OF CIVILIZATIONS

1.

To survey history as a whole, to discover trends in its movement, to seek out its meaning—Professor Toynbee is not
the first to undertake the attempt. He joins the company of
St. Augustine and Bossuet, Condorcet, Hegel, Marx, Buckle,
Wells, Spengler; nor is he the least among them.

Six volumes now lie before us, three published in 1934,
three in 1939 (*A Study of History*, Oxford University Press);
and that another three will complete the work may well turn
out to be an illusion. What we have so far been given is an
imposing achievement. The reading, the learning, are almost
without precedent. Toynbee moves confidently in the histories of the old civilizations of Asia, the Chinese and the
Indian, of Egypt, of America as well. He is thoroughly
acquainted with Roman and especially with Hellenic history.
Classical literature he also knows, and when I say knows
I mean he is profoundly familiar with it and is able to draw
on it freely to evoke a deeper background for his arguments
and his reflections. And indeed for that purpose he has a
great deal more at his disposal, above all, the Bible. Toynbee
lives with the Bible, and its texts lie scattered thickly over
his pages. But from Goethe, too, from Shakespeare and from
Marvell, from Shelley, Blake, Meredith, he quotes liberally.
He knows how to use for his arguments modern ethnological,
sociological, philosophical, psychological concepts. At the
same time he himself writes in a splendid, full, and supple
style, which retains command over this wealth of quotations
by a constant flow of images and with an intense and un-

tiring vividness of argument. And, what is still more important, this rich and variegated abundance serves a majestic vision. He is sensitive to the colorful world of phenomena, to life; but above all he is profoundly aware of the unity of the architectural pattern into which he fits it all. A remarkable mind, unusual in our everyday world of historians.

In his first volume, that is, in 1934, Professor Toynbee announced thirteen parts to be treated successively in his work. Of these, with the appearance of Volume VI, five have been dealt with; the remaining eight will, he expects, demand less space. What a plan! What especially fills one with awe is to see the author from his first volume onward referring to later parts which are to appear after an unknown number of years and of volumes. As he proceeds, there are cross-references backwards and forwards. In his mind the immense structure evidently forms a unity.

His work is intended to be a comparative study of civilizations as a basis for general conceptions about history. Civilizations are for him the real units of history, not States, which he is wont to indicate contemptuously as "parochial," or nations, whose hypertrophied self-consciousness, under the description "nationalism," he detests.

In the six thousand years of which we have knowledge, he lists twenty-one such civilizations. He enumerates them, fixes their mutual relationship—in so far as they were not self-contained, which is a rare occurrence—and observes that they are all decayed or have perished, with the exception of Western civilization, that is, the Latin-Christian civilization, which he represents as having sprung from the Hellenic, in its Roman phase. About the prospects of this, our own civilization, that big swallow-all, Professor Toynbee leaves us in uncertainty; he has already repeatedly touched upon the problem, but only in his twelfth part will he treat it thoroughly. Meanwhile he believes it possible, even at this stage in his investigation, to state rules; sometimes he uses the word *laws;* on other occasions he speaks of *standard patterns of development,* of *tendencies* occurring in certain circumstances.

How do civilizations *come into being?* Not by climate, soil, or situation favoring the process; on the contrary, by overcoming obstacles: thus the shock is administered by which portions of mankind have passed out of the equilibrium of an existence without, or before, civilization, "from the integration of custom to the differentiation of civilization." The author proceeds to examine these adverse conditions at length under a number of headings: "hard countries," "blows," "pressures," "penalizations." "Challenge and response" is the formula in which he summarizes this movement in human history, a rhythm which makes itself felt over the entire field of human action.

Next comes the *growth* of civilizations. There is an increasing command over the environment, in the first place the physical environment; there follows a process of what Toynbee terms "etherealization," in which the physical environment loses its importance and action shifts from outside to within. Progressive differentiation is and remains typical of the process of growth. Here too we are shown in all stages the action of challenge and response. But the author thinks it possible to be more specific: the growth of a civilization takes place through creative persons or creative minorities, whose action is conditioned by a movement of "withdrawal and return." The larger half of Volume III is taken up by illustrations of this process.

In Volume IV the phenomenon of the *breakdown* of civilization is discussed. The vast majority of civilizations known to us have, after a longer or a shorter period, been overtaken by this fate. The duration of growth differs greatly. It is not possible therefore to speak of a normal stretch of time from rise to breakdown, and Toynbee expressly denies that the decline is inherent in an iron law of fate such as governs the physical world. The decay proceeds from the doomed civilization itself, but it must be understood as the result of a shortcoming not decreed by any law; it is a human failure; there is no necessity about it.

The volume is mainly devoted to an analysis of the causes of breakdown. Very emphatically he rejects the view that the downfall can be ascribed to forces from the outside. He finds the causes of breakdown in the retarding force which arises from the mechanical element in the "mimesis" of the majority—that very mimesis through which the creative personality or minority can obtain a hold on them; in the "intractability of institutions," giving them a paralyzing or vitiating effect (he mentions very dissimilar instances, such as those of democracy and industrialism acting upon "parochial" sovereignty, the effect of "parochialism" on churches, of religion on caste systems); in what he calls the "nemesis of creativity," the stiffening or exhaustion following upon creative action, as exemplified in the "idolization" of an achievement or of an attainment, of an institution, of a technique; under this heading he brings the intoxication of successful violence, militarism, triumph—not only in the military sense, though, for, of the historical examples with which he illustrates his argument, none is elaborated at greater length than that of the papacy, which, after having been carried by Gregory VII to the height of power, was ruined by the blind self-conceit of Boniface VIII. (This, by the way, is his method throughout: a large number of particular cases, from antiquity or from modern times, from alien and distant civilizations and from our own, is always adduced to prove the theses presented.)

Breakdown is followed by *disintegration*. This process is studied in Volumes V and VI. Nowhere else in human history has Professor Toynbee found so fixed a regularity. The "creative minority" changes into a "ruling minority," the masses into a "proletariat"—a word by which Toynbee, detaching it from its now usual narrower meaning, understands a group which has no longer any real share in the civilization of its society. This is the "schism," for him the first sign of a civilization's having broken down—a schism into three parts, for besides the ruling minority there emerges "an internal and an external proletariat," which latter clashes against the frontiers of the State or the Empire of the ruling minority. The course of history proceeds by the rhythm of challenge and response; but, whereas a growing society has always been able to find the right answer and is therefore faced each time by a different challenge, a broken-down society can no longer really succeed; it is at best able only to put off the evil day and finds itself after some time confronted again by the same problem. In the souls of men, too, the schism can be observed. Social disharmony creates a feeling of impotence, of sin; the standards of style and of behavior get out of order; ways out of the unbearable present are tried through "archaism"—back to the past, or through "futurism"—a leap into the future; or an attempt is made to detach oneself from society by means of philosophy or of religion. Toynbee here discerns the working of another form of challenge and response, "schism and palingenesis:" a higher religion is founded by the proletariat segregating itself from society, although the creation is only apparently due to the majority. The external proletariat reacts through the formation of "war bands" and "heroic poetry." In any case, this movement does not touch the now doomed society. Its history is governed by another variant of the rhythm, "rout and rally." The rout takes the form of ever more violent wars between states conscious only of their independence; this is "the Time of Troubles," another sign of a broken-down civilization. The rally materializes in a "universal state," the best creative work of which a ruling minority is capable. But the breathing-space of the *pax œcumenica* is of short duration; the universal state brings in its train only an "Indian summer." Soon it is troubled again—another rout, followed by another rally, until the rout, each time worse than before, can no longer be stayed and leads to dissolution, to ruin. This is not, of course, the end of all things. A new civilization has been preparing itself, chrysalis-like woven into the Universal Church, a creation of the Schismatic Proletariat, and this now unfolds itself.

As for the action of individuals in these circumstances, however brightly the creative spark may glow within them, it is doomed to failure. Professor Toynbee distinguishes four methods for Saviors of Society—for this is the shape in which the great man now appears. The sword, or power; the appeal to the past or to the future—these are the attempts to save society itself: Then there are the two by which man is to be saved *from* society: here we meet the founders of a philosophy who, however, work only for the ruling minority, and the founders of a religion, whose empire is not of this world.

Professor Toynbee believes he has observed in history that this decline of a civilization after its breakdown follows a much more regular course than the growing process, to which no inescapable limit has been set. He has been so much struck by the uniformity with which the various "institutions" and phases—Time of Troubles, Universal State, Indian Summer, Universal Church, External War Bands and Heroic Age—spring from the body of a disintegrating civilization that he has reduced it all to a table.[1] Stronger still is the similarity of the psychological condition of men in disintegrating civilizations. The general tendency can be characterized by the word "standardization:" the result of all this violent movement is therefore exactly the reverse of that in growing civilizations, where it leads to differentiation. And it develops, in rout and rally, sub-rout and sub-rally, down to catastrophe, in three and a half beats.

2.

Here we have the dry bones of a system to which the author gives flesh and life. The idea inspiring him is that of Christianity. It is true that Toynbee at times recalls Spengler, and his view of history is in fact not unrelated to the *Untergang des Abendlandes*. He expressly rejects Spengler's identification of civilizations with animate beings, which are born, are young, grow older, and die: when *they* break down it is by their own act alone. Similarly, he speaks emphatically against Spengler's connecting of civilization with race. But though he insists on the freedom of choice, on the spiritual factor unrelated to blood or to the perishable flesh, he too carries to great lengths the presentation of his civilizations as well-rounded units. Above all, during the centuries-long process of disintegration following upon breakdown, he sees them subjected to a regularity of decay hardly less rigid than Spengler's parallel with the biological process.

In any case, however much he may diverge from Spengler, his system is even more diametrically opposed to historical materialism. He may speak of laws, his mind may be stocked richly with scientific notions, from which his language is ever borrowing terms and images; in reality the sovereignty and the freedom of the spirit are his main concern, and his Bible texts are more than a mere decoration of his argument, for in them he finds his profoundest truths foreshadowed and confirmed. God become man in Christ is to him the veritable sense of history. Of the great constructors of systems, St. Augustine is most closely related to him in spirit, and Professor Toynbee himself, in the preface to his second series, written in that gloomy year 1939, brings respectful homage to the bishop who completed *De Civitate Dei* while the Vandals were besieging his episcopal town. Material advantage is nothing in Toynbee's view; it is obstacles which rouse the spirit to consciousness. Violence he detests, he is a searcher after "gentleness." He meets history with ethical appreciations. The spirit, the highly gifted individual, the small group, these are the sources of creative force. Power is an illusion if not a boomerang. As a civilization grows, it etherealizes. What exactly does he mean by this? He expresses it in morphological, in biological, in philosophical, and finally also in religious terms. No doubt all the rest for him is comprehended in the phrase belonging to the last-named category, according to which etherealization means: "a conversion of the soul from the World, the Flesh, and the Devil, to the Kingdom of Heaven." [2]

But of what use to us is his system? To what extent does it clear up our insight into history, help us in disentangling its mysteries, contain the solutions which, each in our own particularist or parochial sphere, we have so far looked for in vain? A system is presented to us as springing not from the author's mind or imagination or faith but from the careful course of empirical research—for this, we are told all through the voluminous work, is its method: we are the spectators of an expedition in quest of the norms, the regularity, the laws, of the historical process, and before our eyes the traveler gathers his data, from which, so he maintains, each time assuming our assent, his conclusions impose themselves. A system thus presented ought to render to all of us these very services. But to me at least it does not do so. Splendid as are the qualities of the work, fascinating as I have found it, grateful as I shall ever remain to the author for profound remarks, striking parallels, wide prospects, and other concomitant beauties—the system seems to me useless.

My most essential criticism, the criticism which embraces all others, is connected with this claim that the entire argument is based on empirical methods, in which it seems to me the author is deceiving himself. Had he really examined history with an open mind, merely formulating the theses supplied him by the observed facts, phenomena, developments, he could never have printed that imposing announcement of the division into so many parts in the opening pages of his first volume, nor could he in his references, as early as 1934, indicate what he was going to say about various chief problems in part nine or in part thirteen in 1950 or in 1960. Not that this is the ground of my doubting the genuineness of his empirical method; that is to be found in my examination of the six volumes themselves. The learning is miraculous, the wealth of examples and parallels overwhelming. But alas! the wealth of human history is ever so much greater. On looking closely, after having rubbed his dazzled eyes, the reader will see that Toynbee does not after all serve up more than a tiny spoonful out of the great cauldron. But no! this is a misleading comparison. When you fish in a cauldron you cannot select, and to select is exactly what Toynbee is doing all the time: he selects the instances which will support his theses, or he presents them in the way that suits him, and he does so with an assurance that hardly leaves room for the suspicion not only that one might quote innumerable others with which his theses would not bear company but especially that those cases he does mention can be explained or described in a different way so as to disagree no less completely with his theses.

3.

So to me the rules, the laws, the standard patterns laid down by the author after he has expounded examples and arguments at length and with never-failing gusto do not seem to possess more than a very limited validity. At times they are no more than truisms. In any case, all these formulas of regularity, these distinctions alleged to present themselves

in a fixed order, and these schemes of parallel development
do not seem to be of much practical use. Personally, at least,
I do not know how to work with them, let alone (and this,
strictly speaking, ought to be possible) to make them
operate unerringly.

Take even the striking formula of challenge and response.
This—or its application from the science of psychology to
history—must be pronounced a find. It hits off happily a
form of movement in human communal life. There is no
question here of a law, there is merely an observation of a
frequent occurrence. But it will deepen our insight when, in
coming across a case of this description, we are conscious
of its belonging to one of the usual categories of life. However, Professor Toynbee cannot stop there. He thinks he can
state as a general rule that the easier the environment the
less is the incitement to civilization man finds in it. And
indeed one can hardly imagine the Land of Cockaigne becoming the cradle of so active a thing as a civilization. But
now this lover of systems begins to ask whether perhaps the
stimulus to civilization becomes stronger as the environment
is more arduous. He therefore applies "our now well-tried
empirical method" [3] and in fact is able to adduce a number
of striking instances. Art and labor had to be expended in
making the valley of the Yellow River habitable, and even
then it remained exposed to devastating floods; in that of
the Yangtse, where the soil is equally fertile, no such terrible
inconvenience is to be feared; and yet Chinese civilization
came to birth not on the Yangtse but on the Yellow River.
There is also the well-known contrast between the fat land
of Bœotia and stony Attica—and everybody knows to which
of the two Hellenic civilization owes the greater debt. Twelve
more such cases are expounded, and, later, after having
shown by a number of instances how blows, pressures, and
penalizations evoke similar reactions, Toynbee writes that one
might incline to the view that "'the greater the challenge,
the greater the stimulus' is a law which knows no limits to
its validity. We have not stumbled upon any palpable limits
at any point in our empirical survey so far." [4]

To my ears this has a rather naive sound. But just as I
am on the point of arguing that fourteen cases of "hard

countries," and perhaps a few dozen of each of the other kinds of obstacles, do not really amount to very much and that it is hardly permissible to speak of empiricism unless the readers can test this so-called "law" by the hundreds or thousands of other cases they can dig up out of history— the author surprises me by announcing with an air of triumph that under the heading of "hard countries" he has not even mentioned two of the most striking examples, Venice and Holland. "What challenge could be more extreme than the challenge presented by the sea to Holland and to Venice? What more extreme, again, than the challenge presented by the Alps to Switzerland? And what responses could be more magnificent than those which Holland, Venice, and Switzerland have made? The three hardest pieces of country in Western Europe have stimulated their inhabitants to attain the highest level of social achievement that has yet been attained by any of the peoples of Western Christendom."

"Oh land wrung from the waves!" Every Dutchman has heard innumerable times his people's sterling qualities explained from their age-long struggle with the water. And nobody will contest that here is one factor in the building of our special type of society. He who has kept hold of the thread of Toynbee's argument, however, will reflect that our author is really engaged in a discussion of the *origins* of civilizations, and of civilizations in the sense in which he calls them pre-eminently "fields of historical study," those twenty-one civilizations of his. The civilization of Holland, however, is no more than a parochial part of the great Western civilization. Of the *originating* of a civilization in the hard conditions of the Dutch soil there can be therefore no question. I note in passing that Professor Toynbee repeatedly commits this error—an error against his own method. But even if we overlooked this and permitted him to adduce *national* instances, we would still have to remark that even within the Netherlands community the form peculiar to Holland (the Western seaboard province of which Toynbee is obviously thinking) cannot be regarded as original. If one looks a little more closely, one will observe that within the European and even within the Netherlands cultural area the rise of Holland was fairly late, and this no doubt as a result of these very conditions created by sea and rivers. If in the end it overcame these conditions, it was not without the assistance of the surrounding higher forms of civilization (even the Romans and their dyke-building had an important share in making the region habitable). But, even after that initial stage, can the continued struggle with the water be decisive in explaining the later prosperity and cultural fecundity of the country? Is it not indispensable to mention the excellence of the soil, once it had become possible to make use of it, and, above all, the situation which promoted the rise of shipping and of a large international commerce? Was the case of Holland then wholly due to hard conditions after all? Is it right to isolate that factor from among the multifarious complexity of reality and to suppress the favoring factors? And, we cannot refrain from wondering, what would remain of the majority of Professor Toynbee's few dozen cases if they were subjected to a similar examination?

It would carry me too far if I attempted this.[5] It is well known that demonstrating an error demands more time than committing it. Let me merely make the general remark that each of the instances discussed by Professor Toynbee of "blows" which had an invigorating effect is necessarily related by him in an extremely simplified form. But in the presentation of history simplification means, if not falsification, at least emphasis of one particular side of a matter which in reality had an infinite number of facets. Every historical fact—he himself mentions the objection he knows very well will be raised against his method—is unique and therefore incomparable with other historical facts. His reply is that the facts, in some respects unique, and in so far incomparable, belong in other respects to a class and are in so far comparable. There is truth in this—else no general ideas about history could ever be formulated—but isolating the comparable elements is ticklish work. In a certain sense, no historical fact is detachable from its circumstances, and in the elimination of the latter violence is done to history. There is hardly an incident or a phenomenon quoted by Toynbee to illustrate a particular thesis which does not give rise to qualifications in the reader's mind—if the reader is conversant with the matter! Most of the time our author is writing about Greek or Arabic or Hittite or Cretan or Japanese history, where we—where I at least—find it more difficult to check him.

Professor Toynbee himself, however, feels that he cannot raise the intensity of his "challenges" indefinitely. It is in fact very simple; one does not need to conduct a learned, allegedly empirical, historical investigation. If I give you a blow on the head it is very likely that your energy will be strongly roused and that you will strike back with vigor; but the blow may prove so powerful that you will not have anything to reply, that (to put it in the style of Toynbee) the source of your energy will dry up forever. In the world of communities it is likely enough that things will pass off in a similar fashion. So we see Professor Toynbee soon meditating "an over-riding law to the effect that 'the most stimulating challenge is to be found in a mean between a deficiency of severity and an excess of it,'" after which we get another 130 pages or more—under a chapter heading "The Golden Mean"—with instances of succumbing under pressure all too heavy or blows all too hard. One cannot refrain from the liveliest admiration for the rich variety of his knowledge, for the ease with which, after having sounded the causes of the downfall of Irish civilization, he does the same for the Icelandic, only to proceed with unflagging vivacity to Arabic history; until at long last he ventures to conclude: "There are challenges of a salutary severity that stimulate the human subject of the ordeal to a creative response; but there are also challenges of an overwhelming severity to which the human subject succumbs." My observation with regard to the blow on your head has a less impressive sound, but does it not convey precisely the same meaning? Yet our author is not yet satisfied. He repeats the phrase coined at the outset of his argument, "a mean between a deficiency of severity and an excess of it," and this time introduces it with the magic words: "In scientific terminology . . ."

So here we have a "law," scientifically established, or at least scientifically formulated. But what next? When we try to apply it, we shall first of all discover that in every given historical situation it refers to only one element, one out of many, one which, when we are concerned with historical presentation, cannot be abstracted from the others. Moreover, is it not essential to define what is too much and what too little, to stipulate where the golden mean lies? As to that, the "law" has nothing to say. That has to be defined anew each time by observation.

4.

Before Professor Toynbee sets out in his third volume to treat the problem of the growth of civilizations, he disposes of the arrested civilizations known to history. These constitute a heterogeneous group: the Polynesians, the Eskimos, the Nomads, the Osmanlis, and the Spartans. The general explanation is that in these cases the challenge was so serious —a challenge of nature in the first three, of the need of keeping large subject populations under control in the latter two—as to impose a system of defense which through its demands or its artificialty used up all energies; an equilibrium was thus brought about, from which there was no getting away. One is struck by the immense ingenuity. The circumstances are in each of the five cases related not only vividly, but with a subtle sense of distinctions. Yet all this hardly makes it convincing. The heterogeneousness alone— Eskimos and Turks!—raises doubts in the mind. As far as the Eskimos are concerned, the explanation adduced is certainly plausible. But in the case of the Turks? That slave court, that peculiar method of fighting and governing by means of a special class, and slaves at that! and kidnapped boys of alien origin!—here is indeed a system we can well imagine did not allow of cultural development. But why should it arrest the civilization indefinitely? Why was it not possible to get away from it or, when it was got rid of, why did not something better take its place? In the case of the Eskimos, struggling with the unchanging conditions of the Polar sea, this immutability is not surprising, but in the other case it is, and so a formula intended to cover both cases does not help much. Let us take another example of our own.

Take the German Order in the Baltic lands. Here too we have a most artificial institution, built for fighting and for ruling. Yet here the populations were Christianized and Germanized and, with the dissolution of the Knightly Order, merged into the great German civilization.

The usefulness of these general explanations, of this tabularizing, is not very apparent. Within the subdivisions the similarity is not only vague but at times forced, and we feel that it is just the differences which matter.

Extremely dubious also, it seems to me, is the withdrawal-and-return theory with which the remainder of this volume is taken up. This is the movement by which personalities and minorities prepare themselves for their creative task in a growing civilization. Even at first glance we wonder what the author will be able to make of the twenty-six or twenty-seven personalities he has selected as examples—men of all times and of all lands, princes and statesmen, saints, historians. What, we ask, can be the connecting element between Peter the Great and Emile Ollivier (and was the latter a great personality?), between St. Paul, Machiavelli, the Buddha, and Dante? A more careful reading only strengthens the doubt. This chapter is hardly an example of valid method. In some cases Professor Toynbee gives complete life histories, full of particulars which have nothing to do with the point at issue; in others he is very brief. The difference in treatment seems wholly arbitrary. But even the point all his heroes have in common, that they withdrew and after a while returned, is governed by arbitrariness. The withdrawal of one was compulsory, of another voluntary. Peter the Great set out to travel in order to learn and coming back he put into practice his newly acquired knowledge and ruled; Emile Ollivier had to expatriate himself after 1870, remained outside politics for the rest of his life, never was able to free his mind from the tragedy of the Second Empire, and, in his old age, having long before returned to France, wrote a book in many volumes about it. Professor Toynbee also mentions Kant and in a few lines describes the philosopher living quietly at Koenigsberg while his thought radiated over the world. But how precisely did he "return"? In this way one can include anybody to whom one takes a fancy. Not that it would not be easy to add more typical cases to the list: there is William the Silent (1567-72), Napoleon (Egypt), Luther (the Wartburg), Guido Gezelle, the Flemish poet (the exile at Bruges and at Courtrai)—but why continue the search? It cannot on the other hand be maintained—nor does Toynbee try to do so—that in all great lives there occurs such a period of interruption. I should not know how to include either Raphael or Vondel in the list, nor most of the great princely rulers: neither Louis XIV nor Saint Louis, neither Philip the Good nor Charles V. Is it that in these cases the rule is suspended by the peculiar conditions attached to hereditary leadership? But De Witt, too, never paused to take breath, and when he withdrew it was not to return. Nor did Shakespeare: the one was murdered, the other spent his last years peacefully as a landed gentleman. What law can we discern in all this?

Things do not improve when minorities are discussed. Professor Toynbee first mentions some penalized minorities, to observe how they acquire particular strength in their retirement and arm for their return to play important parts. Thus for instance the English Nonconformists, who after having their share in the commotions of the middle of the seventeenth century withdrew—rather, were excluded from everything!—withdrew into the world of business to return omnipotent and to become the authors of the Industrial Revolution. No doubt, there is something in this. In Dutch history, too, the Baptists toward the close of the Republican period, during which they had been kept out of the government, were among the greatest capitalists. One is at first inclined to point to the Dutch Catholics as forming an objection to the theory. Here you have a group who had also been compelled to throw themselves into nonpolitical activities, but who even after their emancipation were not able to play more than a fairly modest part in economic life. One reflects, however, that the ever-growing power of the Catholics in present-day political life in Holland might well be connected with their exclusion in the past, for that is what taught them to prize their cohesion and organization. But other doubts are already assailing the reader's mind. Is not that peculiarity inherent in the spirit of Catholicism? Of modern Catholicism at least, and one thinks of Trent: is not this militance of modern Catholicism the response to the challenge of the Reformation? The Toynbee terminology comes to mind very readily. But it never gets one very far. The differences will not be denied. Here comparable developments go faster, there more slowly, here they are stronger, there weaker, or they take this direction and elsewhere another direction. And the exceptions! Professor Toynbee mentions the English Nonconformists. Why does he not mention the English Catholics? These, when they "returned" after their long exclusion, were certainly not "omnipotent"!

But Professor Toynbee now attempts to bring certain decisive developments in Hellenic and in Western history within the scope of this same motive. In his view—and he is not the first to make the observation—there is a similarity between Athens, which made herself "the education of Hellas," and Italy, which filled the same part with respect to Western Europe. When he pictures Athens withdrawing from the eighth to the sixth century B.C., and Italy from the thirteenth to the fifteenth century, and argues that in each case this minority in its retirement devoted the energies released by relinquishing its share in foreign entanglements to the task of solving the problem facing the whole of its society (that is, of Hellas and of Western Europe respectively) by an original solution of its own, the construction strikes me as hopelessly far-fetched. And indeed the whole of Western European history (to confine myself to that) has to be bent askew so as to allow the thesis to be carried through. The thesis is, that in Italy there was developed the modern State, albeit on the city plan only, which became for Western Europe the model in its struggle to free itself from feudalism. True, there were city-states on this side of the Alps, in Germany, in Flanders: as early as the middle of the fourteenth century "the feudal darkness of the Western world was thickly sown with constellations of city-states." [6] In fact, Toynbee here sees the same motive in action: "a creative minority extricated itself from the general political life of the Western Society by building city walls and learning to live a new life of its own behind them." Italy, however, was a decisive factor, and this we are to view as the return of Italy. Is it not evident that a development proper to Western Europe as a whole was at least as important, and that Italy, moreover, did not so much return as was sought out in her seclusion?

But the train of thought is continued, this time with Holland, Switzerland, and more particularly England as the protagonists. In the new chapter of European history opened in the sixteenth century the problem was: how can the entire Western world take over, albeit on the scale of kingdom-states, this new Italian and Flemish way of life? "This challenge was taken up in Switzerland, Holland, and England, and it received eventually an English answer." [7] We are here given, it must be said, a very peculiar and personal and certainly most incomplete view of European history in the post-mediaeval period, and that it should be necessary to begin this way in order to bring in the withdrawal-and-return motive hardly inspires confidence. And how is it introduced into the picture this time? Holland behind her dykes, Switzerland in her Alps, England behind the Channel, were able to stand aside and thus to prepare their contribution. In the cases of Holland and of Switzerland, our author continues, the safeguards proved in the long run ineffective. (I state in passing, without laboring the point, that in the case of Holland at least, at a time when Amsterdam was the great international banking center, Dutch merchant fleets covered all the seas, Dutch diplomacy was active, and Dutch intellectual life giving and taking incessantly, there was not the slightest question of seclusion; whereas neither of the two countries can justly be described as a very striking instance of a free state which had at the same time solved the problem of modern state organization!)

But now we are left with England alone. That the peculiar English form of government, which in the nineteenth century was to exercise so wide an influence, owes something of its development to England's relatively safe situation, is a current and indeed altogether acceptable view. But there are of course a good many more factors to be taken into account, and the picture of a creative minority in quiet and retirement devoting itself to that problem strikes one as somewhat overdrawn. Professor Toynbee, however, is still not satisfied and starts systematizing in a really dizzy fashion.

It is true, he argues, that it was against their own inclination that the English were released from their entanglement in the affairs of the continent. (He places the event between 1429, when the death of Henry V and the intervention of Jeanne d'Arc brought about a turn in the Hundred Years' War,[8] and 1558, when Queen Mary lost Calais.) But subsequently they came to realize that this had been "a blessing in disguise" and fought as hard to save themselves from new entanglements as they had once done to keep them: see their resistance to the successive attempts of Philip II, of Louis XIV, and of Napoleon to fit England into a continental European empire. (An untenable simplification of at least Louis XIV's intentions; but let this pass.)

Might it not be said with equal justice that the English in that second series of wars, besides being moved by the most natural of all instincts, that of self-preservation, were still striving, though in another way, after power outside their island? Were not the true isolationists in England—and there were such, in the sixteenth, in the seventeenth, and in the eighteenth centuries—intent on keeping out of those wars? And was the loss of positions on the continent really recognized as a blessing in disguise? Yes, in so far as the view gradually gained ground that dominion over part of France was an illusion. Yet Cromwell got hold of Dunkirk, and a generation or more afterwards England seized Gibraltar, which she was never to let go. Malta, moreover, may not be situated on the continent, but the clue to England's possession of that island is hardly to be found in her anxiety to live in seclusion.

Professor Toynbee goes on imperturbably building up his system. These periods of relative isolation (which in England, according to him, began with the loss of Calais, with the accession of Elizabeth) generally fall into two phases. "The first, or originative phase is a youthful age of poetry and romance and emotional upheaval and intellectual ferment; the second, or constructive phase is a comparatively sedate and 'grown-up' age of prose and matter-of-fact and common sense and systematization." For Italy he exemplifies the two phases in Dante and Boccaccio respectively (although Dante was certainly not lacking in systematizing capacity and his high poetry is as far removed from youthful emotion or romanticism as from common sense and matter-of-factness!). In Athens he discerns the dividing point in the disaster of 404 B.C. (when, it seems to me, the time to speak of isolation was long past). In England, finally, the first phase runs from Elizabeth down to the Restoration of 1660, and the second from then on to about 1860 or 1870.

One imagines that the characterization of the two phases was primarily inspired by English cultural history (not that Shakespeare or Milton, the latter expressly mentioned by Professor Toynbee, can really be lumped together in the description "youthful romanticism"). The constructive phase of England's creative isolation, at any rate, to let Professor Toynbee put it in his own words, has

. . . to its credit such solid achievements as the foundation of the Royal Society and "the Glorious Revolution of 1688" and the peopling of the North American Continent with an English-speaking population and *The History of the Decline and Fall of the Roman Empire* and the invention of the steam-engine and the passage of the Reform Bill of 1832 and the establishment of the Indian Empire and the *Origin of Species* [which was published in 1859] and the invention of the British Commonwealth of self-governing nations [an invention which dates from the creation of the Dominion of Canada in 1867].

What is one to say of such a passage in this brilliant work? Does England really owe all these heterogeneous achievements to her isolation? England, Professor Toynbee writes, was dragged back into continental European entanglements by the war of 1914. I have already remarked that the wars against Philip II, against Louis XIV, against Napoleon, were just as much evidence of England's uninterrupted community with the rest of Europe. The whole of this suggestion of an isolation lasting from 1558 to 1914, or at least to 1870, is completely untenable. The Glorious Revolution is indeed a fine example of the great deeds which

England was able to achieve through her seclusion! Have William the Third and his Dutchmen been forgotten? Professor Toynbee seems here to have strayed into an extreme insularity such as Macaulay could not have improved upon: one would have thought this had become impossible since Ranke. And now take cultural life. How deeply imbued with Italian influences were Shakespeare and his contemporaries! How strong were the spiritual ties connecting the Puritans, and Milton, with the Reformed confessions on the continent! Was not French influence a dominating force after 1660? and, inversely, how directly did English influence make itself felt on French, and, generally speaking, on Continental thought in the eighteenth century! Toynbee mentions Gibbon; but can Gibbon be imagined without French "philosophy"? Read Hammond's *Gladstone and the Irish Nation,* and you will see how intensely a great mid-nineteenth-century Englishman took part in European intellectual life.

One cannot help asking, furthermore, whether it really was only in the second half of the nineteenth century, or even in the twentieth, on England's "return," to use Professor Toynbee's expression, that England's contribution to Western civilization, allegedly prepared in isolation during that lengthy period, reached the rest of the world. I have hinted already how very far from true this was for the eighteenth century; but no less great and no less fruitful was the "Anglomania" in the first half of the nineteenth century. Yet another question presents itself, whether other nations, which had not withdrawn themselves, which throughout that period were in the thick of European entanglements (to follow for a moment this unacceptable thesis of England's aloofness), whether in particular France, did not by any chance make a creative contribution? The question is absurd. But all these pages of Toynbee's are fantastic.

5.

We come to Volume IV, which deals with the breakdown of civilizations. Professor Toynbee begins with an attempt to prove that these breakdowns are not in general brought about by external forces. On looking closely we soon discover that the author does some violence to the facts to make them fit this thesis. We have only to look at his list of sixteen defunct civilizations (sixteen out of the twenty-one, to which are to be added five arrested and four abortive ones) to think at once that it will be difficult in several cases to escape the verdict: death by external violence.

Leaving aside the old Arabic and Hittite civilizations (about which more in a moment), this suspicion arises in connection with the old American civilizations, that of the Incas and the Mexican and Yucatan (or Mayan); also with the Turkish (not the only, but certainly the most striking, case of an arrested civilization long ago broken down and now decayed) and with the Scandinavian and old Irish (broken down before birth and now dead). Professor Toynbee admits that the ruin of the Inca civilization is often quoted as an example of ruin through external interference. He proceeds to argue, however, that the destruction by the Spaniards of the *empire* of the Incas is not the same thing as the destruction of their civilization. That empire was nothing but a "universal state," that is, according to his own system a late incident in the disintegration of a civilization which had already broken down. After that "Indian summer" winter *had* to come. With the additional help of an interpretation of the oracle of archaeological finds Professor Toynbee concludes that the civilization of the Andes had received its self-inflicted death blow before ever the Spaniards came.[9]

As far as the two Central American civilizations are concerned, these found themselves in an earlier stage of the fatal downward course; they were still in their Time of Troubles, the universal state was only just coming into sight; but here too the irresistible process of decay through internal shortcomings of the civilizations themselves had already started.

It will be observed that Professor Toynbee introduces his own theoretical construction into his argument as an established datum. This method is open to grave objection. It will not carry along the reader who has preserved his independence toward the system.

But even greater are the liberties the author allows himself with respect to the arrested and the abortive civilizations. What does it matter, he says of the first, whether it was the thrust of an alien hand that caused their final collapse? Had they been left to themselves, their ruin simply as a result of exhaustion would have been merely a question of time. That is, if one assumes their arrested equilibrium to be in fact so fatally unshakable as our author has been trying to make out! As for the latter category, he says:

It is true that in each of the four cases the intractable challenge has been delivered by some human neighbour or rival or adversary. Yet this does not entitle us to pronounce that the abortive civilizations have been deprived of their prospect of life by an external act of violence. The truth may be that these miscarriages have been due to some inherent weakness in the embryos, and that the pre-natal shocks by which the miscarriages have been precipitated have simply brought this inherent weakness out.[10]

After such subtle and speculative reasoning the author thinks himself justified in leaving the cases of arrested and abortive civilizations aside and concludes (concerning the American three as well, he now no longer admits any doubt) that of the ruined civilizations only the Hittite and the Arabic appear to have met their end as the result of alien interference; and even here in the end he expresses some doubt.

I have retraced this argument, not only because it is a daring piece of special pleading, well fitted to put us on our guard against the entire work, but also in order to introduce the question: why is it that Toynbee is so anxious that civilizations should come to an end not by external violence but as the result of their own shortcomings? Obviously because the whole of his outlook postulates this view. The idea that the spirit should succumb to violence is distasteful, it is to him a lowering of the grandiose drama of history.

Of course the scene of history lies thickly sown with cases of brute force triumphing over right, over delicate humanity, over innocence. In Professor Toynbee's six tomes one can indeed find a good many such discussed, especially when in Volume III he wants to illustrate the possibility of a "challenge" being too strong. But these cases are only of nations or states, subsections of the large units which in his view are really the exponents of civilization. Although detesting the militarist, the conqueror, whose activities he considers to be one of the factors helping to wreck a civilization (that is, the conqueror's own; a little chapter of Volume IV is entitled "The Suicidalness of Militarism"), and letting no opportunity pass to bring out the transitory nature of military success and the retribution by which it is closely followed—he sacrifices national communities with equanimity.[11]

After this the fourth volume, as might be expected, deals with the internal causes leading to the breakdown of civilizations. The subdivision of these is extremely ingenious. No doubt the results of the ingenuity at times seem far-fetched, but here as everywhere one comes across very striking ideas and extraordinarily fine pages. A most interesting view of the nineteenth century, for instance, is given in a discussion of the illusions and miscalculations of Cobden, who was firmly convinced that democracy and industrialism would secure peace.[12]

One of the weaknesses through which a civilization can go to its ruin is, according to Toynbee, "the nemesis of creativity," the loss of flexibility, the exhaustion, the self-conceit, frequently following upon a creative effort. No doubt this is a fruitful idea, yet again it cannot bear the far-stretched systematization to which the author subjects it. I could demonstrate this by a number of points. I confine myself to one.

In the same section where he deals with cases of extreme nationalism—that is, in his view, the allowing oneself to be hypnotized by the achievements of a previous generation—Toynbee devotes a lengthy argument to the history of the Italian *risorgimento* in order to bring out the fact that this resuscitation of a people which had in past centuries played so glorious a part was in reality confined to a region which had no share in that earlier achievement. Venice especially, he wants to show, was still too much under the spell of the memory of its glorious past to co-operate effectively in the movement which was to make Italy free and one; but the same is true, according to him, of all the ancient city-states which had in the old days stood at the head of Western civilization, of Milan, Florence, Genoa. So it came about that a new country took the lead, Savoy-Piedmont, which had once as an old feudal territory let itself be passed by the astonishing social and cultural development of these now nerveless towns, but which for that very reason was at this juncture able to show such freshness and such energy.

This belongs to a class of explanations often loosely offered by historians: explanations which, when gone into a little more carefully, take so much for granted about the secret workings of the communal life of mankind as to stand in need themselves of elaborate elucidation. In the ordinary course, however, they are not gone into carefully, nor as a rule has the author himself so much as thought of the problems he fails to discuss. Of the same sort is the favorite remark, when an obscure phenomenon presents itself, that it springs from the *nature* of a particular people, this being itself an entity incapable of exact observation or definition. This kind of explanation merely begs the question. Now the interesting thing about Toynbee is that not only has he carefully systematized a number of such theories, but he has also attempted with subtle historical arguments to demonstrate them. We have, however, already come across several instances of the attempt collapsing completely at the touch of independent criticism.

It makes admirable reading, this paragraph.[13] One follows the author with the excitement with which one watches an incredibly supple and audacious tightrope walker. One feels inclined to exclaim: *"C'est magnifique, mais ce n'est pas l'histoire."* The grace and daring with which the facts are handled are astonishing, the capacity of coining striking phrases is uncommon. What a knowledge, what a wealth of general cultural backgrounds, how splendid the characterization of the unusual, non-Italian-Renaissance, feudal society of Savoy-Piedmont! But at the same time, what the author leaves unsaid is at least as important and essential as what he mentions, and by its means one can reveal his thesis in its incompleteness, arbitrariness, and untenability.

I cannot touch upon all the points I might query. There is a fascinating description of the deadness which had overtaken eighteenth-century Venice; but the explanation that all energy had been used up in the senseless attempt, inspired by faith in tradition, to keep alive a Mediterranean empire against the Turkish attacks, and that the lightheartedness and frivolity of Venetian life were nothing but the psychological counterpart to that grim effort, seems to me one-sided. Was there really a large percentage of the Venetian aristocracy that bled in the Turkish wars? Should not the author have said at least a word about the concentration of all power in the hands of a tiny group from amongst that aristocracy? For it can hardly be doubted that this left a mark on the minds of the rest, just as the weaknesses of the eighteenth-century French nobility are in part to be explained by the setting up of an administrative apparatus in which they had no share. And when Professor Toynbee contrasts the bright colors of an English flag flying from a ship in a Canaletto painting with the muffled tones of the setting formed by the harbor of Venice, should he not have recalled the discovery of the sea route round the Cape of Good Hope and of America, and the displacement of trade from the Mediterranean to the Atlantic Ocean?

How is it—to confine myself to the chief point in the writer's argument—that it was precisely Savoy-Piedmont which proved itself capable of that great political feat, the unification of Italy? He examines only the events of 1848-49. In that crisis Milan and Venice, both of which rose against Austrian rule, exhibited the greatest heroism; Savoy-Piedmont's military performance against Austria was on the contrary far from distinguished. "Yet this Piedmontese disgrace proved more fruitful for Italy than those Milanese and Venetian glories;" ten years and seventeen years later the work of liberation was performed (in conjunction with the French, it is true) by the Piedmontese army, while Milan and Venice remained passive.

The explanation is that the Venetian and Milanese exploits in 1848 were virtually foredoomed to failure, however magnificent they might be in their intrinsic worth, because the spiritual driving force behind them was still that idolization of their own dead selves, as historic mediaeval city-states, which had been defeating the finest efforts of Italian heroism and Italian statesmanship since the time of Machiavelli.[14]

"The explanation is . . ." Apart from other considerations, so simplistic a view arouses in the historian an instinctive distrust, which is not lessened by the apodictical delivery. Professor Toynbee continues:

The nineteenth-century Venetians who responded to Manin's call in 1848 were fighting for Venice alone and not for Piedmont or Milan or even for Padua; they were striving to restore an obsolete Venetian Republic and not to create a new Italian national state; and for this reason their enterprise was a forlorn hope, whereas Piedmont could survive a more shameful disaster because the nineteenth-century Piedmontese were not fast bound in the misery and iron of an unforgettable historic past.

It should be noticed that our author no longer makes any mention of Milan. And, indeed, in Milan the rebels had formed a "provisional government" which set itself no other object but fusion with Piedmont on the one side and with Venice on the other. In Milan at least it appears to have been possible to get away from the fascination of the historic past, and the freedom of spiritual movement which Toynbee observes in the new land of Piedmont was not so unique as he wants to make us believe.

But when even the Venice revolt is examined more closely, it will appear how lacking in the complexity of life is his presentation of the facts. Manin had proclaimed the Republic at Venice; but he had done so before the rising of Milan and the advance of Carlo Alberto of Savoy-Piedmont were known there; the Piedmontese consul himself had given his approval to the decision.[15] Nor did Manin ever conceal his opinion that the unity of Italy must be the final goal. It is true that he resisted the pressure which was soon put on him from Piedmont, and even from Milan, to let Venice be merged into the Piedmontese kingdom without delay. It goes without saying that he was afterwards severely blamed for this by Italian historians who, after the bad habit of historians, used the event as the measure of all things; but if one looks more closely at the circumstances of the moment, one begins to understand his attitude. One sees that it is incorrect to put forward a historically conditioned particularism as his only motive, or even to assert that he could not do otherwise because the Venetians would not have followed him. The Italian idea lived in Venice. But at the same time there were feelings of suspicion with respect to Carlo Alberto, feelings which were shared by Manin himself: his ability to live up to his promises was doubted. Especially that proud slogan, *L'Italia farà da se,* behind which in reality there lurked the King's fear of the French revolution, was objected to in Venice. Manin and his friends realized that nothing could be achieved without France. And as a matter of fact in the end the great aim was only achieved with France.

Could not the question of why Italy's liberation failed to emerge from the heroic initiative of Milan and Venice in 1848 be answered thus: *The explanation is* that feudal Piedmont under a reactionary King was striving not so much after Italian unity as after the expansion of Piedmont, and in particular that this king rejected the help of revolutionary France? The statement would surely be no more one-sided than the solution presented to us by Professor Toynbee, his imagination afire with that striking idea of "the nemesis of creativity." For, although our author of course imagines he is here also proceeding empirically, of true empiricism, of an objective observation of the facts whatever the conclusions they may suggest, this passage again is hardly an example.

There are still so many data which have been neglected! Savoy-Piedmont was able to play its great part, even after the failure of 1848-49, because it was independent and moreover was by its situation in a better position than any other Italian region to co-operate with France. These simple facts might at least have been mentioned before the Middle Ages were called in to explain the failures or the passivity of Milan and Venice.

On the other hand Piedmont was certainly not the strongest spiritual radiating center of the new Italian sentiment. Alfieri, who dreamed of Italy in an earlier generation, was a Piedmontese, but *dépiémontisé.*[16] Massimo d'Azeglio, one of the great intellectual as well as political leaders of the *risorgimento,* also came from Piedmont, but he was married in

Milan, where he lived for many years; without the Milanese atmosphere he would not have been the man he became. Silvio Pellico and Leopardi were Milanese. Garibaldi was a native of Nice, which belonged to Piedmont, but it was as a sailor and outside Piedmont that he became acquainted with the Italian idea. Mazzini came from Genoa, and Genoa was one of those towns with a great past, which had in fact offered embittered opposition to annexation to Piedmont in 1815. Mazzini, the prophet of the unitary Italian Republic, had his following scattered over the whole central and northern portions of the peninsula, but in monarchical Piedmont it was perhaps weakest. The older *Carbonari* were merged with his new organization *La giovine Italia:* those pioneers of Italian unity again had certainly not been most numerous in Piedmont. But all this is passed by in silence by Professor Toynbee, and this is, it must be admitted, the most convenient method when one wants to subject history to a system.

I shall make one more remark—out of many which present themselves—and this because I can here invoke Toynbee against himself. In those years 1848-49 another sensational event happened—the rising in Rome, the proclamation of the Republic there, and the resistance led by Mazzini and Garibaldi against the French army besieging the town. In Volume II Professor Toynbee assures us that Rome's heroic perseverance, even though it ended in defeat, made the profoundest impression on the national imagination.[17] He mentions the incident there merely to argue that it supplied the decisive consideration for the choice, later on, of Rome as capital of the new Italy—in itself a disputable view. Was it not the fact that Rome, by her ancient glory, appeared as predestined for that position which had inspired Mazzini and Garibaldi to plant their banner there? But, however that may be, in his second volume Professor Toynbee gives to Rome's behavior in the crisis of 1848-49 an emphasis which makes it all the more remarkable that, two volumes later, intent only on bringing out the providential part played by the new land of Piedmont, he has not a word to say about it.

6.

Volumes V and VI are concerned with the process of disintegration, that fatal downgrade course to which a broken-down civilization is irretrievably committed. I shall not continue subjecting passages to detailed criticism: the examples already tested will have to suffice. I shall rather try to survey the system itself and discuss one or two chief points.

Professor Toynbee himself furnishes his readers with announcements and repetitions or summaries, and it is thus easy to survey the system. It all appears to fit together closely and precisely. But when we try to apply it to the multiform world of reality we fare like little Alice at the croquet game in Wonderland. The mallet turns out to be a flamingo, which twists its long neck the moment we want to strike; the ball is a hedgehog, which unrolls itself and runs off; while for hoops there are doubled-up soldiers, who rise to their full height and get together for a chat just when you are aiming in their direction.

Professor Toynbee writes in his sixth volume:[18]

In a growing civilization, as we have seen, a creative personality comes into action by taking the lead in making a successful response to some challenge . . . In a disintegrating civilization Challenge and Response is still the mould of action in which the mystery of creation takes place, but . . . [while] in a growing civilization the creator is called upon to play the part of a conqueror who replies to a challenge with a victorious response, in a disintegrating society the same creator is called upon to play the part of a saviour who comes to the rescue of a society that has failed to respond because the challenge has worsted a minority that has ceased to be creative and has sunk to be merely dominant . . . A growing society is taking the offensive . . . [and wants its leader] to capture fresh ground for its advance, whereas a disintegrating society is trying to stand on the defensive and therefore requires its leader to play the more thankless part of a saviour who will show it how to hold its ground in a rearguard action.

"*As we have seen.*" Is that indeed what we have seen, and are we in the two latest volumes seeing the rest? As for me, no! Undoubtedly, I have been shown leading or creative personalities in one and the other function; I had indeed seen the like before. But how do I know that the difference is caused by the triumphant creator acting in a growing society and the hopelessly struggling one in a society in disintegration? I have not been convinced of the essential difference between the phases of civilization, and still less have I been convinced that a period of growth is irretrievably cut off by a breakdown, so that the stricken civilization, with its "members," the creative minds included, must from then on have got on to the fatal slope which will carry it to its ruin in three beats and a half and in an unknown number of centuries—irretrievably; with this qualification, however, which can hardly be considered a mercy, that it may stay somewhere suspended between life and death in a state of petrifaction.[19] To me, even after the fourth volume of Professor Toynbee, this great event of the breakdown, which is supposed to lead to the fatal process, remains a mystery; and after his third and fifth and sixth volumes the conceptions of growth and of disintegration retain so much that is fluid, vague and uncertain that I find it difficult to use them for the subdivision of history, especially in conformity with his rigid system. I can sympathize more with the modesty of Huizinga, who, in comparing successive centuries of civilization, came to the conclusion that the conception of "a rising civilization" will escape us as soon as we attempt to apply it: "the height of a civilization cannot be measured." I know very well that these are no more than very simple remarks occurring in an unpretentious essay[20] and that they are very far from exhausting the subject. But when placed beside Toynbee's omniscient positiveness, they seem to me instinct with profound wisdom.

It is noteworthy that our author himself, after having written two heavy volumes about disintegration, and after having in every imaginable way subdivided and analyzed and even tabulated [21] the phenomenon, cannot tell us whether we are experiencing it at this moment. In order to explain that uncertainty he regales us with a wealth of metaphor,

yet it remains curious. At first glance one should think that
the two phases of growth and of disintegration, as sketched
by the author himself, present a contrast like that between
day and night, which cannot remain hidden from the observation of contemporaries. The creative personalities in a
growing society triumphantly find the right answer, and the
new challenge to which this gives rise with its once more
triumphant response can be compared to the taking possession of fresh territory. There you have growth; whereas,
on the other hand, in a disintegrating society the leaders are
doomed to a veritable Sisyphean labor. At best a respite
can be gained, but after every apparent victory there follows
a worse setback. And we, who may have been living in that
wretched condition for the last four centuries (for that is
the possibility suggested by Professor Toynbee)—should
we not know it?

There is an indication here that the author is less rigid
and doctrinaire in the application than in the exposition of
his system. The instances in which this appears can be
brought up against him to show him in contradiction with
himself. They can also be placed to his credit. In any case,
the fact remains that innumerable remarks and illustrations
scattered over the volumes do not agree too well with the
strict lines of the system, but at the same time contribute
not a little to the color and the fascination of the work.
Especially when our Western civilization is under discussion can this be observed.

He seeks, for instance, to establish the existence in our
Western society of a proletariat (in his sense of the word)
and of a dominating minority, and of other equivalents of
phenomena belonging typically to the disintegration process in civilizations which he indicates have run their course
to final dissolution. There are, to mention only a few points,
the loss of style, the aping of alien and barbaric forms of
art, the tendencies to archaism and futurism. I have no room
to follow his disquisitions on all these points. I will only say
that they are frequently to the highest degree stimulating,
but that as frequently they leave one completely unsatisfied.
Wide prospects seem to be opened by his discussion of the
danger threatening our civilization from the sudden assimila-

tion of large areas with other cultural traditions, with all the consequences of "standardization" and leveling.[22] On the other hand, the discussion of the twin tendencies of archaism and futurism strikes me as disappointing, meager, and so incomplete as to become lopsided. To bring National Socialism and Fascism under the heading "archaism" is to belittle the historical significance of these evil doctrines overmuch. And is it possible to overlook the fact that both archaism and futurism can be considered disintegration phenomena only when in excess, that both are among the indispensable forms of life of any civilization, of a growing civilization as well, that they need each other and are often found together?

But there is one point to which I want especially to draw attention. In the theoretical development of his system Professor Toynbee poses a dilemma: a civilization is either in growth or it is in disintegration. When, therefore, one sees him noting so many grave symptoms in our Western history, one is surprised at his leaving open the question as to the stage in which we find ourselves. For, with the signs of disintegration to which he draws attention, he also mentions phenomena as occurring in our modern history which *per definitionem* belong to the period of growth. It is sufficient to recall the (in certain respects somewhat fantastic) description of England as a creative minority living in retirement and of the great achievements resulting therefrom. I do not see how to solve these contradictions. But I am quite willing to rejoice that Toynbee does not in practice keep growth and disintegration so strictly separate as might be expected from his program. Could we but lay aside his system, with its precise subdivisions and sequences, we should find in his analyses and parallels, in his interpretations and even in his terminology, so much to stimulate thought and to activate the imagination!

But of course the system, the doctrine, belongs to the essence of the work, and we cannot after all do without it if we want to follow Toynbee in his reflections upon our own civilization. We shall have to wait for the twelfth part before we see his diagnosis and his prognosis concerning it fully expounded, but in the meantime he has repeatedly touched upon the subject. The element of uniformity in the rhythm of the disintegration process, he says,[23] looking back on his own examination of the histories of the most widely varied civilizations, "is apparently so definite and so constant that, on the strength of its regularity, we have almost ventured to cast the horoscope of one civilization that is still alive and on the move." Even more suggestive is the passage in which he toys with the possibility—for here again he refrains from speaking positively—of Western civilization having broken down as long ago as the wars of religion of the sixteenth century. The minds of some readers instinctively revolt against the idea of our possibly being caught up in a disintegration fatally proceeding to ruin or petrifaction. So Toynbee's disintegration theory has been misread, especially by some of his most fervent admirers, who were fain to think that even in case we are already broken-down he still leaves us the hope of finding "the right answer." [24] But this is not so. For Toynbee everything turns upon the question: has the breakdown actually taken place, or not?

At first glance one is inclined to say: how is it possible to single out the sixteenth-century wars of religion as having such fatal significance? Indeed, to me the suggestion that our Time of Troubles began with them seems completely arbitrary. There really had been no lack of wars in the preceding centuries, not even of socially destructive wars: the crusade against the Albigensians, the Hundred Years' War, to mention only these.

But for Professor Toynbee the evil thing about the wars of religion is their being of *religion*. He is struck not only by the rending asunder of Christendom, but by the atrocious paradox that from the highest good, from the belief in the one God, there was distilled that suicidal poison of intolerance. (Of course, without leaving the plane of his argument, one might remind him of the fact, with which he is certainly familiar, that even this was far from being a new development, although undoubtedly so violent an explosion of religious hatred had never before ranged the Christian nations in opposing camps.) Suspecting that it was these events that marked the beginning of our Time of Troubles, our Christian philosopher finds confirmation in the fact that the appeasement he observes in the third quarter of the seventeenth century proceeded, not from the only true motive, the religious—not from the recognition of all religions as a search for the one spiritual aim—but from an even more cynical temper than that which in the fourth century had underlain the religious toleration policy of the Roman Empire, from weariness and indifference, from *raison d'état*. When Professor Toynbee describes the principle of *cuius regio eius religio* as "a monstrously cynical principle," [25] he knows exactly what he means—even though the question may well be asked whether justice is done to that age by a judgment based so wholly on later considerations. The expulsion of the Huguenots from France long after the termination of the Wars of Religion was a particularly barbaric application of this same principle; but even the milder forms of the Caesaro-papism which was now in the ascendant, of that domination of the lower over the higher, have, so the argument continues, weakened the foundations of our civilization. The barbaric, the despotic aspects were not the worst, or, rather, from them sprang as a fatal consequence a new factor leading straight to the abyss, namely, scepticism, contempt for religion. He writes in an Annex to Volume V:

In our time this repudiation of a spiritual principle which is no doubt exposed, in human hearts, to the danger of being poisoned or perverted, but which is none the less the breath of human life, has been carried to such lengths in all parts of a Westernized "Great Society" that it is beginning at last to be recognized for what it is. It is being recognized, that is to say, as the supreme danger to the spiritual health and even to the material existence of the Western body social—a deadlier danger, by far, than any of our hotly canvassed and loudly advertised political and economic maladies.

Here we have, I think, the hard core of Professor Toynbee's view of history. In this spirit it is no doubt possible—although really I am now anticipating that twelfth part which we may not receive from his hands for a number of years—to construct a downward line with the sixteenth-century religious wars as a point of departure.

Must that line infallibly lead to the final catastrophe? According to the system, undoubtedly. I merely remind you of the cases of the three ancient American civilizations which were apparently in disintegration and whose ruin was therefore, according to Professor Toynbee, so wholly a question of time that he will not admit the forcible interference of the Spaniards as proof that a civilization can be destroyed by an external power. And yet . . . now that our own civilization is involved, he seems to shrink back from the iron consistency of his fatalistic construction. On this point as well the published volumes contain several indications as to what he is likely to say about the problem in his promised fuller treatment. There is in particular a passage in Volume V, whose splendid eloquence comes straight from the heart.[26]

His starting point is "the miracle" of the conversion of the Negro slaves in America to their masters' ancestral religion. Here, he says,

. . . we can see the familiar schism between the Proletariat and the Dominant Minority being healed in our Western body social by a Christianity which our dominant minority has been trying to repudiate . . . The eighteenth century Methodist preachers who sowed that seed . . . were at the same time converting . . . the neglected slum-dwellers in . . . Wales and Northern England . . . In our post-war generation [the writer is of course referring to the generation after the *First* World War], in which the lately brilliant prospects of a neo-pagan dominant minority have been rapidly growing dim, the sap of life is visibly flowing once again through all the branches of our Western Christendom; and this spectacle suggests that perhaps, after all, the next chapter in our Western history may not follow the lines of the final chapter in the history of Hellenism. Instead of seeing some new church spring from the ploughed-up soil of an internal proletariat in order to serve as the executor and residuary legatee of a civilization that has broken down and gone into disintegration, we may yet live to see a civilization which has tried and failed to stand alone, being caught in the arms of an ancestral church which it has vainly striven to push away and keep at arm's length . . . Is such a spiritual rebirth possible? If we put Nicodemus's question, we may take his instructor's answer.

The reference is to John III: "Marvel not that I have said unto thee, ye must be born again.—The wind bloweth where it listeth, and thou hearest the sound thereof, but canst not tell whence it cometh and whither it goeth: so is every one that is born of the Spirit."

What is the meaning of this? It means that Professor Toynbee in his heart believes that our civilization has fallen a prey to the disintegration process; but in spite of the inexorable sentence which according to his system therefore holds sway over us, he leaves us one possibility yet: the grace of a conversion, or of a return, to faith.

7.

Professor Toynbee does not address himself to fellow believers only. Occasionally he alludes to the "neo-pagan" intellectuals of the modern world in a tone of mild sarcasm, at times a little less mild, although not unmixed with pity. But in at least one passage he invites them into the circle of men of good will as rightful claimants to a share in the Western cultural inheritance. His *method* at any rate is not intended to be that of the religious prophet. Utterances from which it appears that he expects salvation from faith only drop from him out of the fullness of his heart, but, as it were, in passing. His method he presents as empirical.

Now the last question I want to examine is—what has this method to give us for the better understanding of the history and the inextricably related present-day problem of our own Western civilization? That Toynbee's system is to me unacceptable I have already stated clearly enough. But his work contains more than the system. Does his method, which undeniably yields striking results every now and again, promise an important contribution to that subject which concerns us all so closely?

It is perhaps unfair to the author if, in conclusion, and after so much criticism, I confine myself to expounding two objections to his method in this particular connection. Let me at least remark with some emphasis that, in spite of all that may be urged against it, the work here too is immensely stimulating, and that the volume in which his views on our own troubles and prospects will at last be systematically set forth promises to be profoundly interesting. But on two points I shall advance a formulation of my doubts.

If Professor Toynbee has not so far given a set analysis of this particular subject, in his own opinion the comparison with the other civilizations whose course he *has* investigated is already of the greatest importance for the right understanding of what we are living through ourselves. In a certain sense this is a thesis no one will contest. An insight into any historical process trains the mind for the grasping of other processes. But that does not satisfy Toynbee. His idea is that it is permissible to conclude from analogies, and to this view, which underlies the whole of his work, I shall now, at this late stage, without absolutely rejecting it, attach a label, "Handle with caution."

I am not going to attempt an examination of the problem in its full extent and its first principles. I shall only point out that, generally speaking, parallels in history, however indispensable and frequently instructive, are never wholly satisfactory, because each phenomenon is embedded in its own circumstances, never to be repeated, from which it cannot be completely detached. This warning must be especially taken to heart by anyone setting out to compare this civilization of ours with other and older civilizations. The circumstances have in many ways undergone so profound a change that we seem to be living in another world from the ancient Egyptians, or the ancient Chinese, or Iranians, or whatever peoples provide Professor Toynbee with his rules and laws, in another world also from that of the Hellenized Romans, whose decline and fall have obviously strongly influenced his mind in the construction of his system.

I realize perfectly that *he* will be little accessible to this consideration. His view of history is pre-eminently a spiritual one. I am far from being a believer in historical materialism, but for all that I do not think that material changes can, in this argument, be simply ignored. Bookprinting; telegraph, telephone, radio; incredibly increased speed of transport; productive capacity immensely heightened; unfortunately, powers of destruction also raised to an unheard-of degree—

all this has created conditions which have not left the processes of spiritual life uninfluenced and on which the possibilities of development and degeneration, the tendencies
and powers of resistance of our present-day society are to
such an extent dependent that it must be a particularly ticklish undertaking to draw its horoscope, as Professor Toynbee
puts it, from the experiences of earlier ages.

The other point is concerned with one particular shortcoming which I seem to discern in the eloquent author's
disquisitions on our civilization: his attitude toward the
national varieties within the wider unit of Western civilization. I have already remarked upon the unruffled serenity
with which, while insisting so strongly on the impotence of
external violence with respect to his "civilizations," he accepts the cases without number in which violence has triumphed over national communities. National independence
inspires him with distrust, national ambitions he rejects. He
does not really do justice to the historical reality of national
life, of national desire for self-expansion or even for preservation.

A striking instance is to be found in his treatment of the
downfall of the Boer Republics in 1902. In his view the
statesmen of the British Empire were driven to make use
of their overwhelming military superiority because the
national ambitions of the two backward independent miniature States made their preservation inconsistent with any
other solution; and, indeed, at the cost of a small local war,
it proved possible subsequently to pursue a constructive
policy within the Empire, which gave satisfaction to Dutch
nationalism. A surprisingly idyllic presentation of the episode!
Surprising especially as coming from this same Professor
Toynbee who is so much governed by the idiosyncrasy of the
apostle of gentleness that he attaches the name of "hang-
man" to the conqueror as representative of a dominant
minority—and this with Caesar for an example! [27]

The fact is that this particular idiosyncrasy of his is here
overruled by that of the hater of nationalism. It is under
that heading, or, in his terminology, under the heading of
"the idolization of an ephemeral self," one of the mental
attitudes leading to the breakdown of civilizations, that the

South African case is cited.[28] The writer's opinion, by the way, that it presents a contrast with that of Ireland, where the nationalists go on fostering their hatred of England, and with that of Serbia, which caused the dissolution of the Austro-Hungarian monarchy, is an error. The cult of super-annuated grievances and the raising of particular rights to the level of the absolute, so characteristic of a wronged nationalism, certainly belong to the dreariest and most dangerous phenomena of the modern age; Professor Toynbee sketches them, in the cases with which he is acquainted, with the insight born of loathing. But when he asserts that South Africa has now become a peaceable multi-national state, after the pattern of Switzerland, and that this proves a new country to possess a greater psychological plasticity as compared with the petrifaction in its obsessions characteristic of old Europe, this only shows, as do other passages also,[29] that he is not well informed about the Afrikander national movement. These mistakes spring from, or at least are not unconnected with, this same inability to appreciate nationalism; perhaps it is wiser to avoid that ambiguous word in -ism and to say that Professor Toynbee here shows in small things the same lack of understanding for the reality of the national factor in history.

This constitutes one of the serious shortcomings of the entire work. If the destructiveness of nationalism when driven to extremes by oppression or even by fancied wrongs is an undeniable fact, it still cannot be overlooked—although Professor Toynbee does overlook it—that in the cultural construction of our Western world national foundations are of essential importance. This does not in the least amount to throwing doubts on the reality of the greater civilization of which the European nations, to use Professor Toynbee's word, are "members." But we are faced by a problem here which is not to be solved by a one-sided negation. In the very first of Professor Toynbee's volumes he placed himself in an untenable position. It is all to the good that the writers of national histories should be reminded that their subject does not form a self-contained whole, that it has to take its place, and this without any well-marked delimitation, in a greater whole. It is all to the good to make an attempt to survey the greatest whole of all, so that the sense of the dependence of the parts may not only be strengthened but may take shape. When, however, Professor Toynbee considers himself so far superior to the distinction between "parochial states" as to ridicule professorial colleagues who set the diplomatic relations between two of these ephemeral units as thesis subjects, he exaggerates not a little. And when he poses the civilization, in the sense of one of the twenty-one, as the smallest "intelligible field of historical study," he is putting forward an impossible, an impracticable demand.

I have pointed out that he himself, every now and again, when speaking not only of our own Western Civilization but also for instance of the Hellenic, cites phenomena which are particularist or national. This is of course quite inevitable. But since he has done nothing but belittle the national factor instead of accurately defining its relationship to the larger whole, he is all the time coming into conflict with his own impossibly universalist system. Wherever possible he adduces examples of "parochial" phenomena as illustrations of the tendencies of a civilization in its entirety. This is certainly a great convenience to him in his argument: it becomes easy in this way to prove anything. Our Western Civilization in particular offers a rich variety of choice. It is only once or twice that he so much as mentions the problem, and not many of his readers will go along with him when he extends an observation made in the case of one people without further ado to cover all.

The case in question is that of National Socialism in Germany.[30] "Germany's troubles in the present generation can be ascribed, without dispute, to the contemporary *Zeitgeist* of the Western Society of which Germany herself is a fraction." The "without dispute" does not make the statement any more convincing. In another passage he even writes: "Italy and Germany are no alien appendages to the Western body social; they are bone of its bone and flesh of its flesh; and it follows that the social revolution which has taken place yesterday in Italy and Germany under our eyes may overtake us in France or England or the Netherlands or Scandinavia tomorrow." The thesis I accept unhesitatingly; but the conclusion seems to me unjustified. Why? Because, with the cohesion of the large civilization area, there goes the variety of national traditions, of national history. It is these that settle the question whether tendencies, which will no doubt be present in several countries, without how-ever constituting the whole of the *Zeitgeist,* will in one particular country gain the ascendance or not. Toynbee's unwillingness to recognize this fact, by which nonetheless his argument in practice is repeatedly ruled, his failure to make up his mind about this, one of the chief problems of the Western civilization area, strikes me as a serious weak-ness.

Considering this, taking it together with the doubtful applicability of his comparisons—doubtful especially in this particular case—I can, after all the other indications as to the necessity of caution, have little confidence any longer that Professor Toynbee, when later on he undertakes a set examination of our civilization and its prospects, will prove able to enlighten our perplexities; or should I not rather say that we need not let ourselves be frightened by his darkness? We need not accept his view that the whole of modern his-tory from the sixteenth century on has been nothing but a downward course, following the path of rout and rally. We need not let ourselves be shaken in our confidence that the future lies open before us, that, in the midst of misery and confusion, such as have so frequently occurred in history, we can still dispose of forces no less valuable than those by which earlier generations have managed to struggle through their troubles.

VI PROPHETS OF DOOM
(*Sorokin and Toynbee*)

1.

Pessimism about the prospect of our civilization is wide-spread. It is unnecessary to recapitulate the circumstances of modern life and the symptoms of its unrest which form the stock in trade of the pessimists. One might say the disturbances fall into two categories. There are the social phenomena which accompany the immense social transformation through which we are all passing—the disintegration of the middle classes and the rise of the working classes: two sides of the same leveling process in which it is possible (it all depends on the point of view one takes) to discern above all the spread of material welfare and cultural opportunities among the masses of mankind. And there are also the shifts in the relationship between the colored peoples, the Asiatic peoples in particular, and the white world. Their assertion of independence, their insistence on a voice in the international discussion, together with the rising power of the working classes, strike many of the once dominant minority as a threat not only to their position but to the natural order. It is seen as the uprising of the mob, "the revolt of the masses," as Ortega y Gasset put it in his famous book. My quotation of this well-known phrase will serve as a reminder that the mood of pessimism which I am discussing was no product of the war; it existed among intellectuals before the war, although there is no doubt that the war intensified it. Not only have both world wars heightened this sense of futility—wars usually have the effect of speeding up the process of history—but they have, moreover, created difficulties and dangers and fears of their own.

But it is not my intention to go into these problems independently. What I want to do is discuss one favorite method of the prophets of woe—the historical method, the appeal to the past.

It is, I suppose, an ingrained habit of the human mind —and indeed it is a noble ambition—to try to construct a vision of history in which chaos, or apparent chaos, is reduced to order. The historical process is made to conform to a line, a rhythm, a regularity—a movement, in other words, which obeys definable and intelligible laws and whose course can, therefore, be predicted by the observer beyond the moment of his own life. It used to be fashionable in the eighteenth and nineteenth centuries to do this in a spirit of optimism. People were sure then that history was but the record of steady progress. They were entirely complacent about their own time when they looked back at the past, but they had no doubt that succeeding generations would be even happier, even richer, and even wiser and more enlightened than they were themselves. The spirit of optimism has somehow evaporated, but the men who give expression to the now prevailing mood, frequently, like their optimistic predecessors, base their views on a contemplation of the past. Only, the past for them takes on a rosy hue, and its interpreters like especially to take their stand on some historical system which no longer shows the straight line of progress but is generally composed of recurring cycles. Their important point is to demonstrate that our generation, our civilization, has reached about the last and lowest stage of one such cycle and that, consequently, disaster lies immediately ahead.

What I propose to do is to examine the methods employed in some of these demonstrations, and especially to test the way in which history is made to serve the purpose of the demonstrators.

2.

I shall deal with two well-known contemporary writers only: namely, with Professor Sorokin of Harvard, and his enormous four-volume work, *Social and Cultural Dynamics*, and with Arnold Toynbee and his no less enormous (but far more readable!) six-volume *Study of History*. Both men were profoundly influenced by Oswald Spengler, whose *Decline of the West* made such an impression after the First World War.

It is tempting to say something more on that powerful work, but I will only point out that the influence I am concerned with is not so much the general one of the great synthesis buttressing up a gloomy view of the future as, more particularly, the way in which Spengler pictures civilizations as independent and mutually impenetrable entities. This is one of the basic elements of his system. He compares civilizations—one might almost say he identifies them—with living organisms. Like these, they pass through the stages of youth, vigorous middle age, old age, and senility, to inevitable dissolution. A civilization is made to appear a living being with an identity and a history of its own, its human components no more able than are the blood particles or the tissues of a human body to stop or to deflect this course laid down by the inexorable laws of nature. Comparisons are, of course, always permissible and they are a powerful aid to the imagination, but there are peculiar dangers attached to them; they should be handled with caution. Nothing can be more misleading than the suggestion that an identity exists between the processes of history and those of organic nature. In that identification the human factor is overlooked, and it is with the human factor that history is, above all, concerned—or should be.

When I suggest that Sorokin and Toynbee have been influenced by Spengler in this matter, I do not mean that they have been blind to this particular pitfall.

3.

Professor Sorokin tries in his four bulky tomes to establish a system of the dynamics of culture. This impressive work is an attempt to apply the methods of sociology to the past. He arrives at a classification of civilizations which falls into two main types: the ideational and the sensate. The first posits reality as nonmaterial and everlasting, its needs and ends being mainly spiritual; the sensate culture, on the other hand, thinks of reality as becoming, progress, change, flux, evolution, transformation, its needs and aims being mainly physical. Each of these civilizations traverses, according to Sorokin, a number of stages, from adolescence to maturity and decay.

One is very forcibly reminded of Spengler here. Yet at first Sorokin seems to make large concessions to the objections which are bound to come from the historian—the historian who has his attention primed for the endless variety of reality, for the particularity or singularity of each country, of each age, and, more than that, of each incident or phenomenon within these larger frameworks. Sorokin admits that there is an infinite number of cultural types which can be empirically observed. But, he says, this is chaos. His classification, which he asserts is logically satisfactory, helps to arrange the phenomena in an order. But none of his types (he admits this too) has ever existed in a pure form. He even goes so far as to deny the existence of civilizations as really cohesive systems, subject to change in their entirety. These considerations, which he develops with great acumen and sociological learning, cut at the roots of any attempt (or so one should have thought) to make the movements of cultural phenomena conform to regular and predictable lines.

Yet this does not prevent Sorokin from ending on a very positive note. He has by then, to his own satisfaction, identified our present-day civilization as "a typically *sensate* culture in its post-mature stage," and, apparently basing himself on all the statistics, graphs, and analyses in the preceding two and a half thousand pages, he formulates a very definite and depressing prognostication.

"Rude force and cynical fraud"—I quote from the predictions which he lists in his conclusion: this is the fifth one—"will become the only values in all inter-individual and inter-group relationships."

"Freedom"—this is his sixth point—"will become a mere myth for the majority."

Of course everybody with some perception of the present world and not willfully blind to disagreeable symptoms knows that these are our dangers, although the historian will soon reflect that it is by no means the first time the world has been threatened with them. But there were always cross-currents, signs of resistance, of recovery, of fight. And are there none such today? Why should we not look to *these* phenomena for the true indications of our future? If Professor Sorokin thinks he is in a position to prophesy, is it not because in the end he has succumbed to his own classification, and has accepted as absolute and compelling in objective reality what he began by telling us was only a device intended to bring clarity into the appearance of chaos which history presented to his mind?

It was only the other day that I came across the following passage in the prewar book of an English historian. After some sceptical remarks on "philosophies of history," Mr. E. M. Young admits the existence of facts "which dominate the system" (of history). He continues:

But if we ask what this system is which provides our canon of valuation, I do not believe we can . . . go further than to say, it is the picture as the individual observer sees it. If we trespass across this boundary, we may find ourselves insensibly succumbing to one of the most insidious vices of the human mind; what the Germans in their terse and sparkling way call: the *hypostatization of methodological categories,* or: the habit of treating a mental convenience as if it were an objective thing.

I am afraid that this is exactly what Professor Sorokin is doing, and the impression is much strengthened when one takes a critical look at the structure of fact and argument on which he bases his conclusions. Nobody can help being awed by the immense labor that is involved. Scores of scholars all over the United States and Europe have assisted in compiling statistics. The numbers of casualties in wars over twenty-five centuries have been estimated and compared, and so have the numbers of books or of paintings showing a prevalent percentage either of *sensate* or of *ideational* characteristics in any given period.

I must say that these immensely elaborate tables strike me as entirely unconvincing. To me it seems an illusion to think that so complicated, so many-sided, so protean and elusive a thing as a civilization can be reduced to the bare and simple language of rows of figures. The idea that by such a device the subjective factor in the final judgment can be eliminated, is the worst illusion of all. The criteria by which the classifications are to be made cannot really reduce the humblest assistant to a machine (for much work is often left to assistants as if it were something mechanical or impersonal). When it comes to comparative statistics ranging over the whole history of the human race, does not Sorokin forget how scanty are the data for some periods, how unmanageably abundant for others? Is it possible, in the statistical method, to guard against the difficulty presented by the fact that what survives from the remote past are mostly the thoughts and works of art of an *élite,* while in our view of our own age the activities and idiosyncrasies of the multitude take an infinitely larger, but perhaps a disproportionate, place? A balance has to be struck between these and many other aspects of history; that is to say, between the records of human activities in many countries and in many ages, that are so scrappy, or again so full, so dissimilar, and mutually impossible to equate. The question imposes itself: Can anybody, in attempting this, claim that he is guided by the sure methods of science? Can he embrace with his mind the whole of that immense chaos and derive from it a conclusion which would be evident to every other human intellect, as would a proposition in Euclid?

I doubt it, or rather—I deny it. I said a moment ago that Professor Sorokin had fallen a victim to his own system and had ended by accepting his classifications as objective and compelling facts. Is it not rather that he *began* with a conviction and then set out to prove it? Most of his imposing and abundant array of facts and figures, in other words, is really irrelevant. If one wishes a sidelight on the value of Sorokin's statistics, which are supposed to tabulate and fix the evidence of literature as well as all other matters, one has only to read those pages in which he lets himself go and confides to us his opinions about novelists and historians. He appears to *have* private and spontaneous opinions—and of course the statistics never contradict these. But it is interesting to note what he has to say on his own hook.

The decline of literature due to the hypertrophy of the sensate factor apparently began in the eighteenth century, and the lover of old English fiction will be surprised to learn that Richardson and Fielding were pessimists, who could sketch in their novels only insignificant characters, failures, or negative types. What can be the worth of a system of ultimate values when the statistics on which it is allegedly built have not saved the author from misapprehensions so patent to anybody who simply has read the writers in question? Sorokin is much concerned, also, about the debunking tendency in historiography. Even Lincoln, he says, is not spared, and he considers this to be an ominous symptom. But, I am inclined to think, the debunking fashion was never more than a passing phase, from which not too much should be deduced about the state of Western civilization. And as regards Lincoln—we have recently had Sandburg, we are still getting Randall. The debunking phase seems closed, and must we now conclude that Western civilization is saved?

But for Sorokin—and this is the point I want to make—the conclusion that Western civilization is in a decline, owing to a surfeit of materialism and other evils, was the one point fixed and determined beforehand. Modern literature or modern art or the state of modern society do not really compel him to conclude that our civilization is doomed; statistics or no statistics, his conviction that this is so colors throughout his view of literature, of art, of the state of society, and of everything else.

4.

Professor Toynbee has reacted in his own way against the influence of Spengler—and he has reacted very strongly. He rejects expressly and emphatically the master's identification of civilizations with living organisms. The life of a civilization is not necessarily subject to a decline, it is not subject (as he puts it) to the "iron necessity" of dissolution. It all depends

on the energy and the efficiency with which the members of
a civilization respond to the challenge with which that civilization finds itself faced. The human factor, so it would
seem, is given full scope by Toynbee, and in fact he prides
himself on this.

In the debate which I had with him early in 1948—a
radio debate, broadcast by the B.B.C. in London—he insisted
on his belief in man's free will, in man's freedom to respond
when life presented him with a challenge; and again he
denied expressly that he had ever presumed to use history
to tell the world's fortune. "With the awful warning of
Spengler's dogmatic determinism before my eyes"—that
is how he expressed it—"I have been mighty careful to treat
the future of our civilization as an open question."

Of course, one can only note these asseverations with pleasure. I did so in the debate, although I could not help pointing to some features of his great work which hardly seemed
to be consistent with this mental attitude. Toynbee retorted
—a little impatiently this time—that he must be the last judge
of what his own beliefs are. Obviously. And yet this cannot
mean that we should not be at liberty to criticize the system
as he has worked it out in the six volumes of his *Study of
History*; and, in particular, are we not entitled to ask whether
his system does not, on this all-important question, come into
conflict with his professed belief? I believe that it does; and if
I may summarize for you the system in which Toynbee tells
us he has discovered how the life of civilizations is enacted,
I can point out exactly in what way the conflict occurs.

Any civilization—so he teaches us—can progress for an
indefinite period, and if it breaks down it is because of the
failure of its members to respond to a challenge. The breakdown is due, in other words, to human shortcomings. Now,
according to Toynbee, practically all civilizations known to
history—he enumerates some thirty—have so broken down.
But what does he mean by the term? It does not mean *the
end*, it is only *the beginning of the end*. It opens the period
of disintegration, which may last for centuries. According to
the system, during this integration period the leaders of the
stricken civilization are unable to meet challenges success-
fully; they can at best obtain a respite, but after every crisis

the situation re-emerges, worse than it was before, and in the end, the dissolution of the broken-down civilization cannot be averted.

This is the system as Toynbee expounds it; this is the law to which, according to his theory, the life of civilizations has to conform. He explains all this so fully, he illustrates it with such an abundance of instances and cases, he returns to the leading ideas so frequently, that there is not the slightest possibility of a misunderstanding. Now, I submit that it is small use telling one you are a believer in man's free will and particularly in the freedom of the human beings comprising a civilization to respond to challenges when in fact you make an exception for this protracted period of disintegration. A number of successive generations—if we accept Toynbee's own teaching—have every now and again in history to live through these distressful circumstances. Such generations struggle, but their struggles are foredoomed to failure. There is no other end for them than catastrophe, than defeat. They are not free.

There is more involved here than the question of freedom or determinism; there is an immediate connection with the subject I am discussing, the question, that is, of what Toynbee undertakes to teach us from history about the future of Western civilization. Toynbee may assure us that he has never used history to foretell the world's future, and that he looks upon the future of Western civilization as an open question. It is certainly true that he has never said in so many words that Western civilization is doomed. He has not in the *Study of History* so far dealt expressly with the prospects of our civilization—that question is reserved for some later volume. But in many passages he has referred to it, and the careful reader can be in no doubt as to his meaning. He is not perhaps quite sure, but he has the gravest apprehensions, that we are, and have been ever since the late sixteenth century, in that unhappy period of disintegration in which all our efforts are in vain, in which things can only go from bad to worse, until release comes in the shape of dissolution and the way will be opened for some new form of civilization.

This is at least what ought to be our position according to the strict tenor of the system, but now Toynbee is seen to waver. According to the system all civilizations in a period of disintegration are doomed, but now, faced with the problem of our own civilization, suddenly and most unexpectedly, he admits an exception: even if, owing to the mistakes of our ancestors, we are and have been for nearly four centuries on the downward path of disintegration, we have one possibility of reprieve. If only we would return to the faith of our fathers, be reconverted to the Christian religion, the threatening disaster might still be averted.

Professor Toynbee can always appeal to this loophole to claim that he is not a prophet of doom and, indeed, in our radio debate he did so very emphatically. If we will only give heed to his warning and follow his direction, we may still be saved. He is, however, confining our possibilities within very narrow limits, and unless we are able to accept his offer of salvation through a return to the Christian religion, the effect of his teaching must be depressing. As for me, I will own frankly that the chances of a real conversion, such as Toynbee means, appear to me to be so exiguous that to make the survival of our civilization depend on their being realized would almost amount to a sentence of death.

But the relative importance of religion in our civilization is itself a question on which views might differ. Assuming that religion was in a stronger position in the Middle Ages than it has been since, would it be true to say that the sense of social or international security, that the realities of justice and the opportunities for the great masses of people to lead lives capable of yielding some happiness, including even the development of spiritual values, were more firmly entrenched in the Middle Ages than they are now, in an age which, according to Toynbee, is characterized by the corruption or the loss of faith? I doubt it very much, and I think, moreover, a very good case might be made out for the contention that problems of that kind, which most people think have to do with the health and prospects of survival of a civilization, have always been tackled, and will still have to be tackled, on a different plane from that of religion. To my way of thinking, it therefore seems the wrong policy altogether to want to concentrate attention on the issue of religion alone, and to divert it from the many other problems which have to be dealt with if we are to get safely over the troubles and difficulties which beset our civilization (difficulties which I am certainly not inclined to minimize). Toynbee, however, speaks slightingly of "our hotly canvassed and loudly advertised political and economic maladies;" for him the only really "deadly danger" is the loss of faith.

This standard of values, by the way, helps to explain his view—which at first sight will strike most people as a rather extraordinary one—that it was the wars of religion in the sixteenth century that caused the breakdown of our civilization. There have been many wars in Europe, both before and after, which were equally devastating, caused as great a loss of life, were socially no less disturbing. But that the highest good given to man, the belief in the Christian God, led to this horrible perversion of intolerance and war, that is what marks out the wars of religion for Toynbee. Their termination, too, in a system of tolerance which was merely practical and cynical, which had nothing of Christian love in it, by which absolute control over religion was vested in the secular rulers of the various national states—all that seems to him to have cut at the very foundations of our civilization. The scepticism of the succeeding period, the unbelief of a still later age— it all flows from that terrible, that criminal, aberration. There is in this view an undeniable grandeur. It hangs logically together and is intimately connected with that estimate of the loss of religion as the really critical problem of our time.

I do not, of course, dream of denying to Toynbee the right to hold these opinions. One can differ from them, and I will just state that I do differ, that I think these views extraordinarily one-sided. To me it seems, frankly, an amazing judgment of the last three or four centuries of European history to write them off as showing nothing but a losing fight against fate. The whole of American history is included in this sweeping verdict, for of course in his conception America belongs organically to the sphere of Western civilization. On this point I agree wholeheartedly, but the main proposition, that our history for the last four centuries has been one of irremediable decay, becomes only the more amazing.

I just state my dissent from that main proposition without entering into any discussion. My intention is only to point out that a large view or interpretation like this one cannot possibly be proved by history, nor do I believe that it is derived from a study of history—and neither, I hasten to add, can the dissenting view be so proved or is it so derived. Both are matters of subjective conviction, and it is from this conviction that Toynbee's history is derived, not the other way round.

I have a feeling that I am stating the obvious. Yet when you read *A Study of History* you will be struck by the insistence with which the eloquent author asserts and repeats that he is conducting an empirical exploration, and that the conclusions at which he arrives, the whole system which he develops, his discovery and definition of laws by which the movement of civilizations is governed, all spring unaided from facts, facts scientifically observed and scientifically connected.

Now I contend that his conception of what an historical fact really is, of what an historical fact is worth, of what can be done with it, is open to very grave objections. Professor Toynbee does not like professional historians; he is inclined to deal somewhat contemptuously with them. Their perpetually critical attitude of mind and their eternal scepticism make him impatient. I am of course, as the French would put it, preaching for my own parish, but I can't help thinking that it is an altogether precious thing—a bracing thing that our civilization cannot do without—that the professional historian should preserve his scruples and his humility with respect to his subject, that he should be aware of the limits set to his knowledge, and that he should prefer his ignorance and his doubt to attractive but facile generalizations.

I don't mean that the historian should (as he is sometimes advised) stick to the facts. The facts are there to be used. Combinations, presentations, theories, are indispensable if we want to understand. But the historian should proceed cautiously in using the facts for these purposes. It goes without saying that he should try to ascertain the facts as exactly as possible; but the important thing is that he should remain conscious, even then, of the element of arbitrariness, of subjectivity, that necessarily enters into all combinations of facts, if only because one has to begin by selecting them; while next, one has to order them according to an idea which must, in part at least, be conceived in one's own mind.

I am quite ready to admit that academic historiography often sins by employing too much caution. This sometimes leads to a shrinking from the use of that precious gift of the imagination. Academic historians do not perhaps always sufficiently remember the great task of history, which is not, after all, meant to be a plaything for scholars in the seclusion of their study, but rather has a great social function to fulfill. I admit all this, and up to a point I can sympathize with Toynbee's impatience. Yet I believe that the scholarly caution of which I spoke is also one of the high duties of the historian and the essential condition of his usefulness.

Toynbee, with his immense learning, has a multitude of historical illustrations at his fingers' ends at every turn of his argument, and he discourses with never-failing brilliance and never-failing confidence on careers and personalities of statesmen or thinkers, on tendencies, movements of thought, social conditions, wars, customs of all countries and of all ages. Now the critical reader will feel that each single one of his cases might give rise to discussion. Each could be represented in a slightly or markedly different way so as no longer to substantiate his argument. They are not facts: they are subjective presentations of facts; they are combinations or interpretations of facts. As the foundations of an imposing superstructure of theory, they prove extraordinarily shifting and shaky, and this in spite of the dexterity and assurance with which Toynbee handles them.

To me it seems that all these large syntheses of history (and I include Sorokin's) are vitiated by an insufficient appreciation of the infinite complexity, of the many-sidedness, of the irreducible variety of the life of mankind in all its aspects, which is after all the stuff of which history is made. This applies with particular force when an attempt is made to establish the laws governing the cultural life of mankind.

The great Dutch historian Huizinga, who died in the last year of the war, once wrote that the height of a civilization cannot be measured. To me this seems a wise saying. It implies that civilizations cannot with any certainty be divided into higher and lower. Toynbee's rigid classification of the successive stages of one and the same civilization in a period of growth, followed after a breakdown by a period of disintegration, remains to me, after reading the many hundreds of brilliant pages in which he tries to explain and to describe it, utterly incomprehensible. To judge a civilization, or one particular stage of a civilization, steadily, and to judge it whole, is a task which I think will always be beyond the powers of the human intellect. We speak glibly—and I have done so myself and shall no doubt do so again—of a golden age, or of an age of decadence. In fact when one studies a golden age in any detail one is struck by signs of corruption or weakness or distress, at least equaling those which frighten us in our own time. On the other hand, no age of decadence in history is without the redeeming features of effort or of new birth. But to measure the one set of factors against the other is what the historian can never do with any certainty.

It is sometimes thought that we are beset by these difficulties only when facing the mystery of our own time. The historian has before him something that is completed, something that can be turned around and around on the dissecting table. What can help him in his analysis to reach a final verdict, so it is imagined, is that he knows the outcome. Surely that must be a sufficient indication of the trend of the period he is studying? No doubt the historian is often guided by the outcome in his judgments, and he cannot neglect the evidence of the outcome. But to think that it will solve all his riddles for him is to fall into a very dangerous delusion. The factors by which the outcome was brought about are numerous, and they are again dissimilar. How shall one decide whether it was the purely material factors that were decisive? One can guess, one can have one's personal conviction; one cannot prove.

Toynbee, no doubt, tries to simplify the problem by contending that the life of a civilization is completely self-reliant, that its fate is governed by spiritual forces alone. I am far from being an adherent of historic materialism, but this exclusive spiritualism is more than I can swallow. Toynbee elaborately tries to prove, for instance, that no civilization has ever been broken down by outside violence. It is always by the spiritual shortcomings of the civilization itself that the breakdown is brought about. The argument is ingenious, but utterly unconvincing. If the thesis were true, the problem for the historian would still be staggering in its complexity, but it would be simplified. If one has to reject the thesis, as I do reject it, one can say only the more positively that the historian cannot fix the past in an unshakable pattern that will be valid for everyone, and from which conclusions as to the future can be drawn.

I need not, I trust, explain that I am not arguing against history as being of no use for the present. I believe, with Burckhardt, that, although it does not yield lessons for the immediate occasion, its study can make us wiser. And let me say that by *us* I do not mean the professional historians particularly; I mean the community in whose midst history is constantly being studied and written. I believe in the indispensable value of historical insight for civilized society. But we must not expect of history what history cannot possibly give—certainty. I do not quarrel with Toynbee when he soars above the ground of history where we others plod; the spectacle enthralls me even when I remain unconvinced. I admire the sweep of his imagination; I feel warmed by the glow of his enthusiasm; I am ready to regard his confessions of faith as significant manifestations in the struggle of minds that constitutes the cultural life of our time. But I enter my *caveat* when the great work is presented to the public as a work of scientific thought. As a prophet, as a poet, Toynbee is remarkable, and nobody will grudge him his appeals to history; one can only feel the liveliest admiration for his historical knowledge and for the inexhaustible picturesqueness and ingenuity with which he draws upon it. But when he pretends to be conducting a severely logical argument and builds up a system in so many stages and parts supposed to be based on a strictly empirical investigation, then I feel I must demur.

And the more so as it all leads to a conclusion that seems to me a dangerous one. Be converted or perish, Toynbee tells us; and he says it as if speaking with the authority of history behind him. But history does not warrant any such dilemma. Only the mystic will read into it the promise of a mystical salvation. To the rest of us it does not convey a message of despair.

VII TOYNBEE ONCE MORE: EMPIRICISM OR APRIORISM?

Frankly, before I came over to this country I did not wish to discuss Toynbee again. It had been suggested to me that I should, but I replied: "No, I have had my say;[1] I am not interested in Toynbee any more." Now, it is of course a fact that many people *are* still interested in him, and when I found a copy of the abridged edition in my apartment here, I could not help dipping into it. For, although the book is common enough in Holland—there is even a Dutch translation—I had never read this abridgment, not even looked at it.

But when I tackled the abridged Toynbee some weeks ago, I felt my interest quicken at once. I must confess that, even more than when I read the six volumes in 1946, it was the spirit of opposition that was raised in me. But that will become plain enough before I have done.

1.

In a little book on Spengler, the German philosopher-historian, whose gloomy work, *The Decline of the West*,[2] made so profound an impression after the First World War, Mr. Stuart Hughes has, with perfect justification it seems to me, ranged Toynbee among the "New Spenglerians." No doubt Toynbee, fine flower of English tradition and civilization, is in some ways extraordinarily different from Spengler, who was like the eruption of a long-accumulated mass of the more explosive tendencies of German thought. Whereas Spengler is in love with violence and the manifestations of force, Toynbee is the apostle of gentleness. Spengler was the pagan; Toynbee is the Christian. But the fundamental conception that the significant portion of human history is enacted within the unit of a civilization, a larger entity than that of nations or states, and that a comparison of civilizations and their histories will reveal the laws governing their development, which is the significant development of human history—that conception the two have in common. Both are, moreover, subject to the fascination of the idea of decline, of catastrophe—a profoundly human trait, to which I think the wide appeal they make can partly be ascribed. Not that, here again, there is not a difference. With Toynbee this mood is clothed in Christian forms, especially in this—that the *escape* from it is to him the thing that matters. Whereas Spengler seems to welcome the idea with a kind of stoical pride, Toynbee preaches the escape through salvation.

It is interesting to note what Toynbee himself has to say on his relationship to the great German predecessor. When, in 1920, he first read *The Decline*, he says,[3] he was already revolving these large problems, and his first reaction was to wonder whether his "whole inquiry had not been disposed of by Spengler before even the questions, not to speak of the answers, had fully taken shape" in his own mind. After a while, however, he came to the conclusion that at least on the question of the geneses of civilizations Spengler was "most unilluminatingly dogmatic and deterministic," and that there was room "for English empiricism" to make a try "where the German *a priori* method drew a blank."

The distinction in method that he himself indicates here is of the greatest interest. Spengler, with his thoroughgoing contempt for analytical, critical, professional history, drew largely upon his imagination, arrived at his parallels and his generalizations by flashes of intuition or by boldly arguing in the abstract and making deductions from dogmatic propositions—not only that, he owned to this roundly, and gloried in it. Toynbee, on the contrary, presents his work as the result of an empirical investigation. In fact, he harps on this constantly in the work itself. He never lets us forget that he draws his conclusions by severely logical argument from carefully established facts and arrives at his system by moving from one such conclusion to another. I have in my earlier criticisms of Toynbee not forgotten to point out that this is the claim he makes, and I have tried to show in several instances that it is mere make-believe. I shall limit my remarks today to that point, and in order to show the hollowness of the pretension of severe empiricism I shall discuss only the chapter on the Stimulus of Hard Countries in the Part dealing with Geneses of Civilizations, and in that chapter mainly one particular passage,[4] in which the history of the settlement of the North American continent is adduced in support of the central thesis of Toynbee's system —the thesis, namely, that it is difficulties or obstacles which lead to the flowering out of a civilization. As you know, he summarizes this notion in the striking phrase, which has become immensely popular, of Challenge and Response.

Challenge and Response is indeed the central theme of Toynbee's philosophy of history. To him the interest of the study of humanity lies in the indomitable quality of the spirit of man. The significance, the motive forces, the causation—to him it must all be spiritual. The lot of man is cast in a material world, but Toynbee sees his relations with the material as a struggle. Man's *significant* relations at least —his emergence into civilization, his adventures and his triumphs as a civilized being, everything that distinguishes him from the animals and from the barbarians and makes him the protagonist of what we call History—all this can never be *deduced from* the material world; it can be related to the material world only in terms of opposition, and of victory.

A striking idea! And often an illuminating one. But the point that I want to make is that Toynbee has driven it to extremes, and that the system with which he has tried to bolster it up obscures the process of history as much as the idea can occasionally illumine it.

I shall not go into the questions one could raise in connection with Toynbee's preliminary chapters. What must be said quite generally is that he is distressingly brief and apodictic. One would like to hear much more about why we must concentrate our attention on civilizations rather than on states or nations, and about how the twenty-one civilizations which he enumerates, and which for him constitute "the smallest possible fields of historical study," really are so overridingly important, really do encompass the struggles, the efforts, the thoughts of men so completely as he suggests but never in any detail sets out, let alone proves. The chapter in which the set purpose of the discussion is the comparability of these civilizations is not any more satisfactory. The critically-minded reader feels dozens of questions cropping up which are not even touched upon by the confident system-builder.

One difficulty Toynbee admits. He envies the ethnologist, who can draw up his general laws on the basis of data relating to six hundred and fifty known primitive societies, whereas the comparative historian of civilizations has to manage with data from only twenty-one objects of study. But there is another difficulty here, and a much more fundamental one than this somewhat paradoxical scarcity of data of which Toynbee complains. Can civilizations, in the sense that he attaches to the word, really be considered as units in the same way that primitive societies can? This question is never really examined by Toynbee, any more than it was by Spengler. When one tries to visualize his twenty-one civilizations, one is at once struck by the enormous differences between them, in size, in structure. Take our Western civilization, for instance. I shall not deny the reality of its unitary character, but the composite structure is certainly very marked. Toynbee does not waste any words over this problem, which nevertheless must—and does—present itself at every turn in the argument on which he is setting out. But, indeed, he never faces up to it. He takes his data from national histories as if they were indisputably relevant to the history of Western civilization, and he takes them from each part as they suit his argument concerning the whole. In short, the reader must take the whole basis of his investigation on trust; if he cannot do so, he will, from the very outset, follow him doubtfully and reluctantly.

2.

So far I have been looking at what, as I said before, are no more than preliminaries. With the Part on the Geneses of Civilizations the writer comes to grips with his problem, and Challenge and Response makes its entry.

The real explanation of the emergence of a civilization, of the transition of a group of human beings from acquiescence in the settled sameness of primitive life to the active and incessant striving and changing of culture, is to be found, so Toynbee wants to show, in the shock administered by adverse climate or geographical conditions and the energy engendered by the exertion of meeting and overcoming them. He clears the way for his demonstration by discussing and ruling out the ideas, so popular at various times, that civilizations could be explained either by racial aptitude or by a *favoring* climatic or geographic environment. And, indeed, these notions belong to a materialistic or mechanistic view of human life which few scholars will hold nowadays. When Toynbee says that these inanimate forces are not *automatically* reflected in history, that they are not *by themselves* the causes of culture, I for one can wholeheartedly agree. But without giving any warning Toynbee carries his argument a good deal farther. He will never admit that the genesis of a civilization can have been brought about by a combination of causes, that the inanimate factor of geography can stimulate by favoring as well as by hindering conditions, that it has therefore occasionally to be taken into account as a positive contribution toward the coming into action of spiritual forces. Before the inattentive reader is aware of it, he is being carried along on an eloquent homily on the uses of adversity.

Very charming pages these are, flown from an imagination richly stocked with erudition. The world's mythology and the world's great poetry are ransacked for illustrations of the truth that it is obstacles which rouse the spirit to action. One is almost ashamed to be such a Philistine when one feels compelled to object that all the glamour and all the wisdom of Homer, Euripides, and Goethe combined cannot make one give up the conviction that other conditions, favoring ones, must be present also—and will in some cases supply the determining cause. This is only one instance of the art with which Toynbee attempts to awaken in us a *mood* in which we shall be ready to accept his proofs. Looked at with the pure untroubled intellect, these proofs—set forth in very brief accounts of the geneses of a number of civilizations—are but meager. Yet Toynbee opens his next chapter by saying: "We have now, perhaps, established the truth that ease is inimical to civilization."

The "perhaps" is curious. The argument proceeds as if the word had never been spoken. And yet, how very far was the preceding chapter from *establishing* anything at all, and how questionable is this truth on which the entire argument of the following chapters is to be built. *Is* ease inimical to civilization? Is it not just as possible to maintain that a modicum of ease is indispensable for civilization? Did not Hellenic civilization flourish because there was a class set free from manual labor by the slaves they held? Was not medieval culture in Europe largely the result of the leisure and relative safety which the monks enjoyed in their monasteries? A thousand objections rise in the critical mind, but Toynbee sweeps victoriously along on the course of his beautifully simple argument—simple because he follows a single line of thought, but at the same time made attractive and suggestive of broad prospects and profound meanings by the rich stylistic and erudite *decoration.*

3.

I come now to the chapter in which Toynbee discusses the Challenge of Environment in greater detail, giving examples of how it works in practice. I have on former occasions looked a little more closely at some of these passages and shown how very one-sided in each the argument is. I shall now limit myself to the case of America. "The classic illustration of our present theme in our own Western history," says Toynbee, "is the outcome of the competition between half a dozen different groups of colonists for the mastery of North America."

Now the first observation to be made is that the outcome of that competition was not the birth of a new civilization, not, at least, according to the meaning attached by Toynbee to that term. The North American society or civilization as it resulted from the unified control of the continent is not, in his terminology, a new or a separate civilization; it is an offspring, or rather an integral part, of the great Western civilization, one of the twenty-one. "Our present theme," Toynbee said. "Our present theme" is the question of what caused *these* civilizations to spring into existence. The struggle for the North American continent was carried on among a number of nations all belonging to the same Western civilization. When that is remembered, the whole of this digression about North America ought really to be ruled out as irrelevant. We have here one of numerous examples of the completely unmethodical fashion (I have alluded to this before)[5] in which Toynbee uses *national* histories when he thinks they can help him in proving a case in what he proudly calls "the smallest intelligible field of study," the history of *civilization*. But on this I shall not insist. Let us accept the case and test it on its own merits.

Now what does Toynbee set out to prove? He contends that the struggle for the North American continent in the two hundred years between the middle of the seventeenth century and the middle of the nineteenth was due to the fact that the New Englanders lived in a more difficult region, a region less conducive to ease, than did the French settlers in Canada and later on in Louisiana, the Dutch settlers on the Hudson River, the Spanish settlers in Florida and Mexico, and the other English settlers in Virginia. Let us see whether he makes good that contention.

Toynbee wants us to imagine a far-sighted observer in the year 1651 who was asked (as he puts it) to pick the winner. This contemporary spectator might have had the acumen to rule out the Spaniards in spite of "the obvious asset" of their leading position among European Powers;

in fact, he is assumed by his creator to have "discounted Spanish prestige in consideration of Spain's failures in the European war just concluded."

Now this is again very curious. Suppose Spain was still as powerful as she had been; does Toynbee mean to suggest that in that case she might have come out the winner? Does he, in other words, betray a glimmering of understanding that the contest was one not between these settlements but between European powers? But, no, it seems as if he mentions these reflections only to show how utterly wrong was this seventeenth-century onlooker, who judged according to the wisdom of the world because the spiritual wisdom of discerning that the victory was to go to the material drawback of New England's poor soil had not been revealed to him. At least, when the imaginary observer continues to muse about the power positions of the three remaining European countries, Toynbee quite unmistakably suggests that this could only lead him astray. And, in fact, now that our man has ruled out the Spaniards, he bets on the French. The Dutch, he reflects, may occupy an excellent position on the Hudson and have the greatest sea power in the world, but the French hold in the St. Lawrence a still finer water gate and, by using their overwhelming military superiority against the homeland of the Dutch, can always immobilize them. As for the English settlements, the Southern group with its relatively genial soil and climate may survive as an enclave, cut off from the interior by the French; but the New Englanders in their bleak and barren country, cut off from their Southern kinsmen by the Dutch and menaced by the French from the North, seem bound to disappear. So far the prophesyings of the observer in 1651.

Toynbee next transfers us to the year 1701, when his observer is supposed still to be living and "to be congratulating himself on having rated French prospects higher than Dutch; for these latter had tamely surrendered the Hudson to their English rivals in 1664."

Let us stop a moment to consider why. If the argument is to prove anything for Toynbee's thesis, it must have been because the New Englanders, hardy and enterprising as a result of suffering the hardships of their soil and climate, had proved themselves superior to the Hollanders of New Amsterdam living on the fat of their desirable land and consequently sunk in sloth. Note, however, that Toynbee does not expressly say so. He is an adept at avoiding all too-direct clashes between his theory and hard reality. But the fact remains, of course, that this is what his theory requires, and that actually the easy conquest of New Amsterdam is to be explained by an entirely different set of factors. Indeed, the contemporary commentator was not so far wrong in principle when he tried to guess the future of America by looking at the politics of Europe.

The conquest of New Amsterdam in 1664 was undertaken, to begin with, not by the hardy New Englanders, but by the luxurious court of Charles II in London. If the hold of the Dutch on the settlement proved so weak, it was not because the soil and the climate were more genial than those of New England, but because the Dutch West India Company, which managed the colony, had always been more interested in trade than in colonization. Conditions in the mother country, too, offered little incentive to colonization; there was, in Holland, no lack of employment, there was no religious persecution. As a result, the settlement had grown only very slowly, and what is more, there had been, long before 1664, quite a penetration by English settlers moving in from New England—a peaceful penetration which, nevertheless, undermined the powers of resistance at the critical moment. As you may remember, the settlement was recaptured by the Dutch in 1672, in the third war with England, when Charles II was making common cause with Louis XIV against the Dutch Republic. Although in that war the English certainly did not have the better of the Dutch, the Hudson colony was again ceded at the peace in 1674. The reason this time was that the overriding concern of the States-General was for the safety of the home country vitally threatened by the French. So they were only too glad to buy off at least one of their enemies at the price of a colony in which Dutch public opinion took little interest.

Toynbee touches very lightly indeed upon this affair of New Amsterdam. The Dutch tamely surrendered it—that is all. Yet the elimination of the Dutch wedge from between the English colonies in the North and those in the South had enormous consequences for the future of the struggle for mastery in North America as a whole, and it is surely worth noting that it was brought about by factors of an entirely different order from that of the challenge presented by the poor soil of New England. But, in fact, if Toynbee wants to save his argument at least in appearance, he is almost compelled to glide over the episode—and that is what he does.

In any case, now, in 1701, only the English and the French are left, and Toynbee's long-lived observer is sure that the victory must go to the French. Had they not pushed on from the Great Lakes along the Mississippi down to its mouth, and had not a new settlement, Louisiana, been founded there?

It is possible that some people did think so in 1701. But was it really only the factor of the superior hardihood of the New Englanders, .resulting from the poverty of their soil, that they overlooked? Was it not, above all, English sea power that decided the issue between the French and the English settlements in North America? Or perhaps it was (but really this is only the converse of the preceding proposition) the fact that the French, both in the War of the Spanish Succession and in the Seven Years' War, squandered their strength on the continent of Europe, where England kept them busy by supporting now Austria, then Prussia? Indeed, Pitt (Lord Chatham) hit the nail on the head when he boasted "that he had won America on the battlefields of Germany."

But Toynbee has not finished yet. Even in 1801, when the French were long disposed of, there remained the question which section of the United States was going (to use Toynbee's words) to pocket the larger share of this vast estate, in other words, of the vast empty West. And this time (still placing ourselves on the viewpoint of contemporaries), Toynbee suggests there can be no doubt. The backwoodsmen of Virginia were the first to found a new state, Kentucky. The very inventions of the Yankees, the steamboat on the Mississippi and the cotton gin, seemed to be destined to add to the wealth and importance of the *Southern* states more than to those of the ingenious inventors.

But now, Toynbee exclaims, look at the outcome. It was the New Englanders, not the Southerners, who actually did settle the West and tied it to themselves by bonds of interest. Their inventiveness was not exhausted. The Mississippi was relegated to the second plan by the railways. And while the Northerners solved the transport problem for the West, they solved its labor problem by the reaper-and-binder. "By these two Yankee notions, the allegiance of the West has been decided and the Civil War lost by the South before it has been fought."

Is it possible more recklessly to simplify? No doubt these factors counted, but it is not enough for Toynbee's argument to have that admitted. He must needs insist that they were *decisive*. So he does not hesitate to represent the outcome of the Civil War as a foregone conclusion. Lee and Grant, apparently, might well have spared their exertions, and if Lincoln ate his heart out in sleepless nights, it was because he did not understand that the bleakness and barrenness of New England was bound to save the situation.

But it is not only the tragic reality of that terrible struggle of the Civil War that Toynbee sacrifices to the necessities of his pet notion. Let us grant him that the North started with an enormous economic superiority and that the relations between industrial New England and the agricultural Middle West of the pioneers had a great deal to do with the ultimate victory. But does this justify him in suggesting that the economic backwardness of the South was due to the richness of its soil and mildness of its climate compared with New England? He does suggest this. Let me quote the final paragraph of the three pages (in the abridged edition) that I have been analyzing:

It may be said that all the different groups of colonists in North America had severe challenges to meet from their environments. . . . Still, taking all in all—soil, climate, transport facilities and the rest—it is impossible to deny that the original colonial home of the New Englanders was the hardest country of all. Thus North American history tells in favor of the proposition: the greater the difficulty, the greater the stimulus.

Anyone who has not surrendered his critical judgment to the persuasive manner of this master of style and sophistry will reply that North American history does nothing of the sort. In the earlier portions of his argument Toynbee achieved his effect by blandly ignoring what was obviously the decisive factor, namely, the power and action of the respective European mother countries of the settlements in North America. Now, similarly, not only does he all too unconditionally identify the North with New England, but he has not a word to say about the particular disability of the Southern economy, slavery. No doubt the peculiar institution was somehow connected with the qualities of the soil and of the climate of the South, but it is utterly impossible to fit the innumerable aspects of that problem, its causes and effects, into the oversimple categories of Toynbee's scheme: hard and soft countries, challenge and response. That is no doubt why (once again) he has ignored those aspects and the problem itself. But the whole of his argument is thus made to lose its force. "The classic illustration of the theme" of Challenge and Response turns out to be a classic illustration of the charmingly innocent fashion (for I prefer not to call it unscrupulous) in which Toynbee exercises the art of special pleading.

It is not, I think, necessary for me to apologize for having taken up so much of my allotted time in dissecting three pages out of Toynbee's three thousand. My justification is that it is not an isolated, but on the contrary an all too characteristic, case. It is one instance out of the innumerable fallacious arguments and spurious demonstrations of which the whole book is made up.

4.

These are hard words. I think that they are perfectly justified, but I want nevertheless to make it clear that there is much in Toynbee's book that I warmly admire. His mind is a fertile one; it teems with brilliant suggestions and conceptions. His vast learning almost inevitably turns out to be superficial whenever the expert sets to work on the parts in which he has ventured onto the expert's particular field; but certainly his learning is vast, and it has enabled him to survey the history of the human race from a much wider viewpoint than is attainable for the rest of us. And the survey inspires him every now and again to most striking and original perceptions, combinations, comparisons; also, the nimbleness of his imagination and his command of language enable him to throw off a firework of phrases and formulas which are sometimes illuminating to the reader. I mentioned Challenge and Response; but there are many others—and in almost all of them, and in the way in which he applies them, there is something that contains food for thought. He is certainly neither a dull nor an insignificant writer.

But the unfortunate thing is that he wants to bring it all into a system, that he argues as if all these brilliant brainwaves were fixed and sure truths out of which a solid edifice could be constructed. It is this on which I have concentrated my attention and the result is that I can in this essay be only critical. I have sometimes an uncomfortable feeling that the proceeding is unfair to him, but, after all, this is an important aspect of the whole of his book, and he himself invites, as it were, the criticism which I am offering by making this claim of scientific construction when his method is so clearly purely imaginative.

I quoted his own statement in which he contrasted his method as the empirical to that of Spengler as the aprioristic. I must confess that the historian who presents me with large generalizations and in the same breath tells me that he has been proceeding empirically will always arouse my distrust. Nothing is more likely to be misleading than the comparison of the historian's method with that of the scientist. When the scientist conducts an experiment intended to show that a certain reaction is brought about by one particular element, or combination of elements, rather than another, he will take care above all to isolate that factor beyond the possibility of mistake. It will always be hard indeed for the historian to do likewise.

No doubt an analogy may be seen, although never an identity, between his way of arriving at a conclusion of more than individual or singular validity—a law, if you like (dangerous word, however!)—and that of the scientist. Sometimes he will be able to present a number of developments marked by a striking similarity and leading to similar results, in each of which a factor obviously belonging to the same class will conspicuously stick out. He may then conclude: given such and such circumstances this particular factor is likely to bring about such and such a result. It will, however, be wise to be very cautious even then, and not to speak too positively. The circumstances may be similar; they will never be the same. And the factors may belong to one particular class; they too will never be quite the same. Each will always have in its appearance or quality something exclusively its own. Nor will it ever be safe, however conspicuously one may stick out, to be too dogmatic about its having been the really determining cause. Observers will always observe from slightly (or greatly) different points of view, and unanimity among them is hardly to be counted upon, since their estimate of the circumstances, of the result, and of the determining factor may differ accordingly. The measuring tape, or the weighing scales, or the chemical test, which supplies the scientist with objective data, is not for the historian. Nevertheless, given a critical attitude of mind and a sense for the distinctions to be made, the historian will sometimes, by analyzing sequences of events and comparing causes, be able to arrive at general conclusions. These certainly are top moments in his activity. Even though these conclusions will never be of absolute validity, they may still be most valuable.

However, that Toynbee is entirely lacking in the requisite qualities of caution and a sense of discrimination appears very strikingly in the passage about North America; indeed, it appears on almost every page, and the whole imposing work is a travesty of the scientific method.

Mr. Stuart Hughes, the author of the little book on

Spengler that I mentioned, seems at times to suggest that the laws of rational criticism do not apply to a prophet or a visionary. I do not agree that they should be suspended for the benefit even of Spengler, however decisively he himself may have rejected them. I do not agree because I believe that in our human affairs, although not everything (and certainly not the highest good) springs from the reasoning faculty, nothing can claim exemption from the tests it sets. It may be that in the case of Spengler I am particularly unwilling to renounce the criticism that I feel will undermine confidence in his grandiose visions because the purpose and spirit of his writings are so utterly hateful to me. But this is not a reason which it is necessary for me to advance. I believe that in applying this sort of criticism I am merely being faithful to the calling of the historian, or of the scholar. And it is a comfort to me when I discover that other historians and other scholars, starting from an ideological point of view differing widely from my own, agree with me on this essential principle.

I am thinking now particularly of a review written by a professor of the Catholic University of Nymegen, of the Dutch volume in which, in 1950, my original Toynbee criticism was reissued. Professor Rogier, who is a faithful Catholic and a stimulating historical thinker, begins by observing that many of his co-religionists will not admit any criticism of Toynbee, because they are so profoundly impressed with his message, the message of salvation through Christ. But, says Rogier, this does not alter the fact that Toynbee offers as the result of empiricism what is purely apriorism; and even though I know, through God's revelation supported by infallible authority, that his apriori is in a general sense true, it is not, and it must not be represented as, a fact deduced from earthly data. And Rogier appeals to Bossuet, the great French Catholic writer, who stated, three centuries ago, that the concatenation of events which is History is ruled by God's secret decrees. The historian cannot trace that concatenation by his investigations. What he investigates are the ways of men, the acts determined by such freedom of decision as is left to human beings. "How the action of our liberty," said Bossuet, "is comprehended within the de-

crees of Divine Providence, remains hidden to us mortals."
The system which Toynbee has constructed (I am still quoting or summarizing Rogier) may be intended to support
divine truth. But it attempts to do so by presumptuously
arranging verifiable facts as if the mystery of God's plan
could thereby be solved. To show the insufficiency of that
method, to knock away the structure of argument from under
the conclusion, is a service rendered to intellectual honesty;
nor does it touch the conclusion in so far as that is valuable
to Christians, because in fact the ultimate truth rests upon
a different foundation altogether.

I can gladly accept the alliance of the Catholic scholar.
Part of his argument I should, certainly, state in different
terms. But I am glad to find the method of Toynbee rejected,
on the same ground which I advanced myself, by a man to
whom the message conveys a real meaning. I am glad, because it shows that the laws of rational criticism can bridge
a gulf which would be fatal to the unity of our civilization
if it made an absolute separation between us.

That Toynbee cannot claim to be outside the jurisdiction
of those laws should at any rate be self-evident. He is himself eager to assert that he lives by their light. To say that
it is this which I find irritating in his work is really doing
less than justice to the gravity of the case. Spengler, who
openly proclaimed his contempt for those laws, was less of
a danger to the great principle represented by them than is
the man who pays them lip service but in fact uses them as
a subterfuge to foist upon an anxious public his fanciful
construction. Toynbee's system may not be as offensive as
Spengler's in its political implications, but it is essentially
no less irrational and aprioristic. By presenting it under the
guise of scientific method and empiricism he not only revolts
the scholar in me but he rouses me to protest, because I believe that clear thinking is perhaps the most crying need of
our distracted world.

VIII TOYNBEE THE PROPHET
(*The Last Four Volumes*)

The last four volumes of Arnold Toynbee's great work have been issued from the press. I confess that at the sight of those 2500 closely printed pages, duly provided with diagrams and tables, my heart sank. But it was inevitable that I should have to find my way through that strange and yet familiar country. Everybody seemed to expect it of me, and I could not refuse reviewing the volumes.

Once I had overcome my initial reluctance I found myself fascinated. The system of the six volumes which I tried to analyze eight years ago[1] is now practically discarded, but the new system springs naturally from it, and if the pretense of a scientific argument leading up to a rationally irrefutable conclusion has by the change been rendered patently absurd, I was never taken in by that pretense, so the spectacle of this subtle mind deceiving itself in so naive a manner was nothing new to me. In spite of that, my weariness was shot through with feelings stronger than irritation this time too, but also (again familiar!) I could not help feeling an admiration bordering on amazement or awe for the tremendous intellectual energy, which has not flagged under the crushing task of twenty-seven years and which goes on, throughout this long and sustained argument, juggling with the events, the crises, wars, revolutions, state-formations, religious manifestations, of all the centuries and all the races, drawing effortlessly (or so it seems) on libraries of books in I don't know how many languages. If one could only accept the work as a collection of stories, and glimpses of life, and dissertations on aspects and problems, from the history of the world, what a mine of curious and out-of-the-way information (I know that by that phrase "out-of-the-way" I betray myself as the confirmed "parochial" Westerner I am), what flashes of insight, what instructive juxtapositions even —what learning, what brilliance!

But in the author's mind it is all subordinated, and intended to contribute, to a system, a message. It is on the relation that the details bear to the system and the message, and on the system and the message themselves, that the work must be judged. The change which these have undergone (as I already hinted) only brings out their nature more clearly. Reading these volumes has confirmed me in the views expressed in my earlier criticisms; it is all as I said it was, only more so.

1.

Toynbee's thinking is revolutionary, "metaphysical" in the sense in which Burke used that word, abstract. To my view, this is as much as to say unhistorical. For all his wealth of detail, and although the spectacle of the particular obviously interests him in some detached part of his far from simple mind, he is never for one moment captivated by it; not for one moment does it free him from the obsession of his dream. His dream is the unity of mankind in the love of God. Or rather, his dream is to participate in that loving vision and to see it approach realization. He has pretended to "investigate" the phenomena of communal life, within the framework of "civilizations," throughout the course of history. In reality he is the prophet revealing that one, to him all-meaning, idea and trying by his revelation, accompanied by warnings and denunciations, to contribute to its glorious and blessed consummation.

As for me, I am not speaking against the love of God, although I have no doubt that to Toynbee I must appear to be doing so. What I criticize and oppose is, first of all, the pretense of an empirical investigation.

When I wrote my earlier criticisms on the strength of the incompleted work, this was the aspect that thrust itself most prominently upon the attention and that is why I still give it pride of place. Yet, after my exposure of "fallacious arguments and spurious demonstrations" [2] in the first six volumes, it will be hardly necessary to examine particular passages from the four new ones for the purpose of showing up their insufficiency from the point of view of "scientific" (as Toynbee loves to say), or simply rational, argument. It is enough to say that these new volumes are, when considered from this angle, a further instalment of the same maddening profusion of vastly learned examples, stated in an attractive or impressive, but frequently slipshod, fashion and *proving* exactly nothing. It is enough—and yet I shall give three instances, which will at the same time serve me to make a transition to the second objection I have to offer to the work as a whole.

In describing the plight of contemporary Western civilization (post-Modern, in his jargon), Toynbee mentions the trade unions. They were, he says, an outcome of the spirit of Freedom, intended to resist the regimentation consequent upon the new industrial conditions. Unfortunately the trade unions led to the workers' regimenting themselves and so we are left with a self-defeating contradiction. I shall not deny that there is a grain of truth in this observation, but if the matter is left there it is just such a half truth as the many forming the stock in trade of the cheapest political claptrap. Yet Toynbee, without saying a word on the improvement of material conditions nor on the building up of political power, does leave the matter there and imagines that he has now presented us with another fact by which to judge, and of course to condemn, the present state of our civilization.

Extraordinary (but one learns, when reading these brilliant and self-assured dissertations on everything under the sun, to be surprised at nothing) is Toynbee's appreciation of the extermination of the Jews by the National Socialist regime. Of course he abhors it. Yet he places the policy of evicting Palestinian Arabs from their homes, to which the Government of Israel resorted in 1948, on a par with it; at least, he describes this as a more heinous sin than that committed against the Jews, at divers times in the past, by Nebuchadnezzar and Titus and Hadrian and the Spanish and Portuguese Inquisition, for these were not sinning against the light that God had vouchsafed them. As for the National Socialist Germans, "on the Day of Judgment the gravest crime standing to their account might be, not that they had exterminated a majority of the Western Jews, but that they had caused the surviving remnant of Jews to stumble." [3]

I have personally always regarded the Zionist adventure with misgivings, but is it possible to discuss the unfortunate consequences with a more complete lack of balance or with less sense of proportion? And what is it that has moved the writer to this amazing outburst against the Jews? It is neither the love of God nor a scientific survey of the world's history as a whole. It is his hatred against nationalism in every shape and form. Because nationalism, even when it means no more than the recognition of the fact of nationality, a basic fact in the life of civilizations, is to him merely a stumbling block on the road to his idolized unity.

My third instance has to do with a question even more directly connected with the view taken of Western civilization at this moment.

It will be seen that Hitler's eventual failure to impose peace on the World by force of arms was due, not to any flaw in his thesis that the World was ripe for conquest, but to an accidental combination of incidental errors in his measures for putting into execution a nefarious grand design that, in itself, was a feasible scheme for profiting by a correctly diagnosed psychological situation. A twentieth-century World, that had thus, in A.D. 1933-45, been reprieved, thanks only to a chapter of lucky accidents, from a fate which Mankind's patently increasing defeatism and submissiveness had almost provocatively invited, could hardly count upon any future would-be world-conqueror's being so clumsy as to let the same easy prey escape for the second time. [4]

"It will be seen." This refers to the preceding two pages in which the Hitlerian attempt and its failure had been described, and it is, as usual, a gratuitous assertion that this description must carry conviction to the mind of the average unbiased reader, for, also as usual, the facts had been marshaled in accordance with the writer's preconceived conclusion. "Thanks only," "patently"—it all comes out of the bag of tricks, not of the scholar but of the orator out to persuade or, if need be, to bluff. Toynbee *will* have it that we were ripe for conquest and he *will* have it that we are more so now. He *will* have it that Western civilization is in a bad way, and, indeed, why should he care? Western civilization means nothing to him.

2.

I know the weaknesses of the position of the West as well as anybody. I shall not prophesy that it will be able to beat off another attempt to overthrow its badly organized independence. Toynbee is sure that in any case a World Government will be forced upon us by the dangers inherent to atomic warfare. I shall not dispute the possibility, not even the likelihood, of a development in that direction, but the tone of indifference in which Toynbee discusses the future fate of the "parochial states" under a world dispensation is significant. He only remarks in passing that these *peritura regna* (their doom is a matter of certainty) "might be ostensibly preserved instead of being overtly liquidated." [5]

I should have thought that from the point of view of Western civilization, or of civilization, the point of view one could still think that he took when only the first volumes of his *Study* were available, the alternative here stated is one of vital importance—although in fact it cannot be said to have been fully or fairly stated unless a third possibility is added: preserved for more limited purposes. [6]

But there is to me one dominant conviction to be affirmed when viewing these large possibilities hidden in the impenetrable future, namely, that even in the worst case of a direct overthrow by some world-conqueror on the Hitler or Stalin pattern, Western civilization will prove to have sufficient moral and intellectual reserves to continue the struggle for existence and will survive.

I know that I am not now speaking as a historian, although my reading of history comes comfortingly to my support. I am speaking as a son of that Western civilization in which I believe and which I love, and I should consider it base treason to accept with acquiescence this sentence of ignominious extinction which Toynbee, wrapt in his dream of world unity, passes over it with so light a heart. Here come into play feelings that Toynbee has throughout his immense work ignored, and of which he now gives more patent evidence than ever that he is constitutionally unable to recognize the existence.

Nevertheless, they do exist. I remember the summer of 1940, when Holland had just been occupied by the National Socialists and when after the defeat of France the war seemed to offer very little prospect for the one ally still holding out. There were many Dutchmen then who urged us to judge the facts coldly and realistically and to draw the inevitable conclusion, however unpalatable, that we were in for a period in which Germany would rule Europe, if not the world. "We shall have to come to terms," they said; "the Dutch people must live." And at the same time many Frenchmen were saying the same. But there were many others who refused to accept the evidence because they were judging the situation by a faith. And these men felt that they must so judge, that this was the sacred duty laid upon them by the hour. Why should not there be such men again, in every country of the West, if the trial came to be imposed upon our world once more? "Mankind's increasing submissiveness and defeatism" may be patent to Toynbee, and indeed he sets an example of these weaknesses by so blatantly proclaiming them. But there will be resisters upheld by a more manly faith, and as long as there are, it will be premature to talk about the dissolution of Western civilization.

3.

This, then, is the second reason why, after my initial reluctance, I feel an irrepressible urge to testify against this false witness and indeed to criticize and oppose a system productive of such pernicious counsels.

Western civilization, I said, means nothing to Toynbee. This is a new development (although by no means a new departure) in his mental attitude toward his subject, and it must be more closely examined.

The preface to the seventh volume, that is, the first of the four now published, is illuminating on the point. In accordance with the scheme drawn up as long ago as 1927-29, this volume deals with Universal States and in a second part with Universal Churches. When he was at liberty to resume his interrupted task in 1946, the writer, so he tells us, felt constrained to recast his notes.

"The world around me and within me had, indeed, met with a number of challenging and transforming experiences in the course of the nineteen years and more that, by the summer of A.D. 1946, had already passed since the first of the original notes for the book had been written." He then mentions "further discoveries in the field of Archaeology," but also "the horrifying practical demonstration of the moral depths to which the heirs of a Christian civilization were capable of dragging themselves down;" besides, there was the work of the psychologists and that of the atomic physicists. "An Einstein and a Rutherford, a Freud and a Jung, and a Marshall and a Woolley, as well as a Gandhi, a Stalin, a Hitler, a Churchill and a Roosevelt, had been changing the face of the Macrocosm." But, moreover: "my inner world had been undergoing changes which, on the miniature scale of an individual life, were, for me, of proportionate magnitude."

We shall see in a moment that the resultant change in the structure of the system was a momentous one; the whole view of the significance of civilizations is modified. First, however, a somewhat disturbing reflection, but one which does not seem to disturb Toynbee, imposes itself. Does it not follow that the empirical investigation as set out in the first six volumes had not, after all, led to any reliable conclusions about the laws of mankind's historic life, with the help of which the future might be forecast? This was the purpose for which we were assured that investigation was undertaken. Toynbee is still convinced that he can tell us something about the future. He admits the speculative nature of all predictions, he is careful not to be dogmatic either about the period needed for the process or about the exact modalities. Yet the twenty years between 1929 and 1950, so he repeats when starting in his twelfth Part to deal with the Prospects of Western Civilization,[7] make it possible for the historian to speak with much greater confidence about the inevitable merging of parochialism into universality. The Wall Street collapse, the breakdown of France, on the whole "the experience of twenty-one sinisterly illuminating years" makes "relatively sure prediction" [8] possible.

It is startling to see with how little ado the author himself brushes aside the labor devoted to his first six volumes and in effect bases his concluding wisdom on his observations of the world's vicissitudes during the last twenty years, observations such as are indeed the source of innumerable pronouncements on our condition and our prospects in newspaper articles, political speeches, and sermons. To these experiences common to his generation must, in Toynbee's case, be added, in order to explain the views he is now expounding, changes in his own inner world. So we heard him admit in this same preface to Volume VII.

Habemus reum confitentem. I said eight years ago that the study of history cannot supply us with forecasts having universal validity. Toynbee's refreshingly frank confession now implies agreement with that view. I say "implies," for in spite of his refreshing frankness he does not go so far as to admit that his work is not really the scientific investigation for which he has all along tried and is, in the face of his change of front, still trying to pass it off.

What does this change in the writer's inner world amount to? Mr. Martin Wight, who read the chapter on Universal Churches before publication and whose remarks are printed in the book—sometimes but not always having caused the author to modify his text—expresses in an Annex his profound gratitude as a Christian critic to Toynbee for having "abandoned [his] original judgment that all civilizations are philosophically equivalent and for having found that 'civilizations . . . have ceased to constitute intelligible fields of study for us and have forfeited their historical significance except in so far as they minister to the progress of Religion.'" [9] But although grateful, Mr. Wight is not entirely satisfied. Toynbee, while distinguishing religions into higher and lower, is not prepared to grant to the Christian religion a unique place of pre-eminence. "The writer of this study" (as he puts it, for he always uses the third person to describe himself)

ventures to express his personal belief that the four higher religions that were alive in the age in which he was living were four variations on a single theme, and that, if all the four components of this heavenly music of the spheres could be audible on Earth simultaneously, and with equal clarity, to one pair of human ears, the happy hearer would find himself listening, not to a discord, but to a harmony.[10]

Mr. Wight would be completely satisfied only if the writer had come to the conclusion "that the higher religions in their turn cease to be intelligible fields of study and forfeit their historical significance except in so far as they are related to Christianity." It is instructive to see that the admiring critic wants to confine the concept of "historical significance" within still narrower bounds than Toynbee in his changed state of mind is willing to do. Even to him, nevertheless, civilizations are no more than "the handmaids of religion," [11] and he writes, for instance:

We have to think of the civilizations of the second generation [i.e., the Babylonic, the Syriac, the Hellenic, the Indic and the Sinic] as having come into existence, not in order to perform achievements of their own, and not in order to reproduce their kind in a third generation, but in order to provide an opportunity for fully-fledged higher religions to come to birth; and, since the genesis of these higher religions was a consequence of the breakdowns and disintegrations of the secondary civilizations, we must regard the closing chapters in the secondary civilizations' histories— breakdowns which from their standpoint spell failure—as being their justification for existence and their title to significance.[12]

The consequences for his appreciation of Western civilization are set forth uncompromisingly in the Part on its Prospects in Volume IX. The change of heart subsequent upon the completion of the first six volumes led him to discover, as we saw, that the civilizations, between which he had until then assumed a philosophical parity, were unequal. This, by the way, is how he puts it himself: he found them to be unequal *"as a matter of historical fact* on the evidence of an assay in which the touchstone had been the part played . . . in the history of Religion." Can anything be more obvious than that the selection of that touchstone was an arbitrary decision, governed by personal or subjective feeling, and that the slipping in of the words "historical fact" is therefore an act of naive, but very characteristic, presumption? When the civilizations were (on that test!) found to be unequal, "the result was not," says Toynbee, "to re-exalt the Western civilization to the pinnacle on which it had once been placed by a naively vulgar native Western egocentric prejudice." By comparison with, for instance, the Indic and the Hellenic civilizations, which had given rise to, respectively, Hinduism and Christianity, "the Western civilization and its contemporaries of the third generation had been 'vain repetitions of the heathen' (Matth., VI, 7)," and this time he has the grace to add: "from the standpoint of an observer who saw the guide-line of History in a progressive increase in the provision of spiritual opportunities for human souls in transit through This World." [13]

Western civilization does not, it will now be realized, interest Toynbee; I should perhaps add: any more. It is for this reason that he is ready with so much complacency to insist on its defects and weaknesses. He proves to himself, by doing so, his freedom from that "blight of egocentricity," which "had been the nemesis of an act of hybris," from that "intellectual effect of Original Sin." What he seems to overlook entirely is that it is *his* civilization, and *our* civilization, and that he and we can work and think to any purpose only on the lines issuing from it. This is no reason to ignore what has been or is being wrought and thought outside it (in fact, no civilization has been so catholic in its interests as this Western civilization which Toynbee singles out for the reproach of egocentricity); it is no reason either to exalt it above others (and in so far as we are apt to indulge in that somewhat sterile habit it is good to be reminded of the special virtues of other civilizations); but it *is* a reason why we are perfectly justified in giving it special and loving, though not uncritical, attention. Indeed, this is one of the conditions for creative work in the present, and one of the tasks of history as I understand it is to entertain a living sense of tradition.

Toynbee, however, tries to escape into a nonexistent world unity, which he sees as God's idea and purpose. The energy with which that concept has inspired him is impressive; it is indeed almost superhuman. But his vast, global knowledge of history has tempted him into what strikes me as prideful and sinful, an inhuman and at times slightly ridiculous, ostentation of detachment from his own heritage, to which his work nevertheless owes so many of its most admirable traits.

Often one cannot help suspecting that this is spite masquerading as detachment, so incredibly biased is his treatment of Western civilization when he comes to discuss its prospects. Every sign of crisis or of decadence, every flaw, every incidental infidelity to its professed principles, is by him eagerly displayed as evidence of its approaching dissolution. On the other hand, there is hardly more than a grudging word, now and then, about its positive achievements. And, indeed, how can one make much of these when the last four centuries at least are regarded as "a vain repetition of the heathen"? The great European thinkers and poets and artists and scholars serve Toynbee with quotations wherewith to decorate his pages or to strengthen his ideas; but as far as his estimation of Western civilization is concerned they might as well never have existed. The scientists, of whose contribution he makes so much use in his explanations and interpretations, are never valued for what they helped to make of Western civilization; the atom bomb seems at times to outweigh all their merits.[14] The great advance made during that period in the countries of our civilization in the matter of social security and material prosperity (which also have their importance when it comes to "spiritual opportunities"), in humanity coupled with more stable order and more equitable law, weighs as nothing in his scales. The deficiencies in these respects of the centuries when civilization had in Toynbee's view a more real significance are ignored or condoned. The study of history is not to concern itself with men as they lived and strove. The system requires that it should all be viewed and "assayed" by the one test which Mr. Arnold J. Toynbee discovered a few years ago: religion.

Western civilization can hardly expect to pass with honors when it is called before an examiner to whom neo-paganism, beginning with the Renaissance, suddenly blossoming out in the eighteenth century, has no other than the negative significance of a departure from the one vital principle of the West, Christianity. Toynbee consistently refuses to it any value or any strength of its own, except for evil. A High-Powered Enormity, the Abomination of Desolation, are some of his names for it and he holds it responsible for the deadly menace of a third world war waged with atomic weapons. "But this appalling prospect was merely the unveiling of a goal toward which a secularized Western Society had been heading ever since it had erupted out of a medieval *Respublica Christiana.*" Can the simplification, and one might say distortion, of history be carried farther? The *Respublica Christiana* was never more than an aspiration. The people of the Middle Ages waged war, without atomic means, it is true, but with equal ferocity nonetheless, every day of their lives. And neo-paganism has as little to do with the atom bomb as has Christianity or Buddhism or Mohammedanism. A world in which all these spiritual states are mingled together is striving to avert the disaster with which the purely mechanical intrusion of this wonderful as well as awful invention is threatening it; more cannot be said in "A.D. 1954" any more than in "A.D. 1950."

But neo-paganism is Toynbee's butt. Occasionally, in so far as he can represent it as a pale reflection of the religion which it denied, he will condescend to say something for it. As to admitting that among its adherents, too, there may be allies for the building up of a firm defense against the deadly dangers with which he sees our civilization threatened —never! In this single-minded judge of the civilizations' view, it would be absurd to look for moral strength in any principle divorced from positive religion.

Toynbee loves to talk about humility; "a contrite humility the first of the Christian virtues," he reminds us on the very

last page of his Part on the Prospects.[15] He had rejected
Mr. Wight's plea for a recognition of the Christian religion
as (to use Toynbee's own words) "possessing a monopoly
of the Divine Light," and he rejected it on the ground that
in making such a claim, "a church seems to me guilty of
hybris." [16] But in making the claim on behalf of the four
higher religions collectively, or on behalf of his own personal conviction supported by ten volumes of eloquent and
biased interpretation of history, it seems to me that he makes
himself no less guilty of hybris.

I give one instance of the demagogic fashion in which the
impression of Western civilization being undermined by neo-
paganism is supported. Toynbee quotes a long passage from
Frazer's *Golden Bough,* in which the Renaissance is described
as the period marking the weakening of "the obsession" with
"a future life" and "the return of Europe to native ideals of
life and conduct, to saner, manlier views of the world. The
long halt in the march of civilization was over. The tide of
Oriental invasion had turned at last. It is ebbing still." [17]
It is a passage which bears the mark of the time when it
was written, fifty years ago. But now listen to Toynbee's
comment.

It was indeed still ebbing when the present lines were
being written on the 4th March 1948, and, in the act, the
present writer was wondering what that gentle scholar would
have had to say if he had lived to see some of the ways in
which Europe's "return to native ways of life and conduct"
had manifested itself since. [Frazer, Toynbee asserts, has
been proved to belong to] the last generation of Western
neo-pagans of a rational, unenthusiastic, tolerant school . . .
By A.D. 1952 [1932?] they had been swept off the field by
demonic, emotional, violent-handed successors who had
suddenly emerged, unheralded, out of the unplumbed depths
of a secularized Western society. The words of Frazer had
been re-uttered by the voice of Alfred Rosenberg with a
different ring.

But is Alfred Rosenberg now in occupation of the field
off which he has swept these gentle scholars? Is Western
Civilization really dominated by National Socialist theories

of race and culture? One might also ask: Has no nonsecularized civilization ever known outbursts of human devilry? —and recall the Crusade against the Albigeois, or the Inquisition (which, when he wanted to belabor Jewish nationalism, was excused by Toynbee because the Inquisitors naively believed themselves to be carrying out the behests of religion), or the Anabaptists, or the burnings of witches. But the point I want to make here is that once again we see Toynbee making capital out of the National Socialist aberration at the expense of Western civilization. To me it seems the height of irresponsibility to speak as if in the Western world at large the spirit of Frazer had been ousted by that of Rosenberg. But it is all grist to Toynbee's mill.

Once one has grasped the spirit and purpose of the last instalment of the great work, one feels that demonstrations of fallacious arguments, of perversions of the significance of historical data or of their complete irrelevance for the thesis, demonstrations which seemed worth attempting in connection with the first six volumes, have indeed become utterly superfluous. These volumes, especially VII and VIII, again testify to the enormous learning of the writer. However, learning, even when assisted by an acute mind and a sensitive as well as powerful imagination, is not enough to produce history. What is needed, unless all the rest is to go for nothing, is an attitude of mind from which Toynbee's is as far removed as can be.

The historian should take an interest in his subject for its own sake, he should try to get into contact with things as they were, the men and their vicissitudes should mean something to him in themselves. I do not mean that the historian should not have a point of view, that he should be indifferent to the problems of his own time; nor that he, having a point of view, and caring about the present and the future, should try to tell about past events as if they bore no relation to either. But when a man comes to the past with a compelling vision, a principle, or dogma, of such magnitude and emotional potence as Toynbee's unity in the love of God; with a system which causes him to reduce the multitudinous movement of history to one single, divinely inspired current. and to judge civilizations and generations by one single criterion, rejecting most of them, and incidentally his own, as unimportant—that man can write a work full of color and striking theories, glowing with conviction and eloquence, but no history. The *Study of History* is no history. The Student of History, as Toynbee calls himself, may know more of history than I shall ever do, but he is no historian. He is a prophet.

4.

There has never been any love lost between prophets and historians. Toynbee devotes a paragraph of forty-six pages of a chapter on Law and Freedom in History (Vol. IX) to criticizing and ridiculing Modern Historians as a class, and as the air resounds with the scornful reviews[18] that historians are writing of his last volumes (I was the first in the field in 1946, but I have long lost the feeling of doing something adventurous or audacious), it might seem that we are quits. Historians, however—I believe that, although an interested party, I am stating an objective truth—have a better understanding of the rules of the game of polemics than prophets have. And, at any rate, this attack on the Modern Historians and their Antinomianism is a piece of very spirited, but at the same time very questionable, polemics.

Toynbee in this chapter maintains not only that the course of history is governed by laws but also that these laws can, and therefore should, be discovered and defined. He had of course long been aware that modern historians regard this thesis with suspicion and are on the contrary accustomed to stress the infinite complexity and intangibility of the factors of the historical process; and he had also found that they were inclined to criticize his practical attempts in the *Study of History* as utterly unconvincing. So he now denounces them wholesale as purblind worshippers of technique and *minutiae*, indifferent to the great problems of the present and the future, and deaf to the call to action, which is the essence of Life.[19]

No doubt there are and always have been historians whom this description fits. But when applied to the profession as a whole it is no more than a caricature. Because we do not swallow Toynbee's generalizations and systematizations, are we to be charged with lack of interest for the meaning of the facts of history? Because we try to solve problems of less world-wide proportions on the basis of a close attention to the sources, do we bury ourselves in technique? I need only point to the work of the three English critics of Toynbee mentioned in footnote 18, above, to confound that ill-directed counterattack. Are we not interested in the world around us, are we not aware that our scholarship has a function to fulfill to civilization or society at large? The very criticisms leveled against Toynbee are often inspired by that feeling: these grandiose and impassioned, wrongheaded and one-sided prophesyings and pronouncements offend against the spirit of scholarship which the scholar must feel it to be his first duty to the community to uphold.

The real truth of the matter is, of course, that there is an incompatibility between Toynbee's mental attitude toward the past and that of "the historians." They would not care if he wrote as a prophet, but they feel that the best traditions of their profession are insulted when the prophet poses as a historian. I have already indicated the difference. It is not only—not even in the first place—the looking for laws, the generalizations, even the faulty reasonings, that offend; it is the vision itself in which every age and every civilization is judged by a standard foreign to it and its importance restricted to what it contributed to the progress of an arbitrarily chosen principle. The historian believes that history can enrich the civilization of his own age especially by trying to enter into the habits of thought and the relationships of past generations and that only thus can these be understood. He believes, too, that the discipline of transferring oneself into strange surroundings and states of mind has in itself an educative, a broadening, a moderating influence, which should be a valuable component in the spiritual life of his own community. To see a self-styled historian reducing the whole of the wonderful and mysterious movement of history to one single motif, rejecting whole centuries as uninteresting, forcing it all into the scheme of a presumptuous construction, strikes him as going against all that history stands for. This spate of moral judgments, too, this highly-strung sense of impending disaster and contempt for vital currents of thought, does not seem to the historian "humble"; it denotes a hectoring and censorious attitude toward the social phenomena which to him seem an integral part of life, to be explained, but, with life, first of all to be accepted. The modern historian, in other words, is intellectually the descendant of Burke,[20] rather than of Rousseau; with Toynbee it is the reverse. His speaking of modern historians as taking refuge from larger views in the sands of technique is therefore doing less than justice to the far-reaching philosophic difference involved.

In his more direct defense of his thesis about historical laws Toynbee is little more to the point. Here too he follows a well-known, though far from admirable, method of debate. The only professional historians whom he permits to state the case which he intends to demolish do so in a way which few of us will accept as a fair representation of the position. (One marvels, by the way, at the insularity, or parochialism, of Toynbee's reading on the subject: both the historians quoted are British, and so are most of the other modern writers mentioned in this chapter either in support or for refutation. No notice is taken of the important German contribution to the theory of history.)

H. A. L. Fisher's saying that there can be no generalizations, and that the main thing is to recognize in the development of human destinies the play of the contingent and the unforeseen, is patently an overstatement. E. L. Woodward, on the other hand, took up a somewhat too apologetic attitude when he argued that for "a final synthesis . . . the difficulty at present is that the *data* are insufficient." The real and permanent difficulty is rather that the data are so unmanageably abundant. For Toynbee the chance is too good to be missed, and he pokes fun at adversaries who excuse themselves with two diametrically opposed pleas. But in the meantime he fails to advance any effective arguments against the really serious objection.

It is true that he deals with it at some length, but the argument, when examined, turns out to consist of an assertion, endlessly repeated in that inexhaustible wealth of language and of metaphor which he has at all times at his disposal, and enveloped in scientific and biblical and mythological allusions and parallels. The assertion is that the complexity by which historians allow themselves to be paralyzed is of their own making; it is the result of their own nihilistic technique. "While the shivered splinters had become unmanageably numerous and complicated, the intact bones remained intelligibly few and simple. . . . The significant known integral events in the history of Man in Process of Civilization were, not awkwardly abundant, but awkwardly scarce" [21] (until new archaeological finds added to their number).

An amazing statement! There is, to begin with, the familiar confusion in Toynbee's mind as to what constitutes a historical fact. He qualifies his "known events" in this passage by the words "significant" and "integral," apparently without realizing that he thereby introduces a speculative or subjective element that must make all generalization on the basis of these data, not valueless, but uncertain and hypothetical. And the bones of the structure of history simple! If any work is apt to make the reader doubt the truth of that bold assertion, it is Toynbee's *Study of History*. For the feeling created in the mind of the beholder by the picture drawn even by this "terrible simplificateur" [22] is one of bewilderment. One searches one's way desperately through this jungle of arguments, metaphors, digressions, hypotheses, one tries to follow the eloquent (at times one is tempted to say loquacious) demonstrator, but inevitably one loses the thread. The nonsequiturs and the contradictions, the far-fetched comparisons, the dizzying assumptions, are too confusing. And if conclusions are all along drawn with that glowing conviction, with that unshakable self-confidence, one feels that they spring from another source altogether than that of the preceding exposition, which has seldom succeeded in covering up the unruly and indomitable complexity of historical reality.

The simplifications are at their most "terrible" in the Tables (at least they are nowhere else so glaringly patent). One of Toynbee's laws is the recurrence in history of a War-and-Peace Cycle in so many phases. In a table on page

255 of Volume IX he shows these phases—"Premonitory Wars (the Prelude), The General War, The Breathing-space, Supplementary Wars (the Epilogue), The General Peace"— in an Overture and four Regular Cycles between 1494 and 1935. It looks beautifully "simple." I shall say no more than that I have rarely seen a more arbitrary juggling with the known facts of history.

Toynbee, meanwhile, also holds up to the historians the example of the sociologists and the economists, and twits them somewhat laboriously for ignoring the activities of these searchers for laws in human affairs. He never mentions the fundamental difference presented by history, which deals not with one more or less confined and homogeneous sphere of man's communal life but with the whole of it. It is not only the large number of data (all this talk about the "shivering" or "splintering" effect of "technique" and archival research is largely beside the point), but the fact of their belonging to the most diverse and mutually incomparable spheres, including that of events, which makes it so difficult to embrace them all in one fixed and balanced survey. In fact, even the sociologists, in their more restricted sphere, are not finding it easy and have become cautious.

Toynbee's indictment of the historians, then, is a disappointing performance. But the worst remains to be said of this chapter in which he tries to dispose of them. It is that, while obviously seething with resentment, he limits his counterattack to this more spectacular than solid exposition in the field of theory and avoids coming to grips with the concrete criticisms made against his earlier volumes. The proof of the pudding is in the eating. These theoretical discussions have their importance, but after all the theory in the world, when someone comes along with a work even of suspiciously large synthesis I would try to preserve an open mind and judge it on its merits. It is what I did with Toynbee's six volumes in 1946, and, if in the end I rejected them, it was not because they offended me in any dogmatically held theory but because I had found them wanting.

Toynbee makes an allusion to the essay I wrote then when he says that "these distracted latter-day Western historians were appalled" by "the novel universe of an incomprehensible complexity," which they had conjured up themselves and which "made the sheltering sands of technique look like the only practicable refuge from the mental hell of being compelled to play an eternal game of croquet with the unmanageable implements prescribed for the luckless players of the game in Lewis Carroll's fantasy *Alice through the Looking-Glass.*" It was indeed to that game with continually changing and unexpectedly moving implements (the description occurs, by the way, in *Alice in Wonderland*) that I had compared the method of *A Study of History,* and the comparison still seems to me a very apt one. But no other reference to my criticisms is to be found in Toynbee's defense, and I am not alone in thinking that his position is untenable unless he refutes a good many of my precise and cogent demonstrations of the fallacies and inconsistencies and misinterpretations to be found in his "empirical investigation."

This is a good deal more than a question of "technique." Toynbee assures us that his theories about the destinies of civilizations rest securely on the historical foundations he has built up so laboriously. If these foundations are proved to be unsound, as I believe that I have proved them to be, the whole imposing structure becomes a dreamlike fantasy— not unlike (since Toynbee has reminded me of the parallel) the Wonderland through which Alice wandered, with, I must say (and in so far the parallel seems to be defective), her critical faculties very much awake.

But I am afraid that it is too late in the day to issue an express challenge to Toynbee to prove that, for instance, his reading of nineteenth-century Italian history, which according to my demonstration (see pages 131-36) did not warrant the conclusions he built upon it, was right after all; or to do the same for his reading of North American history,[23] which I agreed was hopelessly wrong, so that his laws and large theories fall to the ground (see pages 170-76). He has missed the opportunity afforded him by his chapter in Volume IX to respond to the challenge implicit in my earlier essays, and he is less likely to respond to it now than before. He dwells in a world of his own imagining, where the challenges of rationally thinking mortals cannot reach him.

Prophets will at most traduce and scoff at their critics. As to showing that their critics are wrong, why should they? They know in their inmost hearts that disagreement can only spring from infidelity.

And, indeed, prophets have experiences which more earth-bound scholars cannot hope to share. In the little intellectual autobiography which is to be found in Volume X (and which is from more than one point of view absorbingly interesting) Toynbee relates how on seven occasions, all carefully dated and located, he was momentarily "transported" or "rapt into communion" with historic events or historic personages, generally connected with the outlandish place where he happened to find himself. One of these memorable experiences stands out from the rest.

In London, in the southern section of the Buckingham Palace Road, walking southward along the pavement skirting the west wall of Victoria Station, the writer, once, one afternoon not long after the end of the First World War . . . , found himself in communion, not just with this or that episode in History, but with all that had been, and was, and was to come. In that instant he was directly aware of the passage of History flowing through him in a mighty current, and of his own life welling like a wave in the flow of this vast tide.[24]

5.

The book and the man have an importance altogether apart from the achievement or failure in the realm of history or of scholarship. I suppose that a later student of history will regard them and their immense, though unevenly distributed, popularity as a curious portent of our times. Is it not highly remarkable, for instance, that Toynbee's admirers are to be found not only among Christians such as Mr. Wight, but also among such typically "neo-pagan" and at the same time neo-Marxist scholars as Professor Romein of Amsterdam, who took the chair when Toynbee delivered at The Hague the lecture on "World Unity and World History" which I had shortly before heard him deliver in London? The religious garb can apparently be quietly removed and the preaching of the idol Unity, which is, Moloch-like, to devour national traditions, attract a man stricken with a craving for what his friend, the Amsterdam philosopher Pos, has dubbed: "universalist solidarism." [25]

If I have, in this essay, been primarily critical and destructive, the reason is not that, as I put it before, there is no love lost between prophets and historians. The prophet can be to the historian an exciting and a moving subject. The reason is rather that this prophet usurps the name of historian and, especially, that I regard his prophecy as a blasphemy against Western civilization.[26]

IX THE NATIONAL STATE AND THE WRITERS OF NETHERLANDS HISTORY

1.

The problem I shall here discuss—the problem of the modern State and my own Netherlands history—is one that posed itself before me very early in my career. It is a problem that would bear discussion of a more general theoretical character than I shall venture upon. I shall write as a practicing historian—which is what I am—who has come up against a problem that required some thinking out, some grappling with theory.

The Dutch State resulted from revolution and war in the closing decades of the sixteenth century, but there had been a long history in the Low Countries before it came into existence—a long history when the Dutch language was spoken and Dutch literature flourished, when people felt and thought about religion in ways which still have a meaning today, when churches were built which still dominate our towns and villages and pictures painted in which we can still recognize ourselves.

If there was no Dutch State, there had been, ever since the migrations 'and settlement of the Franks in the sixth century after Christ, a Dutch linguistic area. The extent of this linguistic area has remained extraordinarily constant throughout the centuries. The linguistic boundary separating Dutch from French still runs where it ran when the Frankish colonization was completed some thirteen centuries ago.[1] Expressed in present-day political terms, it runs right through

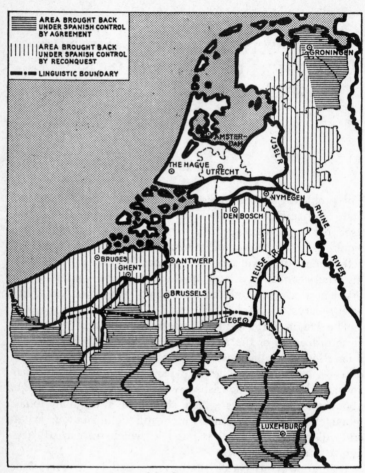

Parma's advance in 1590

(See explanation on facing page)

Belgium, so that the Dutch linguistic area now embraces Holland (or the Kingdom of the Netherlands, to use the official description) and the northern half of Belgium, commonly called Flanders. (Let me mention in passing that this name *Flanders,* historically speaking, belongs only to the western part, the ancient County of Flanders. Flanders in the modern sense of the Dutch-speaking region of Belgium, extends also over the ancient Duchy of Brabant and other districts still further East. Similarly *Holland* is originally no more than the northwestern part of the Kingdom which is now commonly so called. The ancient county was later on only one of the seven provinces constituting the Dutch Republic.)

Now the point that needs stressing is that this ancient (and still modern) Dutch linguistic area is not co-terminous with the Dutch State as it suddenly sprang into existence in the course of the sixteenth-century revolt against Philip II of Spain. It is much larger. The Dutch State comprises not quite two thirds of the Dutch-speaking people in the Low Countries and the region which remained outside at the critical moment in the last quarter of the sixteenth century was the region in which in the Middle Ages—with towns like Ghent and Bruges, Antwerp and Brussels—Dutch literature and civilization had had their earliest and most significant development.

PARMA'S ADVANCE IN 1590

(*Explanation of map on facing page*)

The area left white on the map includes the provinces of Holland, Zeeland, Utrecht, Friesland and the western half of Gelderland.

The Walloon provinces—Artois, Hainaut, Walloon Flanders, Namur—made their peace with the King in 1579; the province of Groningen did the same in 1580.

The area reconquered by Parma includes the provinces of Flanders, Brabant, Limburg, the eastern half of Gelderland, Overysel and Drente.—Den Bosch ('s Hertogenbosch) is the Dutch name for the town generally described by its French translation Bois-le-Duc.

It is a fact deserving careful attention that the linguistic area had never been the basis of any political formation. In the late Carolingian times part of it owed allegiance to the French Kingdom, another part to the German Kingdom; but, as time went on, in both cases this allegiance came to mean less and less. The reality were the feudal principalities—duchies, counties, bishoprics—and these gradually became completely independent. At last, in the fifteenth and early sixteenth centuries, a union was brought about by an outside power, the French Dukes of Burgundy, and their successors the Hapsburg rulers. But in this union the French-speaking provinces—as the old principalities now came to be called—Hainaut, Namur, Artois, and the rest—were combined with the Dutch-speaking provinces, Holland, Gelderland, Groningen, Brabant, Flanders and the rest; and the whole of the Netherlands came, moreover, to be connected with the extensive Hapsburg Empire, and in the end more especially with Spain. The Burgundian-Hapsburg rulers had meanwhile brought the beginnings of a central administration to the Low Countries; the governor and his councils resided at Brussels.

Within the framework thus created it was a natural development for a national sentiment, a sentiment of belonging together, to grow up. But the Burgundian-Hapsburg rule had at the same time introduced subjection to a foreign system, and it was in opposition to this domination, in opposition particularly to the purely Spanish tendencies of the rule of Philip II, that the national sentiment became more keenly aware of itself. It was fully awakened in the revolt in which all the seventeen provinces, with the single exception of Luxemburg, participated from 1576 on, under a States General meeting in a revolutionary fashion at Brussels.

Everybody knows that this union was broken up in the course of the resulting war and that only a group of Northern provinces achieved independence, becoming the Protestant Republic of the Seven United Provinces, while the Southern provinces were reduced to obedience and became, under the sovereignty of Spain, an advanced post of the great Counter-Reformation movement. Today the Dutch Kingdom is still preponderantly Protestant, or at least non-Catholic, and the

Kingdom of Belgium homogeneously Catholic. The great question is: how did this separation, and this divergence in religion, come about?

There is one answer to this question which I am afraid is the one which will occur spontaneously to most of you. It is that it must have been because Protestantism steeled the Northern rebels—the Dutch—to a successful resistance, whereas the Southern rebels—the Belgians—being Catholics, did not have the heart to persevere in the struggle. It is the answer that is still to be found in innumerable English and American textbooks and that indeed until fairly recently used to be given, in various disguises, or to a greater or lesser extent attenuated or qualified, by both Dutch and Belgian historians. But it never agreed with the facts.

You should note, first of all, that at the outset, before opposition had developed into revolt and war had altered the face of things, the Protestants were not more numerous in the North than they were in the South (and everywhere they constituted no more than a small minority). When in 1576 all the provinces united against the King of Spain—by the so-called Pacification of Ghent—it was not long before in all of them, in the provinces of Flanders and Brabant no less than in the Northern provinces, the Protestant minority managed to get hold of the positions of power and actually were in command of the rebellion. How was this possible?

For one thing, the only armed force which was from the start at the disposal of the Prince of Orange, the Sea Beggars, had helped the Protestants into the saddle four years earlier in the Northwestern provinces of Holland and Zeeland. If they managed in 1572 to revolutionize those two provinces alone it was not because their inhabitants were so much readier to welcome them, but because their geographical position invited attack from oversea and their soil offered special advantages for defense against Spanish attempts at reconquest. These partisan bands were composed of the exiles of the abortive rebellious movement of 1566-67; they were drawn from all the provinces; and they were Protestants to a man. The rebellious spirit in the country, however, was by no means exclusively caused by the new religion. It was primarily due to the irritation of a people wedded to their medieval tradition of self-government at the relentless policy of centralization and autocracy pursued by the royal government. But the Protestant minority, placed in a position of power by the armed invaders in 1572, were the most determined, in fact irreconcilable, enemies of the King, and that was in itself another reason why they came to occupy the leading positions everywhere. Revolutions are always led by minorities, and so it was here. It had been so in Holland and Zeeland from 1572 on, and soon after 1576 the Protestants came to the top in Brabant and Flanders as well.

But now the Spanish Government had got ready another army, which under the Duke of Parma, from 1578 onward, set about conquering the rebellious Netherlands. This army started from the outlying province of Luxemburg and in the course of not very many years managed to reduce to obedience a considerable part of the country. The fall of Antwerp (the great commercial metropolis of the Netherlands at that time) in 1585 completed the conquest of Flanders and Brabant. But Parma also took the whole East, up to the extreme North; Groningen made its submission as early as 1580. In 1590 Parma's advance was definitely halted, and the rebels, reduced now to a small group of Northwestern provinces clustered round Holland, set in a counteroffensive, by which they recovered part of the ground lost.

The religious convictions of the populations had little to do with these movements of conquest and reconquest. One glance at the map will show you that Parma's farthest advance, about 1590, was bounded by the strong strategic barrier of the rivers traversing the Netherlands from East to West (the Rhine and the Maas) and by the river Ysel. How strong this barrier is we learned to our cost in September 1944, when Montgomery was held up at Arnhem and the liberation of exactly the same portion of the Netherlands— all the country north of the great rivers and west of the Ysel—was delayed by a terrible eight months. If Parma was never able to cross that barrier, if the rebels on the contrary were able to take the offensive and push him back, it was because he was ordered by Philip to intervene in the French civil war and had to divide his forces. The counteroffensive, led by Maurice of Orange, William the Silent's son, was again conditioned by the geographic factor. It was easy to recover the country east of the river Ysel, but not because the population there were in sympathy with their "deliverers." On the contrary, they were overwhelmingly Catholic—much more so than Flanders and Brabant had been, although today that region, Groningen for instance, is solidly Protestant. But in those years the Groningers clung to the Spaniards as their protectors from the heretics. If they were "delivered," and then Protestantized, it was because the region was too far removed from the base of Spanish power in the South. To push on south of the great rivers, on the contrary, was a task beyond the power of Maurice. It would have meant a head-on attack on the main strength of the Spanish position.

Meanwhile, these military events were deciding the fates of the two religions contending for mastery. As soon as Parma and his Spaniards had recovered their hold on a district, Protestantism was strictly suppressed; most of the Protestants in fact emigrated—the majority settling in the provinces which were still holding out, in the North, that is, where they strengthened the Protestant element. The rebels, on their part, were all the time carrying on a reverse process of Protestantization, in which all means of pressure were used: dissolution of the old Catholic church organization and suppression of Catholic worship, exclusion of Catholics from all public offices, education based on the Heidelberg Catechism, public charity reserved for the Reformed. This was a process, however, for which time was needed, and only where the rebellion survived for a generation or longer could the majority of the population be brought over to the new church.

The true explanation, then, of the division of the Netherlands into a Protestant North and a Catholic South is the exact opposite of the current one. It is not because the South was Catholic and the North Protestant that the rebellion failed here and succeeded there: it is because the rivers enabled the rebellion to entrench itself in the North, while Spain recovered the provinces situated on the wrong side of the strategic barrier, that in course of time there sprang into existence this dual system of the Protestant Northern Republic and the Catholic Southern Netherlands, of Protestant Holland and Catholic Belgium.

2.

I have now given you, reduced to its simplest form, and somewhat dogmatically, an argument which I adumbrated for the first time more than thirty years ago[2] and which I have since set out on many occasions, elaborating certain aspects of it or indicating its implications in connection with a variety of topics. Here I shall discuss something of the historiographical background to the conflicting views on this matter. I never discovered any new facts. The relevant facts were not unknown nor are they in dispute. Is it not remarkable, then, that historians both in Holland and Belgium either completely overlooked them, or at least gave them little attention, failed to draw the obvious conclusion, and commonly wrote as if the separation had been a perfectly natural event and the emergence of a Holland and a Belgium, the one Protestant and the other Catholic, was the consummation of divergent tendencies inherent in the history and character or civilization of the populations?

Seeley, in his little book on *The Growth of English Policy,* refers to "that curious sort of optimistic fatalism to which historians are liable" and which in England caused them to argue (as he puts it) "that the loss of our American colonies was not only inevitable, but was even a fortunate thing for us." It is in that spirit exactly that Simon Stijl, about 1770, in a popular one-volume *History of the United Netherlands,* wrote that "one of the principal causes to which our Republic owes its durability resides in its *correct size.* Had it been smaller, its neighbours would have despised it. Had it been larger, it would have become unmanageable." Remember that this "correct size" of the Republic of the Seven Provinces was less than one third of that of the single state of Pennsylvania. Remember also that this paean to its durability was written twenty-five years before it was overthrown for good and all by the armies of the French Revolutionary Republic. And in fact this was not the first occasion, nor was it to be the last, on which the break-up of the old seventeen Netherlands into two unrelated small states left both helpless in the face of foreign invasion.

Here is another example of the way in which historians dealt with the problem. In 1860 Fruin wrote: "It was no passing misunderstanding that brought about the separation; it was a profound difference between the northern and the southern provinces, in origin, in national character, . . . in religion. . . ." [3]

Now, Fruin is a historian of a very different stamp from Stijl. He is the acknowledged master of the modern, methodical school in Holland, and his work is still very highly regarded. There is no glamour about Fruin. He is pre-eminently critical. He does not paint, he tries to explain. When he was a rising scholar, the reading public in Holland as well as in the rest of the world was captivated by the moving and colorful work of Motley. Fruin devoted to Motley's *The Rise of the Dutch Republic*, and later on to its sequel, two very long essays,[4] small books really, very deferential in tone; but the effect of the story as told anew by the critic is to make the reader realize that Motley had sacrificed everything to his sense of the dramatic and that he had no real understanding of the problems of Dutch history. Today nobody—among Dutch or Belgian historians at least—will any longer take Motley's views and explanations seriously, but everybody will study Fruin's magisterial essays. It is all the more amazing, then, that a scholar of this calibre could go so utterly wrong in discussing the causes of the Netherlands split.

He says that it was due to *difference in origin.* Apparently he was thinking of the difference between the Dutch-speaking section and the Walloons. But the line of political separation did not follow the linguistic boundary. The fact that requires explanation on the contrary is the splitting-up of the Dutch-speaking population.

He says that it was due to *difference in religion.* But, as he knew very well, Protestantism was no less strong in the South than it was in the North. The homogeneous Catholicism of present-day Belgium and the preponderance of Protestantism in present-day Holland cannot have caused a sixteenth-century event.

He says that the separation was due to *difference in national character*. No more is needed to answer this than to quote another English historian, Maitland, who once described national character as "a wonder-working spirit, at the beck and call of every embarrassed historian, a sort of *deus ex machina*, which is invoked to settle any problem which cannot readily be solved by ordinary methods of rational investigation."

In the present case "rational investigation" will yield the solution readily enough, if only it is resorted to. But the most surprising thing of all is that Fruin never once mentions the Spaniards when enumerating the causes of the split. Antwerp held out for a year when Parma laid siege to it in 1584, and yet we find Fruin and a host of writers, both Dutch and Belgian, speaking as if the separation were due to mutual misunderstanding or incompatibility.

How can this be? I think it is essential to remember that the mid-nineteenth-century generation was strongly influenced by the recollection of 1830, when the Kingdom of the Netherlands, reunited under William I in 1814, was broken up by the Belgian Revolution. On that occasion not only did anti-Dutch sentiment and a new and hot feeling of Belgian nationalism triumph and become the accepted and the patriotic thing in Belgium, but Holland herself was swept by a wave of anti-Belgian passion. No distinction was made between Dutch-speaking Flemings and French-speaking Walloons. In fact, when the great experiment of the reunion between Holland and Belgium had been undertaken after the downfall of Napoleon, the Dutch language in Flanders was in a bad way. We can see here the long effects of the catastrophe of the separation of the sixteenth century. For two centuries the Flemings had been isolated, politically and morally, from what had suddenly become the leading region in Netherlands culture, Holland. They had been all that time associated with the Walloons under the auspices of a foreign, but French-speaking, court at Brussels. On top of that they had been incorporated for twenty years, from 1794 to 1814, in the French Republic and French Empire and exposed to an intensive policy of gallicization. As a result especially of that last episode, the Dutch language had been driven out of public life in Flanders and had sunk to the level of a collection of local *patois*. During the reunion, after 1814, the Dutch government had tried to restore Dutch to its rightful position in Flanders, but Dutch public opinion had felt little but contempt for the unfortunate Flemings and their uncouth way of speaking the language. It had the less patience with them because they were "papists."

For here, too, the events experienced since the separation two centuries and a half before made themselves felt. The Dutch were not all Protestants; at least one third of them were Catholics, then as now. Since 1795 these Catholics had been in possession of full political and civil equality. But in reality Dutch society continued to be governed by the tradition set by the minority dictatorship of the time of the revolt, by the tradition which had in the days of the Republic been looked upon as the very life blood of the State; that is to say, articulate Dutch political opinion and active Dutch civilization, scholarship, literature, were still in fact controlled by Protestantism. The Catholics were still regarded as not quite what a true Dutch citizen or patriot should be. Dutch history and Dutch nationality never ceased to be openly identified with the Protestant idea. This tradition had received a tremendous filip from the difficulties experienced with the Belgian Catholics during the short-lived reunion and from the excitement roused by the Belgian Revolution. So it was with enthusiasm that the Dutch withdrew, in 1830, from the association with Belgium on to what was exultingly called "old Dutch soil" and prepared "to be themselves again," heirs to the tradition of the seventeenth-century Republic and of a Protestant ascendancy.

It is this spirit, however much by the middle of the century it may have been mitigated, which helps to explain the state of mind in which even so cool and critical a professional historian as Fruin approached the history of that earlier separation. Seeley's remark on "that curious sort of optimistic fatalism to which historians are liable" clearly does not cover everything. There is also the tendency, against which not even the historian can always guard himself, to transfer the preoccupations and habits of thought of the present into the contemplation of the past. And there is, especially, the desire, unconscious, or half conscious, to justify the State of which the historian is a citizen, the patriotism which it claims, the society, the civilization, the religion which seem to be its distinctive marks. The idea that all this should have resulted from the accidents of war, that the ancestors should not have been the free choosers of their destiny, that the Spanish army was responsible, and that success or failure was determined not by the convictions or the courage of the Dutch people but by the material factor of the course of rivers—that idea seems to have in it something derogatory to the dignity of Dutch nationhood, something almost blasphemous when it is supposed to have decided which section of the Low Countries was to be Protestant and which Catholic. And so the idea was instinctively barred.

The revolt and the separation in the late sixteenth century form critical points in the debate outlined; and if space permitted it could be shown from Belgian writers as well as Dutch how other details came to be misrepresented under the influence of contemporary preoccupations. But it is obvious that the whole course of Netherlands history *before* the separation must present difficulties to anyone placing himself on the modern State point of view.

Yet this was generally done, and the first author to do it systematically and with really brilliant synthetic power was Henri Pirenne, the first volume of whose *Histoire de Belgique* appeared in 1900. Here the past was uncompromisingly subjected to a conception inspired by the modern State. In his preface Pirenne announces quite plainly that it is his aim to bring out "the character of unity presented by the older history of Belgium." Of Belgium? He means, of course, of the regions which were at one time, many centuries later, to constitute Belgium. For in the days of Caesar or of Charlemagne, or even of Philip the Good or Charles V, Belgium really was still far to seek. But Pirenne sees it coming all the time. He does not for a moment conceal the fact that we are in the presence here of an unusual phenomenon: the exchange of influence between, the gradual growing together into one nation of, Germanic and Romance populations, Flemings and Walloons. But he is all the time out to show how criss-cross connections, economic, political, social and cultural, led to a similarity of conditions and bound together the regions on either side of the linguistic boundary.

It is clear to me that there is a large element of artificiality in this conception of Pirenne's. Given the unmistakable present-day political inspiration, one would on general grounds expect this to be the case; but the imposing work actually abounds in passages, as well as in omissions, where the constructive intention can be seen to have done violence to the unruly multiplicity of historic reality. I shall make two criticisms of a general nature.

The first is that Pirenne achieves the effect of a Belgium in existence long before there was a Belgian State simply by leaving the northern provinces out of the picture. Every incident or phenomenon that can strengthen the impression of intercourse and exchange across the linguistic boundary (in other words, between Flemings and Walloons) is made much of; but the intercourse and exchange connecting the various sections of the Dutch-speaking area (that is to say, the northern half of his Belgium and present-day Holland) are passed over. When the crisis of the late sixteenth century comes along, Pirenne can let the North fade quietly out; so well has he prepared the stage for his "natural" Belgian formation that the reader forgets to ask awkward questions. It is a miracle of tact. But once it is noticed that this problem has been evaded, misgivings arise.

The other criticism is that the Belgium which dominates the historical conception of Pirenne is not merely a Belgian national state; it is the Belgian national state such as it was created in 1830. In fact, the whole work was an attempt to bolster up that nineteenth-century Belgium, which already was menaced when he began to write and had to capitulate just about the time when, in the late twenties, his last volume was issued from the press.

Let me explain. The creation of the kingdom of Belgium in 1830 had been accompanied by a violent reaction against the attempt of the late Dutch regime to undo the Gallicization of public life in Flanders effected by the preceding French regime. Dutch was again banned from the administration, from the law courts, from the army, from the universities and the secondary schools—banned, that is, in the Dutch-speaking part of the country, for the monopoly of French in Wallonia had never been touched by the Dutch. But after 1830 French was to be the one cultural and public language in the whole of Belgium; it was to be the medium through which Belgian unity would be realized. The nineteenth century was thus a period of profound humiliation for Flanders. If I regard this state of affairs as a misfortune for the Flemish people, it is not because I do not personally love and admire the French, and French culture, but because of the simple fact that Dutch was the language of the Flemings. The statistics show that only a small percentage of them knew French; and *knowing* did not really mean *possessing*. Only through their own language could the Flemish people absorb, and actively contribute to, culture. The result of the state-supported predominance of French was to create a French-speaking upper class, who could not really, in the domain of culture, compete with the French (or with the Walloons), and who were at the same time incapacitated from fulfilling their natural role of cultural leadership with respect to their own people. As for the mass of the Flemings, they were largely cut off from the sources of culture.

Professor Pirenne was a Walloon, teaching history, in French, to Flemish students at the only public university in the Dutch-speaking part of the country, at Ghent. In other words, he occupied an advanced post in the movement of penetration and conquest which French civilization, under the auspices of the centralized Belgian State, was carrying on in Flanders. He never understood the resentment, or the feelings of responsibility toward their own people, animating the Flemish intellectuals who were behind the countermovement, the movement of resistance, the Flemish movement as it was called, which aimed at the re-nationalization or de-Gallicization of public life in Flanders. On the contrary, Pirenne contributed to the struggle by offering this historical conception of the interdependence of Wallonia and Flanders —under French auspices!

A development by which Flanders and Brabant had become alienated from their co-linguals in the north he represented as natural; and their acceptance of French as "one of their national languages" he made out to be natural, too.

This was a favorite phrase of his, and he did not mean that French was one of the national languages of *Belgium,* which is of course self-evident; French, he meant, was one of the national languages of *Flanders,* in fact, the one through which the Flemings had freely chosen to carry on their public life and the pursuits of the mind. As early as in the Middle Ages, Pirenne tries to show, the situation in Flanders in this respect was similar to what could be witnessed in his own day. This idea runs through the whole of his work, and again I have no hesitation in saying that it cannot be reconciled to the facts. It is no more than a smoke-screen behind which is hidden the stark and incontrovertible truth that nineteenth-century linguistic conditions in Flanders resulted from disasters in the past, namely, foreign conquest and foreign rule, and especially from the twenty years' incorporation into the French Republic and French Empire.

If French-led Belgium was, at the beginning of this century when Pirenne wrote his *History,* more self-conscious and aggressive than ever, it was because it felt itself menaced. Indeed, hardly had it, in the late twenties, greeted the completion of Pirenne's great work, in which it was glorified as the final outcome of long centuries of normal and inevitable development, than it was seen to crumble and give way before the assaults of the Flemish Movement. Pirenne lived to see the day when (in the early thirties) Dutch was introduced as the language of instruction at his own university of Ghent.

But in the first quarter of this century Pirenne's work, which is in any case a great historical achievement, seemed to dominate the scene by means of its political implications as well. Nothing is more remarkable than the eagerness with which it was accepted in Holland. The bitter feelings aroused in 1830 had of course long subsided. The Dutch Catholics were no longer so much relegated to the second plan; their self-emancipation following upon the legal emancipation of 1795 was proceeding apace. Nevertheless, the views which had become traditional under the Republic, and which had received the stamp of historical scholarship in the nineteenth century after the violent disruption of the united kingdom in 1830, survived.

The most striking expression of these views is to be found in a little book, *Nederland en België,* published in 1905 by a young historian, Colenbrander, who was to be one of the leading men of his generation. It was inspired entirely by Pirenne. The Flemings, by Pirenne's theory, had been skillfully and unostentatiously detached from the Dutch, and had been safely, and to all outward seeming honorably, incorporated in a mystic Belgian unity stretching back into the remotest ages. It now remained for Dutch historiography to show that a similar unity had from ancient times embraced the regions which in the late sixteenth century came to constitute the Protestant Republic, forerunner of the contemporary Kingdom. What the argument required particularly was a demonstration of the original and innate difference that had caused Dutch and Flemings to diverge. Colenbrander found evidence in religious movements, in schools of painting, in architecture. The method has been applied many times since, by writers on art, on literature, and on religion, and also by the political historians, to prove that a Dutch nation existed in the midst of the feudal confusion, or in a corner of the Burgundian-Hapsburg State, before ever a Dutch State had been born—a nation already complete with all the virtues which present-day Dutchmen love to regard as being their own: soberness and simplicity, a strong spiritual awareness under a reserved exterior, a nation, in short, of regular little Calvinists before ever Calvinism had been thought of.

How easy a game it is! The civilization of the medieval Netherlands was a rich one and richly diversified; features to suit a particular argument can always be discovered and, if isolated and arranged in a certain way, can be used to produce the desired impression. How easy a game, but how unprofitable! These ingenious speculations might have some interest if the separation of the sixteenth century had indeed been a voluntary one. The assumption that this is so underlies the whole argument of Colenbrander, just as it did that amazing passage of Fruin. Like Fruin, Colenbrander seems to forget about Parma and his Spanish army; and although I have always been ready to meet the speculators on their own ground, the recollection of the way in which things

actually came to pass in the sixteenth-century war of liberation and reconquest is enough to brush their fallacies aside as
so many cobwebs.

That, at least, is my opinion, and some thirty years ago I
began my attacks on what I called "the little-Netherlands
tradition in Dutch historiography," and on the related, or
complementary, "Belgicist" view. I challenged Colenbrander,
and all the leading men of the generation immediately preceding my own, all the men, in fact, who at that moment
dominated the historical world in Holland and in Belgium—
my good old master Blok, and Japikse, and Huizinga, and of
course the master spirit behind them all, Pirenne. The historians of literature in the person of my old teacher Kalff, and
the historians of art, Martin, Friedlander, also came in for
an occasional blow. It was a great fight that lasted over a
good many years. From 1930 on I have been at work on a
History of the Netherlands People, in which I am undertaking to test my theories on the realities of an account based
on the Dutch-speaking area as a whole.[5]

I hope the reader will forgive me if I cannot conceal the
pleasure with which I look back on the great controversy of
the twenties and early thirties, and my conviction that I introduced into the history-writing of both Holland and Belgium a point of view that has proved fruitful. Let me at
least make it clear that I do not attribute this to any exceptional perspicacity or originality of my own, nor do I attribute to my unaided powers of persuasion the fact that my
views are now finding a large measure of acceptance. My
views, too, were up to a certain point the product of the
times, and the times had changed and were still changing.

It had been my good fortune, as a young man, when I was
just finishing my studies at Leyden in 1911, to come into
contact with the Flemish Movement at a Flemish Students'
Congress in Ghent. I was deeply impressed by the moral
fervor that met me there; I felt that this was not merely a
manifestation of nationalism, but that these men were conscious of a great social task, which they could fulfill only
when the abnormal language conditions in their country
were righted. I noticed that they looked upon Holland, in
spite of the indifference of the leading circles there, as a

great asset in their struggle. But I felt that we of the North had an active obligation toward them, for what was at stake was the future in Flanders of our own, of our common, language and civilization. These impressions were never effaced, and they led me to question the spirit in which the history of our common past was generally written; to question the Belgicist view which tried to imprison Flanders in a fundamentally anti-Dutch conception; and to question the Little Netherlands, or Dutch State, view, which amounted to a denial of the Flemings, and as it seemed to me, of our own duty consequent upon the vigorous and healthy state of Dutch civilization in Holland.

And if my views, after their rough reception at the outset, are now making smooth headway, it is because, while the controversy was proceeding, both Holland and Belgium kept on changing. The Catholics now pull their full weight both in the political and in the cultural life of Holland. The Protestant conception of Dutch nationhood, which had been decaying for so long already, has become frankly untenable. Meanwhile in Belgium the Flemish Movement obtained the redress of most of the old grievances. During the last twenty years nothing less than a social revolution has taken place in Flanders.

Not only in the elementary schools, which it had been impossible to "de-Flemify," but also in the secondary schools, Dutch is now the only medium of instruction, and new generations of Flemish intellectuals are being formed at the Universities of Ghent and of Louvain by means of their own language, in the same way as Dutch intellectuals had all along been formed at the Universities of Leyden and of Utrecht.

It has now become impossible for the Dutch to ignore the value of our cultural tie with Flanders; nor does Belgium, in which Flanders has now its full say, look askance any longer at Dutch-Flemish intercourse. The way is open for a view of Netherlands history in which attention is not given exclusively to points of difference, but which proceeds from the principle of community.

3.

The moment has come for some more general reflections. What is the moral of the story that I have been telling?

I should not be surprised if some of you were disturbed to notice how profoundly the views of historians are influenced by contemporary political circumstances or considerations. I think we shall have to accept this—up to a point—as one of the inevitable limitations of history. History cannot be conceived, and it cannot be written or communicated, except from a point of view conditioned by the circumstances of the historian. One can even argue that, human beings being what they are, history can benefit by a close contact of the historian's imagination, or awareness, with contemporary life.

But I do not therefore believe that any point of view supplied by political or religious (or anti-religious) passion or prejudice is as good as the next for all that history will care. Nor do I think that the historian should allow himself to be turned into the obedient servant of his point of view, however acceptable it may otherwise be. He should constantly watch himself, he should try to get away from his point of view, even though he must return and be faithful to it if he wants to produce something that will hang together.

There exists a point of view from which indeed the difference between the systems that I have been opposing, of the modern State, or the linguistic or cultural area, must appear negligible. I am thinking of H. G. Wells and of Toynbee, although in fact there is a fundamental difference between the two. For Wells the world was a unit. It may have been so in his dreams only; the result was that for him national subdivisions became meaningless. For Toynbee it is "civilizations" that form "the smallest intelligible field of historical study;" that is to say, the histories of France, of the Netherlands, and of the United States are not worth writing; or, rather, they cannot be written in a satisfactory way, they cannot be isolated from the context of Western civilization and make sense.

Now in this latter proposition I think there is a measure

of truth. I think the reminder that we are all parts of a larger whole, not of a shadowy and unarticulated *world,* but of Western civilization, a spiritual organism, the life of which pulsates in the veins of each of us, is a very useful one. In these days of the North Atlantic Pact, the writers of national histories, who often had an inkling of the underlying truth when dealing with purely cultural matters, will perhaps be more ready to admit that even in the sphere of international rivalries a victory of their country may have been less important than the weakening of the Western European family. In any case the value of their presentation will gain, if they remember that its subject is not something completely self-contained and that there are outside standards to which it must be subordinated.

But this does not mean that, even in a possible future of much closer organization on these larger lines, national histories will become obsolete. In so far as Wells, and even Toynbee, reject the principle of history being written on the basis of nations, or states, I for one part company with them. Western civilization I can accept as a real unit, but it is a composite unit and the component parts are no less realities than is the whole. To say that the civilization is "the smallest intelligible field of study" is to set an almost impossible standard. Is not that field so large as to elude the grasp of the mind? Nothing is more natural than to study it in the smaller patterns of nations and state structures, through which its life manifests itself to the observer more immediately and more intimately.

But it was not in order to justify national histories that I write now. I am taking their right for granted. I have wanted to draw attention to a conflict that arises in some cases—the case of the Low Countries is by no means singular, although there is not often so glaring a discrepancy—between the history of a linguistic group, which is at least potentially a national group, and the modern states established in that area.

A friend of mine, who has a knack (as some friends have) of laying his finger on one's tender spots, once said to me: "You are just Pirenne reversed." I might have felt flattered, for I have the warmest admiration for Pirenne's great historical qualities. But the intention was not complimentary, and

I have often remembered the remark as a challenge to my historical conscience. Am I? I think not. I think there is all the difference in the world between trying to fit the past into a conception completely contemporary (Belgium), and starting with a conception which has had a foundation in objective fact ever since the sixth or seventh century after Christ (the Dutch linguistic area), in order to conduct an inquiry as to how far, on that basis (after a pattern usual in Europe), national consciousness has developed; and if it has not, why not?

But I must not wander off into an apology of my own work. And indeed I do not mean to offer the solution that I am attempting—a history on the basis of the linguistic area—as the only one that will meet the case.[6] No doubt, to use the territory of the modern state as the framework, say, of a history of medieval architecture is to fly in the face of history. One may be tempted to do so by the fact that the modern state has a bureau which carries out investigations and assembles data concerning all old buildings within its frontiers. But this demarcation, which had no meaning whatever in the Middle Ages, must distort or disrupt the vision of the student of medieval architecture who allows himself to be shut up in it. For the later period the situation becomes more doubtful. Since they came into being in the sixteenth century, the Dutch State and the Belgian proto-State have been themselves the creators of national sentiment and the directors of political and cultural life, without, however, uprooting the older and larger identity. There are, from then on, several points of view possible from which to survey developments. The choice will always be a delicate affair of personal preference and of adjustment to subject matter.

But the important thing seems to me that one should be aware of the existence of a problem. That is perhaps enough to guard against the danger of becoming enslaved to one's point of view. There is not, at any rate, a worse slavery than the illusion—not unlike that to which, Carlyle tells us, the goose falls a victim when you draw a chalk circle round him —that one is not free to cross the boundary of one's sentiments or prejudices, that there is no choice involved, that one's point of view is the one immovably set by history itself. And it is that illusion which has been so often fostered by the modern state, with its high claims to total allegiance, and with its efficient machinery to assist, but at the same time gently to guide, the historian. I preach no hostility to the modern state (or to any modern state). But I do warn the historian, and the national historian, not to surrender his mind to it unquestioningly.

X THE FRENCH HISTORIANS
AND TALLEYRAND

In the purely political sphere—apart, that is to say, from personalities such as Madame de Staël and Chateaubriand, who hold their own beside him in the realm of thought—only one figure has in the view of history maintained its rank beside Napoleon: Talleyrand.

And Talleyrand remains as problematical as Napoleon himself. Could any life present more striking contrasts? Aristocrat, *grand seigneur* even, he rushes into the Revolution; a renegade bishop—a man, one would think, who has irretrievably lost class. Nevertheless, he rises to a great position, and not under the always somewhat questionable regime of the First Consul and Emperor only; the real surprise is that he manages to retain it under the Restoration, under the Bourbons, and again after 1830 under Louis Philippe. And yet, within him, the rift between idea and practice goes even more deeply.

He *had* an idea. At the very outset of his career he gives striking and clear expression to it. In 1792—he was thirty-seven years old—Talleyrand was staying in England on a dim diplomatic mission; he had really gone there to be safe from the increasing violence of the Revolution. Here it was that he wrote a memorandum on the foreign policy which the new France should pursue. Let France liberate the peoples (this was his bow to the prevailing temper at home), but let her rest content with her frontiers. The entire paper was an argument for the futility of all this striving after expansion of territory. I quote Talleyrand's own words:

All extensions of territory, all usurpations, by force or by fraud, which have long been connected by prejudice with the idea of "rank," of "hegemony" . . . , being only the cruel jests of political lunacy, whose real effect is to . . . diminish the happiness . . . of the governed for the . . . vanity of those who govern.

This is a confession of faith such as one would hardly expect from a man destined to become the Foreign Secretary first of the Directory and later on of Napoleon as Consul and Emperor. For under those regimes extensions of territory were the order of the day. But Talleyrand was also the man who in 1814 was to lead France back within the old frontiers and who did it without reluctance, rather in the style of a wanderer returning after untold dangers to the ever-regretted safety of home; and as late as 1830 he did his bit toward the avoidance of war over Belgium. Yet in the intermediate period, how zealously had he co-operated in the wild excesses of the policy of conquest.

But *had* he been zealous? No doubt he had congratulated Napoleon, in 1797, upon the bartering away of the Venetian Republic of Austria. But first he had pleaded against it. It was he who in 1803 penned the threat to England that the young ruler (then First Consul) might venture out and found a great Western Empire. But was it not rather a warning, which he hoped would result in peace being preserved and the policy of adventure nipped in the bud? It was he who had drafted the decree establishing the Continental System, intended to exclude English commerce from the Continent of Europe, and after Austerlitz he had assisted in drawing up the humiliating peace treaty imposed upon Austria. Yet in the decree he had inserted fine-sounding words about a European peace—did he perhaps mean them? And before the defeat of Austria (in a memorandum which has remained as famous as the one of 1792, I should say, has *become*, for at the time neither the one nor the other was known to the public) in a memorandum written at Strasbourg in 1805, before Napoleon came to grips with the Austrian army, Talleyrand had implored the Emperor to use moderation after the expected victory because driving Austria to despair could only breed more wars and expose Western Europe helplessly to the Russian menace. More, after the victory he had repeated this advice, although the victor plainly did not relish it. Only after his counsel had actually been brushed aside did he again lend a hand toward the policy he had spoken against.

When in his memoirs Talleyrand discusses his acceptance of the Foreign Secretaryship under the Directory, he disclaims all calculations of personal interest. It is a sacrifice, rather, he says, when one consents to act as the responsible editor of somebody else's works. Egoism or fear are not likely to counsel such a course of renunciation of self. I remark in passing that Talleyrand, even if he was not moved by considerations of self-interest into accepting, certainly saw to it afterward that he was well paid for his self-sacrifice. His secretaryship enabled him, by means of a venality which became a by-word, to build up an enormous fortune. But let us hear what more he has to say for himself. In days when everything is in ruins (he proceeds), a refusal to act amounts to giving further opportunities to the architects of destruction. Much good could be done, much evil be prevented.

The apology of the *collaborateur!* In a certain sense Talleyrand can be regarded as the illustrious patron of that class of men which we have come to know so well on the continent of Europe during the German occupation. We owe it to him, however, to remember that his case was one not of collaboration with the foreign conqueror but only of serving a national government, thrown up by Revolution but universally acknowledged. The fact remains that he was separated from that government by a sharp divergence of opinion (never openly admitted), and also it is very questionable indeed whether all his serving and urging ever caused either the Directory or Napoleon to swerve from their path by as much as an inch.

His service to Napoleon especially had frequently placed him in very questionable situations. It has never been proved, but many times been asserted—by Napoleon himself among others—that Talleyrand had given advice tending to the execution of the Duke d'Enghien, a cold-blooded murder really, by which the First Consul had, in 1804, meant to show the Bourbons in an unmistakable manner that their time was over; and three years later Talleyrand is again said to have counseled the deposition of the Bourbons still reigning in Spain. Later he naturally denied having been an accomplice on either of those two occasions, and he did so with that imperturbable self-assurance of which he possessed the secret. Chateaubriand assures us in his memoirs that he had with his own eyes seen documents which indubitably proved Talleyrand's guilt with respect to the Spanish drama; so that when the old man in 1823, in the Chamber of Peers, coolly denied having had anything to do with it, he, Chateaubriand, listened hesitating between horror and admiration. "Has nature given this man the power to remake or to destroy truth?"

However this may be, long before the close of the Napoleonic intermezzo Talleyrand had himself come to the conclusion that he was not able, by collaborating, to direct or deflect the course of events. In his memoirs he puts it very strongly. As early as 1803, he tells us, he had come to be convinced that Napoleon no longer pursued a French policy, but rather a personal one—that, in other words, a conflict had arisen between Napoleon and France, between Napoleon's lust of conquest and French interests. Yet it was not until 1807 that he resigned the Foreign Secretaryship. Or should I say that Napoleon dismissed him? In any case, his departure from the ministry was surrounded with new conspicuous (and profitable) honors. As *Vice-Grand-Electeur* and *Prince de Bénévent* he entered the small circle of the greatest dignitaries of the Empire, and, moreover, the Emperor continued to consult and employ him in the weightiest affairs of foreign politics. Immediately after the fateful measure of ousting the Spanish Bourbons from the throne, in which Talleyrand was in any case somehow concerned, Napoleon took him along to Erfurt, where, surrounded by a crowd of more or less dependent German rulers, the Emperor was to meet his new great ally, Alexander of Russia.

We touch here the critical point in Talleyrand's career. He now went beyond giving advice that he could be sure would not be taken—beyond, also, dropping critical remarks in drawing rooms, grains of venom instilled in the syrup of praise which everyone was bound to administer to the Emperor and which *he*, Talleyrand, certainly did not stint. He now suddenly proceeded to action; he put a spoke in the wheel of Napoleon's chariot. He did it, let there be no mistake, in the dark. The Emperor was much upset and surprised by the poor results of the Erfurt meeting, but he never knew that this was Talleyrand's doing.

What Napoleon had wanted to get from Alexander was a firm promise of concerted action with regard to Austria. Austria, humiliated in 1806 against Talleyrand's advice, was plucking up courage now that the Spanish embroglio proved so embarrassing to Napoleon. It was all-important to Napoleon to be safeguarded against surprises from that quarter. But he could not, at Erfurt, get the Czar, who might have restrained Austria, to pledge himself. What was the reason? It was that Talleyrand had suggested a different policy to Alexander in intimate conversations which had been screened from Napoleon's watchful attention. Do not mistake (was what he had said): Napoleon is not France. The French people are sick of these endless wars. Help the sensible Frenchmen to tie his hands. See in the French nation an ally for a policy of European stability. These suggestions had impressed the Czar the more as they were not new to him. In 1804 the underlying ideas had already been the basis of negotiations conducted between himself and Pitt.

The actual obstruction experienced at Erfurt in that critical juncture remained, as I have said, hidden from Napoleon. Yet it soon became plain to him that the Prince of Benevento had grown to be a European figure at his court, a center of whispered opposition, which his enemies outside France, too, were observing. Against the background of the startling triumphs with which that extraordinary man even yet put to shame the expectations of an early collapse, this position of Talleyrand became a great European fact. What is amazing is that the Emperor, whose system was so intolerant of independence, who had a Minister of Police for the purpose of warning him of all symptoms so that the menace might be suppressed in its initial stage, should have left Talleyrand unmolested through all these final years. He was conscious of the opposition all the time; the whispering campaign irritated him. At times the tension found vent in one of those fits of passion which made his surroundings tremble. In January 1809—affairs in Spain were going badly, the attitude of Austria became threatening—the Emperor suddenly, in the presence of a number of ministers and high officials, began to inveigh against Talleyrand. Gradually he worked himself up to the most scathing abuse. "You are a thief and a coward, you don't believe in God. You have deceived and betrayed everybody; nothing is sacred for you, you would sell your father. I have heaped riches upon you, and there is nothing of which you would not be capable against me." The accusations became more pointed, and also cruder. After having charged him with political intrigues, the Emperor taunted Talleyrand with the (all too notorious) infidelity of his wife. A truly miserable scene— and what made a deeper impression than Napoleon's passionate screaming was the perfectly impassive countenance of Talleyrand, who stood listening and, on account of his crippled leg, leaning against the wall. On leaving he said, in an expressionless voice, to his colleagues (and it is of all that was said on that occasion the phrase that has survived until today): "What a pity that so great a man should be so ill bred." The next day he appeared at court again as if nothing had happened, and relations went on as before.

Napoleon managed to defeat Austria once again. He now even married the defeated Emperor's daughter. When in 1812 the rupture with Alexander came about and he invaded Russia, the whole of continental Europe supported him, or seemed to do so. But now the catastrophe came down upon him, and was reinforced at Leipzig in 1813. The whole of continental Europe was now with England against Napoleon. Against *Napoleon?*—or against *France?*

It was Talleyrand who suggested the answer. The distinction which he had already made in his own mind for so long and which he had expressed, at the height of the Emperor's power, to the Czar and also to Metternich, Talleyrand now, in the crisis when the Allies occupied Paris, succeeded (soon in the capacity of Louis XVIII's minister) in having accepted. For France this distinction between the usurper and the

French nation proved a blessing, and the man who could present it with such quiet conviction, a precious asset.

At least that is what one should think must be the general opinion, but the fact is that foreign historians seem more ready to admit it, and generally to appreciate the statesman-like qualities of Talleyrand, than the French. There are two books in which Talleyrand has of late years been pictured as a great European, as a man able to rise above the hatreds and passions which proved the undoing of the European society of nations and especially of France. One was by an Englishman, Duff Cooper, well-known conservative politician; the other by the anti-Fascist Italian Ferrero (now dead).[1] And at the same time the hostile view which was customary among French historians, which is to be found in the older works of, for instance, Bourgeois, Driault, Sorel, and even of Talleyrand's devoted biographer, Lacour-Gayet, has persisted—witness a new book by the veteran writer on Napoleon, Madelin.

Of course the elements for a hostile picture lie ready to hand, and those who want to write sympathetically about Talleyrand, and set him up as a pillar of wisdom among statesmen, have a good deal to explain away. There is his notorious venality to begin with. Let me add at once that although I do not want to play the apologist for financial immorality, yet I must say that human nature is a complex thing and that a man can be unable to resist the temptation to line his pockets and yet have clear-sighted and sound ideas about international politics and about the hollowness of wars of conquest; and, moreover, he can hold these ideas tenaciously and believe in them profoundly. The more serious charge against Talleyrand, the one which creates a more real difficulty for his admirers, is that his career shows him up as a time-serving opportunist—that he was never prepared to risk his tenure of office for his convictions; that he allowed both the Directory and Napoleon to use him for their own purposes.

Ferrero gets round this difficulty by ignoring it, although he makes an important point when he says that in the last years of Napoleon's power Talleyrand risked more than office;

that he risked his head, every day, by his underground opposition. The interest of Duff Cooper's book is that he does not extenuate the shifts and tricks to which Talleyrand found himself obliged to resort, and that he yet manages to suggest a faithfulness to certain high conceptions of European solidarity. You are made to feel that here, even though this wisdom had to remain on the shelf for so long while the secret devotee trafficked in the rowdy market place of politics as he found it—*here* you had the real Talleyrand, who in the end, in 1814, made his effective contribution.

But now the problem that I want to discuss particularly is: Why is it that this view is so rarely set forth by French historians? Are the French more inclined to detest inconsistency of action and deceitfulness? Have they less patience with the witty and charming intriguer, the shifting, evasive character? I do not think that we shall find the solution by looking in that direction. I think it is something in the make-up of the political mentality of the French that explains their attitude toward Talleyrand. I may perhaps say that this lecture is really a postscript to my book, *Napoleon, For and Against*,[2] in which I tried to show how the appreciations of Napoleon as you will find them in French historical literature are always closely connected with the particular author's political outlook, or, if waves of *pro* and *anti* can be detected, then with the general phases of political temper or tendency through which France passed after Napoleon's downfall. The presentation of history is subject to these influences. And so it appears again in the case of Talleyrand.

Mr. Duff Cooper has also discussed this phenomenon of the bad press which Talleyrand has had in his own country, and he puts it down to the cult of Napoleon. Naturally, veneration of Napoleon must be incompatible with admiration for Talleyrand's political wisdom. To the Napoleon worshipper, not only Talleyrand's conduct at Erfurt in 1808 but even his independent action in 1814 must appear simply treacherous; and indeed Talleyrand is more often called *the traitor* than *the far-sighted statesman* in French historical writings. Only, as will be seen in my Napoleon book, the pro-Napoleon mentality is by no means universal among French historians, and that Duff Cooper's explanation is incomplete appears very clearly from the fact that even those Frenchmen who take a very critical view of Napoleon the despot and of Napoleon the egotist who in his foreign policy sacrificed French interests to his own insane ambitions—even those Frenchmen cannot stomach the activities of Talleyrand. No, the real explanation seems to me to lie in a feeling which is far more common among Frenchmen than that of veneration for Napoleon (although certainly that is by no means dead) —I mean their strong feeling for the State.

To make a distinction between Napoleon's policy, interests, views and those of the French people—that is what Talleyrand did, and in the reality of that distinction if anywhere was his justification. But even those French historians of a later age who realize that Napoleon was dragging France along on a dangerous course shrink from the conclusion that an individual could therefore be right in conspiring with foreign governments against the Emperor, who after all represented the lawful government of the country. Sometimes, no doubt, they try to rationalize their disapproval by arguing that Talleyrand's underhand action at Erfurt, and even the bold independent line he took in 1814, had disastrous results in actual fact. As far as 1814 is concerned it may seem curious to the non-French observer that this can be seriously maintained. France, one is inclined to think, was let off surprisingly lightly after the commotions which she had created in Europe for a generation past.[3] But it was until recently an article of faith with most French historians that their country had a right to its "natural frontiers"—that is to say, to Belgium and the German Rhineland!—and it was often argued that Talleyrand by recklessly and precipitously preaching peace played into the hands of the foreign powers whose real desire was to rob France of those regions. But, quite apart from argumentation, one seems to notice an instinctive, unreasoning shrinking from the deed as such. "Don't let us play upon words," writes Driault (and he wrote it in the phase when he was far from being an enthusiast for Napoleon); "to betray Napoleon was to betray France."

One certainly does not need to be a Frenchman to understand that attitude. Everybody will find it easier to recommend to the citizens of another country resistance to a dictator as their true national duty than to put that doctrine into practice when the case presents itself at home. Yet one would expect a historian to realize that the short and positive formula in which Driault summarizes the opposite view did not fit the reality of those awful years when Napoleon was paving the way for the catastrophe. And, in fact, Talleyrand's independent action was by no means an isolated phenomenon. There was Caulaincourt, who is charged by some with having abetted Talleyrand at Erfurt and who in any case acted in a strikingly similar fashion in 1813. Marshal Berthier was not a politician, but had he been one he would not have acted differently; and the same applies to most of the marshals. It seems undeniable that there had come into being so sharp a divergence between Napoleon's policy and the interests of France, felt so painfully by most Frenchmen who had any capacity for forming a judgment, that the conflict of contradictory obligations simply could not be suppressed.

A historian such as Driault should have realized this. But precisely in the modern period, in the nineteenth and early twentieth centuries, French opinion was decidedly averse to juggling with the claims of the State. The idea had taken firm root that the State, represented by whatever government happens to be in power, has rights before which individual dislike, individual criticism or dissent, have to give way. French history was presented in such a way as to teach the young Frenchman that very lesson. The wars of religion of the sixteenth century, when the Catholics had their connections with Spain and the Huguenots with England, were viewed preferably from this standpoint. After that crisis the State, victorious over national dissension, was incarnated in Henry IV; it was more firmly established by Richelieu; and again, after the episode of the Fronde, which had been accompanied by other (and this time very frivolous) party intrigues with the foreigner, Louis XIV had appeared as the restorer of national unity. These were the aspects, rather than those of despotism or stifling centralization, that were stressed and applauded by modern historians. Richelieu and Louis XIV were not shown as the suppressors of freedom, but as the builders of the strong national State. In 1789 there began the aristocratic emigration and the attempts of the emigrants to overthrow the revolutionary regimes with the aid of foreign countries. Their miserable failure had seemed to drive home the conclusion that there was no greater folly than to set individual preference or party above national unity as represented by the government. And now the nineteenth century, with its rapidly changing regimes, each one established by revolution, had served to familiarize Frenchmen with the view that one's loyalty was due to the government actually in power, irrespective of one's personal feelings as to its desirability.

And note well that, in spite of all the excitement attendant upon each of those many changes, in 1830, in 1848, in 1851, in 1870, people were gradually beginning to lose the experience of really profound ideological contrasts or despotisms extending over every department of life, such as the religious conflicts of the sixteenth and even of the seventeenth century had brought in their wake and such as had prevailed in the period of Great Revolution. This made it even harder for the generations of the Liberal Age, of the age before the rise of the totalitarian creeds of National Socialism and of Communism, to understand situations in which the obvious claim of lawful authority might be less valid than the conscientious conviction that the moment had come for resistance. And as regards the *methods* of resistance—that ruse and deceit and dissimulation could be the only ones possible in the struggle with a dictatorship and a reign of terror, was not this a tenet of political wisdom that had somehow been lost from sight in those seemingly stable times before the Great Wars? All of this of course militated against nineteenth- and twentieth-century historians' viewing the career of Talleyrand with sympathy or understanding.

I was thrilled, not long ago, on reading the latest volume of Mr. Churchill's *War Memoirs*,[4] to come across a passage containing this same view of the force of the French tradition of the individual's duty of submission to whatever regime happens to have been thrown up by the accidents of policy.

Mr. Churchill discussed this characteristic of the French political mind (and he did it very strikingly indeed) in connection with an actual war problem. The passage occurs in a speech made by him in December 1942 in a secret session of the House of Commons, for the purpose of allaying the irritation and indignation aroused in England by the policy which the Americans were at that moment pursuing in North Africa. General de Gaulle, the leader of the Free French, was kept completely in the background, while General Eisenhower co-operated with Admiral Darlan. You may remember that very dubious figure, who was originally sent by Marshal Pétain and to whom there still clung the somewhat unpleasant odors of Vichy.

Mr. Churchill's speech was meant to make the House of Commons understand that the Americans were not actuated by leanings toward Vichy or dictatorship. Their policy of supporting this man was simply dictated by the circumstances of the case, among which the overridingly important one was that of the political outlook of the Frenchmen with whom they had to deal in North Africa. The Prime Minister examined

. . . a peculiar form of French mentality, or rather of the mentality of a large proportion of Frenchmen, in the terrible defeat and ruin which had overtaken their country. [He did not defend that mentality; he only wanted his audience to remember that] the Almighty in his infinite wisdom did not see fit to create Frenchmen in the image of Englishmen.—In a state like France, which has experienced so many convulsions—Monarchy, Convention, Directory, Consulate, Empire, Monarchy, (Republic), Empire, and finally Republic—there has grown up a principle founded on the *droit administratif* which undoubtedly governs the action of many French officers and officials in times of revolution and change. It is a highly legalistic habit of mind, and it arises from a subconscious sense of national self-preservation against the dangers of sheer anarchy. . . . Much turns in the minds of French officers upon whether there is a direct, unbroken chain of lawful command, and this is held by many Frenchmen to be more important than moral, national, or international considerations. From this point of view many Frenchmen who admire General de Gaulle and envy him in his role, nevertheless regard him as a man who has rebelled against the authority of the French State. . . .

So far Mr. Churchill.

Mutato nomine! . . . In the eyes of Frenchmen of this way of thinking, though Talleyrand might be ever so clever and enterprising, he was outside the law; legality was represented by Napoleon, and as for questioning the Emperor's claim to the obedience of every Frenchman on the ground of his policy being mistaken and threatening the country with ruin, that was dangerous individualism which could lead heaven knows where.

Mutato nomine! . . . Another name might also be changed, and we might get involved in the controversy that is going on in Germany as to the patriotism or otherwise of the men who conspired to overthrow Hitler and to come to some sort of arrangement with the Allies. The mere mention of the case will be enough to make it even clearer that the problem which I have been discussing is one of an interest far exceeding the limits of the career or of the personality of Talleyrand—not only in time but geographically as well. The German parallel does not of course imply that I am overlooking the enormous difference between Napoleon and Hitler. But they were both dictators, and to use the term of Ferrero, adventurers. The parallel seems to me to be enlightening, in that it helps us on the one hand to realize that this reluctance to admit the right of the individual to act in a crisis against his government, which I have shown to be typically French, is by no means confined to the tradition of that country; on the other hand, as regards Talleyrand, the German parallel will remind us—if we need that reminder: the present generations are becoming ever more familiar with the idea that under the regime of a dictator-adventurer the social order is partially dissolved and resistance cannot be judged by the rules of normal times.

XI LATTER-DAY NAPOLEON WORSHIP [1]

There are few periods in the life of Napoleon that have been so copiously recorded as that of his last years, spent in captivity. There was quite a little group of men (some married) —four military officers dignified with high-sounding court titles, doctors, a priest, attendants and servants of varying ranks and varying functions—cooped up with him in the privacy of Longwood. For on that solitary rock of St. Helena, lost in the ocean, thousands of miles from anywhere, Napoleon, with indomitable fortitude and unbreakable will, managed to establish himself as the ruler of a little court, completely distinct from the English society of the island. It was a purely illusionist affair, but a desperate reality in the lives of all concerned.

The great pastime of nearly all the more important members of that terribly artificial and secluded little community was keeping diaries. In them they jotted down expressions of their boredom, of their regrets and longings and disappointments. But although they were so completely cut off from the world, which they felt was going on without them and without heeding or caring what had become of them, it was not as if nothing happened in that funny little world of their own.

There were, for one thing, the doings of the master. And if he no longer took decisions that affected the fate of nations, his commands, and even his moods, were important to *them.* Besides, there was his talk. Napoleon was a great talker, especially now that talk had to serve as a substitute for action. Reminiscence was its prevailing trend. His life, which had set the scene for all their lives, and for the life of the world, suddenly come to a stop, and, as it were, set before him and them to contemplate, seemed absorbingly interesting. But there was more at St. Helena. There was the never-ceasing feud with the hapless Sir Hudson Lowe, the governor, the jailer, carried on with passionate zest by Napoleon, and no less passionately watched by his companions. And then these had their own jealousies and ambitions, their own rivalries and quarrels, which could at times, in so confined a space, loom maddeningly large.

Lord Rosebery, in his book on Napoleon's captivity, which is still, after more than fifty years, the wisest, the most detached and at the same time sensitive, and the most readable account of that tragi-comic episode, in introducing General Bertrand, Grand Marshal of the Palace (no less!), says: "Bertrand has one agreeable singularity, he wrote no book, and tells us nothing; which is in itself a pleasant contrast to the copious self-revelation of Gourgaud and Las Cases."

But here we have Bertrand's book to add to the collection after all. The occasion of my talk is the appearance in English of his journal for the months of January to May, 1821—the final phase, for Napoleon died on May 5th, and this is only a part (the part which was published in France some years ago) of the enormous mass of notes which Bertrand turns out to have left behind him. Tucked away in a strong-box, and passed from one generation to another of Bertrand's descendants, his papers were at last, in 1946, discovered by the Secretary General of the Napoleon Institute in Paris.

M. Fleuriot de Langle is one of those *érudits* whom nothing can daunt in the service of their chosen subject. And he needed an almost superhuman determination and perseverance. For the Grand Marshal had made his day-to-day entries not exactly in cipher, like Pepys, but in a kind of stenography, jotting down only the initial letter or letters of most words. The result set to the eager twentieth-century reader problems which could be solved only by supreme ingenuity, familiarity with the men and the circumstances of the period such as only long and assiduous study can give, and an inexhaustible patience. When the passage which is given in facsimile as a sample of the manuscript is compared with what the editor has printed, one does not doubt the correctness of his completed version, but one marvels that it has been possible to establish it.

M. Fleuriot has been sustained in his labors not only by the self-sacrificing devotion of the antiquarian: in his case this is reinforced by the enthusiasm of the Napoleon worshipper. How very curious, and how very French! How startling, and at the same time how fitting, how apparently in harmony with the nature of things, to find in M. Fleuriot's preface proof that the race of the Frédéric Massons and of the Octave Aubrys has survived not only the horrors which the First, but the catastrophe and humiliation which the Second, World War brought to France. Napoleon is the incomparable "Hero", he is "He"—again the capital letter is called in to express the writer's feelings of awe—"whose countenance posterity is never tired of scrutinizing, whose secrets it indefatigably tries to penetrate." The writer and a friend "spend a moment of silent meditation in front of the marble shaft and the sarcophagus of porphyry where, with the sun streaming down through the gilded windows, the Emperor reposes *in aeternum* in his Glory."

The translator has been a little shy in rendering these effusions. The "Hero" guarded by his "Victories" has lost some of its impressiveness in his English because he has balked at the initial capital with which the word victories was adorned in the original, and he has altogether omitted the concluding paragraphs of the introduction. Here the impression of "the grandiose and of the pathetic," which is said to emanate from Bertrand's unadorned and realistic tale, is likened to "a sky during a thunderstorm, the ashy coloring suddenly animated when traversed by a shaft of fire which lends an unforgettable set-off to human beings and to things. That purple and gilded ray is the ray of Glory, torch of the living, sun of the dead."

I do not blame the translator—this sort of thing does not go down with an English public nor was it meant for them. I confess that, as for me, while it irritates me and moves me to ridicule, it delights me at the same time: it is so precious a specimen of a mood and a style which I really believed to have become extinct.

But the journal, not the introduction, is what matters. And one can on the whole agree with M. Fleuriot's estimate of its value and of the quality of its author. From its soberness and matter-of-factness the figure of the selfless and faithful servant comes out unimpaired. It has done Bertrand no harm that we have his book after all. His admiration for Napoleon is of the wholehearted, unquestioning kind, so much so that he is not tempted to extenuate or to embellish. He is apparently undisturbed by anything the master says or does and he records it as it comes along.

There are not, of course, any startling revelations: we know so much about Napoleon already. But it is fascinating to meet him again, and to be able to listen in to confidences certainly not intended for our ears. It is often a book which he has just read that sets him talking. The arrival of a fresh supply from Europe was an event, and often there were memoirs or histories about himself or the recent past dominated by him. Starting to point out the injustice or inaccuracy of a certain passage, he would be led far beyond the point originally at issue, tell the story of a campaign with a wealth of detail, lay down the law on the politics of the Baltic or on what was to be done for Corsica, or speak his mind with a complete absence of reserve about all his nearest associates: for instance, about Murat, about Bernadotte, about Joseph, his brother.

Most interesting is what he has to say about Josephine. He had loved her, he says, although he had no respect for her. In a book about Josephine the old story had been repeated that she had begged him to spare the life of the Duke of Enghien. Quite untrue, said Napoleon. I am quoting Bertrand's report of his words:

Like everyone else she wept and said that she had spoken to me about it, whereas in actual fact she never mentioned the matter to me. She took no interest in anyone. . . . She was kind in the sense that she would have asked anyone to lunch, even [and here he mentioned two notorious women, the Empress's dressmaker and an actress]. She gave freely. But would she have gone without something so as to be able to give? No. Would she have sacrificed anything in order to help someone else? That is real kindness. She gave, but she got it all out of the bag. [She was a congenital liar, he also said.] The real reason why I married her was because she had got me to believe that she had a large fortune. . . . I found out the truth about her finances before I married her, and in any case the marriage with a woman of a good old French family was an excellent thing for me. I was a Corsican, after all.

There is about all this a downrightness, and also a psychological truth, which are positively staggering. Napoleon often saw the world distorted by his imagination, his fervent ambition made him discount obstacles, his overwhelming egotism made him despise opposition. And yet with that dangerous visionary and subjective quality he allied a piercing perception of facts and a natural hunger for them. So he tore away the veil of romance that covered his first marriage and seemed to revel in the naked and sometimes very ugly truth. He does it coolly, too. One does not feel that he is moved by rancor. It is the past, it does not matter any more, except in so far as facts are always interesting.

Nothing is more amazing in Bertrand's notes than the pages-long record of a close questioning to which the Emperor subjects an English doctor—about his pay, his rank, the respective behavior of English and French wounded on the battlefield (which cried out loudest?), the efficiency of French methods of surgery compared with English, etc. It is especially amazing because he collected these facts when he had not another fortnight to live, in an interval between attacks of pain and vomiting.

His illness adds poignancy to the whole of this record. Through all these months the eager talker, the cynical commentator on life, the tenacious upholder of his dignity, the kind master (for he could be truly and charmingly kind), was ill, during the last six weeks or so desperately ill. What makes the relentless account of his long-drawn-out agony particularly horrifying is the crass ignorance of his doctors and their insistence that he should eat, that he should take medicines which made him even more wretched, and, down to the very end, that he should submit to treatment which was positive torture.

Once, speaking to Bertrand, the dying man whispered: "I am glad I have no religious faith. It is a great comfort now. I have no chimerical fears. I am not afraid of the future." The utterance is in direct conflict with the statement in his will that he died in the Catholic religion; and, obviously, although he did accept the services of the priest, this was only for the public. It does not seem to me farfetched, however, to detect behind the patently sincere confession to Bertrand the stirring of an uneasy conscience.

How bravely had he proclaimed in his will that he had nothing to reproach himself for in the death of the Duke of Enghien! He repeated now, but also for public consumption, that on the brink of the grave his conscience was clear on that score, that he would do it again. All through his career he had proclaimed the right of the dictator to ensure order, and incidentally his own power, by acts of terror. What did guilt or innocence matter, what did justice matter, when the interest of the state (or of the master) was in question? His conversation at St. Helena was full of reiteration about this very principle, on which his rule had been built. He still spoke with all the accustomed contempt of liberty, of ideology, of theory. He loudly proclaimed that the party wronged was *he,* that the English oligarchy were murdering him instead of extending generosity—to him who had never been generous to the vanquished. And yet, in the view of death he had to seek comfort in the conviction that his soul would not survive. And why? Apparently because otherwise it might meet its punishment for a career of violence and for the systematic denial of that moral law which he seemed in this last whisper of defiant satisfaction to acknowledge.

The problem of Napoleon's guilt is one on which no fellow human being should lightly pronounce. Pity will creep in on the thoughts of every reader of this story of his last months. And when thus moved, one is almost ready to accept the supramoral verdict of the Spirit of the Years in Thomas Hardy's great epic drama:

> Such men as thou, who wade across the world
> To make an epoch, bless, confuse, appal,
> Are in the elemental ages' chart
> —Like meanest insects on obscurest leaves—
> But incidents and grooves of Earth's unfolding;
> Or as the brazen rod that stirs the fire
> Because it must.

XII THE AMERICAN CIVIL WAR AND THE PROBLEM OF INEVITABILITY

The quarrel which broke up the Union in 1860-1861 was about slavery. It had been gathering strength for a long time and at last erupted with elemental violence. The North and the South, divided by a moral issue of the first magnitude, the one detesting slavery, the other glorifying it as the basis of its social system, were unable to understand each other and the Civil War came as an inevitable result.

This is a fair summary of what was once the view taken by most American historians of the origins of the great crisis of the sixties. The picture was presented in different colorings: all sorts of admissions or reservations were made and complications introduced. Nevertheless, this is in the main the impression that one will gather from Rhodes and Woodrow Wilson, from Channing and Morison, from Lord Charnwood, from James Truslow Adams, and from countless others.

For some time now this interpretation has been subjected to attack. First, the proposition that the quarrel was about slavery came under fire. Charles and Mary Beard, true to their system of economic interpretation, transposed the whole matter from the moral sphere to the sphere of the struggle of interests, and placed in opposition, instead of slavery and liberty, agrarian economy and capitalism, free trade and protection. Their view has had a profound influence, and rightly so, for they emphasized phenomena which had not, indeed, been completely overlooked, but which had not received the attention which they deserve. It is only when the Beards attempt to substitute the economic factor for the moral issue that one feels bound to part company with them. One notices, on looking critically at their argument, that they glide over the awkward fact that at the moment of decision the most powerful capitalistic interests in the North were all for compromise. One reflects that the hysterical excitement and self-glorification of the South can hardly be understood as a reaction to a merely economic menace, especially not as the country happened to be doing so well in a material sense. This mood cannot be explained except as the reply to a moral indictment. The accusation of the Abolitionists was such a painful hit because in it there spoke the spirit of the times. Behind that little group of fanatics there stood the silent condemnation of the free North, of Europe, of the world. By clinging to its "peculiar institution" the South cut itself adrift from the modern development of Western civilization, isolated itself in an obstinate and willful self-righteousness, and fell under the spell of its wildest, blindest, and most reactionary elements.

A good deal more could be said about the economic explanation as presented by the Beards, but the point that I propose to deal with in this essay is the other one on which for some time now the critics of the traditional interpretation of the origins of the Civil War have concentrated their energies, that of the inevitability of the conflict. Here the Beards did not depart from the tradition. To them the economic forces seemed to be as ineluctable as had the moral issue to their predecessors. Yet I think that their view, and the despiritualization of the whole episode which resulted from it, contributed to bring about the state of mind in which others soon proceeded to question the traditional conception of an "irrepressible conflict."

I shall not try to trace the emergence of the rival view that the Civil War was a mistake which could have been, and ought to have been, avoided. I came across this new interpretation years ago in a little book that I picked up in the shilling box of a shop in the Charing Cross Road in London, a somewhat irresponsible little book, but one which I found very illuminating and which is indeed not only amusing but written with ability. It is *The Secession of the Southern States* (1933) by Gerald W. Johnson. I have never found it mentioned in any bibliography, but it has played a part in my education. "The fatalistic theory," Mr. Johnson writes, "grows more and more unsatisfactory to modern writers." And he goes on to quote from the well-known book by Dwight L. Dumond, *The Secession Movement* (1931): "That idea implies that the American people were incapable of solving a difficult problem except by bloodletting, and confuses the designs of party politicians with the art of statesmanship."

Many books have appeared since in which the period preceding the outbreak of that war is studied, and in several this line of argument has been pursued. Prominent among them is, of course, the work of Avery Craven; but for the sake of clearness I shall concentrate on the writings of J. G. Randall, in which the thesis of the avoidability of the conflict forms a central theme. I shall deal mainly with the first two volumes[1] of his *Lincoln the President* (1945), but shall also glance occasionally at his earlier work, *Civil War and Reconstruction* (1937), and at his volume of essays, *Lincoln the Liberal Statesman* (1947).

I admire the work of Professor Randall, and I am conscious of my own status as an amateur in the field in which he is an acknowledged master. If I venture upon a discussion of his view, it is because I feel that his argument springs from a philosophy of history—or of life, for it comes to the same thing—against which I am tempted to pitch my own; and the more so as I have to do with a man who not only places a wealth of historical documentation fairly before his reader, but who presents his case with a vigorous and practiced historical dialectic.

Randall detests the thesis of the irrepressible conflict, and his work is a sustained attempt to refute it. He argues that we cannot do justice to the prewar years if we will see them only in the light of the war *we* know was coming. There were expressions of antagonism no doubt, but if we compose our account of the period preceding 1860-1861 by simply combining those, we subject the past to a mere literary device. One should not read back from the fact of war to the supposition that war-making tendencies were the nation's chief preoccupation in the fifties. "In those years shipowners were interested in the merchant marine, writers in literature, captains of industry in economic enterprise; if any class was concerned chiefly with factors of sectional antagonism it would seem to have been certain groups of politicians and agitators."

The warning that a period can be torn out of focus by interpreting it too resolutely with the help of the familiar outcome is one after my own heart, but that does not mean that criticism will have to disarm before every attempt at putting the implied principle into practice.

No, Randall says elsewhere, there was no irreconcilable contrast between North and South. The very concept of two sections was an oversimplification. A further trick was played: the politicians and the agitators, in their pamphlets, their speeches, and their newspaper articles, pictured the two sections as hopelessly antagonistic. There were influences making for peace; only they attracted insufficient attention. Alarms tending toward war, on the other hand, whose appeal was not to reason, were loud and vociferous. Their menace was in a kind of emotional unbalance. Their language was that of name-calling, shibboleths, tirades. In that way normal life could be upset, and a conflict could be precipitated, that no majority in any section would have deliberately willed. "One of the most colossal of misconceptions is the theory that fundamental motives produce war. The glaring and obvious fact is the artificiality of war-making agitation."

There we have the thesis, and, in order to establish it, Randall marshals his evidence with inexhaustible energy and ingenuity. His material consists largely of incontrovertible facts. It is the great advantage of such a mental attitude as his that it is perceptive of the rich diversity of life. Randall discerns an infinity of shadings where most historians had been content with clear-cut contrasts. He is himself very much aware of this. He refers repeatedly to his historical revisionism, although he prefers the terms "realism" or "historical restoration." This latter word strikingly reveals his faith in the attainability of objectivity. He does not seem to realize that it is not *the* Civil War that emerges as a result of his revisions, but that, in spite of the undoubted finality of some of his fact-finding, it is still *his* Civil War and *his*

Lincoln. His judgments of persons and of actions—and he works with judgments as well as with facts—are governed by a definite attitude of mind, the same, in fact, as that from which springs his thesis itself. Even incontrovertible facts can be used for arguments that are not equally acceptable to all of us.

It can readily be conceded that in no part of the country did there exist at any moment before the actual crisis a majority for extreme solutions. Lincoln's two-fifths share of the poll of 1860 no doubt comprised a majority of the votes cast in the North, but Lincoln, for all that the South pictured him as the secret ally of the Abolitionists, consistently did what he could to reduce the conflict to the smallest proportions. Of the Northern electors who cast their votes for him, the large majority, therefore, never meant a pronouncement in favor of war, either to liberate the slaves or to establish an economic domination.

As regards the South, Breckinridge, the candidate of the extreme state-rights party, remained in a minority there compared with the aggregate of votes cast for his rivals. But Breckinridge himself was comparatively moderate: he never mentioned secession, as did Yancey and Rhett. No more than the North, therefore, did the South pronounce in favor of secession in November 1860. And when suddenly, starting from South Carolina, the secession snowball was set rolling, it was because people saw in Lincoln's election a victory of the spirit of John Brown and because they attributed to the new President the most evil designs against the South— because, in other words, people labored under grievous misconceptions.[2] At the same time, moreover, the opinion was propagated that the North would stand by inactively when the slave-holding states seceded. As a matter of fact, some Abolitionists had on occasion shouted for a separation from the immoral South, and there were moderates, too, who were prepared to say, with the old commander of the Union army, Winfield Scott: "Wayward sisters, depart in peace!" Yet it was an idea completely divorced from reality to think that the North would allow the Union to be broken up without resistance. The prospect had the immediate effect of causing the Northwest to feel itself one with the Northeast.

It was an intolerable thought for those new regions that the lower course of the Mississippi, their main outlet to the outside world as long as the overland connections with the East were defective, would come to be situated in foreign territory. But in the entire North, Union sentiment, quite apart from the feelings about slavery, was strong.

So it was fear, and at the same time it was illusion, that dominated men's minds in the South. But even so the secession had to be forced through in a manner which was denounced as dictatorial by its opponents. The Convention of South Carolina refused to have its decision subjected to a referendum. Yet, once proclaimed, the secession immediately created ambitions and a loyalty of its own. Jefferson Davis, who had lately had leanings toward unionism and who had tried at the last moment to put on the brakes, nevertheless accepted the dignity of the presidency of the Confederation. Alexander Stephens, who had grumbled bitterly at the excitability of the crowd when in state after state the Conventions were passing the secession resolutions (several against considerable minorities), let himself be elected Vice President as soon as the issue was determined. In the slave states on the border, which were still sitting on the fence, feverishly discussing schemes of compromise and negotiating with Lincoln, it was only the shots fired on Fort Sumter which brought about the decision.

How different a picture can be constructed out of all these complications and divisions from that of the inevitable war arising out of a clear-cut contrast. One seems to discern all sorts of side paths and ways out to a very different future from that of these four terrible years of war, followed by that miserable episode of Reconstruction. And the impression is strengthened when one looks more closely at the North after the rupture and observes how weak were the foundations of Lincoln's position, in his own section, now that as War President he admitted no other aim than that of the restoration of the Union, ·that is to say, of a continuation of the struggle down to the complete subjugation of the states in revolt. It is true that not all the criticism, not all the opposition which he had to endure came from the moderates or the doubters. There were, too, the violent, the impatient. The Abolitionists now felt themselves carried along by the tide of events and urged and pushed Lincoln on. But the moderates and the doubters were a powerful party for all that. The accusation of the South, describing Lincoln as the despot trying by brute force of arms to do violence to free American states, found echoes in the Northern press and in the Congress at Washington. "Negotiate!" was a loud clamor, not merely an underground murmur. After the early death in 1861 of Douglas, Lincoln's Democratic rival, who had loyally stood behind the elected President, the entire Democratic Party in the North adopted that cry, and in 1864, when the presidential election came along, it looked for some time as if its candidate General McClellan would win. In that case the fate of the country would have been entrusted to the man whose tenderness for the interests of the slaveholders had been a difficulty when Lincoln in 1862 contemplated his Emancipation Decree, the commander who had been suspected of not really wanting to beat Lee.

But why go on piling up instances and particulars? I am quite ready to concede the point. The American people had suddenly found themselves in the Civil War and the majority in none of the sections had deliberately willed it. But what does this prove? Does it prove that the war might therefore have been avoided? Is it not rather one more proof of the general truth that the course of history is not governed by the conscious will of the majority? Jefferson Davis was a believer in this truth. In 1864 two Northerners came across the lines under a white flag and laid a proposal before the President of the Confederation—which had not, however, Lincoln's sanction. They suggested that a truce should be concluded in order to hold a referendum, and that both North and South should promise to abide by the result. But Jefferson Davis was not interested. "Neither current events nor history," he said, "show that the majority rules, or ever did rule. The contrary I think is true."

And is not this indeed what can be read on every page of the book of history? Did the majority of the Netherlands people will the complete rupture with Philip II and with the Roman Church, the independence and the change of religion? Did they will these things in 1566, in 1572, in 1579, in 1581? There can be only one reply (even though we cannot for the sixteenth century, as for the nineteenth, rely on election statistics): no. Did the majority of the English people will the overthrow of the monarchy and the execution of Charles I, in 1642, in 1649?—no. Did the French people will the Republic and the execution of Louis XVI? In 1789, in 1790, even in 1791, those who had ever thought of these developments as within the sphere of possibility must have been a tiny minority; but in 1792 and 1793 as well: no. Did the majority of the Belgian people in 1830 will the break-up of the union with Holland? Till the very last moment the leaders themselves spoke only of an administrative separation, but even when it happened—did they will it?—no. Did the majority of the German people in 1933 want Hitler, did they will war?—no. When the English people in 1939 took up the challenge of the Third Reich they already found themselves in a position of compulsion. Or, if one wants to look at it from a different angle, one can say that the bulk of them had no notion yet of what they were letting themselves in for, and at any rate in 1940, when their eyes were opened, the position of compulsion was there beyond a doubt. But who does not remember the storm of cheers that greeted Neville Chamberlain and Munich in 1938, and not only in England, but in Germany, in France, in a country like Holland? The large majority wanted peace. "The ship-owner thought of his ships, the writer of his books, the manufacturer of his machines." Here, there and everywhere peace was what men wanted, "and the war came." [3] The instinctive aversion of the mass of people is no evidence that it might have been avoided. It is possible to believe—note that I am not saying, one can prove—that there were forces at work stronger than individual desires or fears, or than their sum as resulting from the ballot box, which made it inevitable. How striking in this connection is the example of recent American history. I need hardly recall the way in which the United States entered both the First and the Second World Wars. This is a controversial subject, but to me it seems that in the light of his own country's experiences,

Randall's postulate of a strict majority democracy as a fixed standard of historical judgment comes to wear a somewhat ghostly look of unreality.

"Forces? indeed!" Randall will say: "Name calling, shibboleths, epithets, tirades." An appeal not to reason or to true interest but to the emotions. And who will deny that sentiment, passion, extra-rational conviction, supply a fertile soil to the monster growths of misunderstanding and exaggeration, misrepresentation, hatred and recklessness! The question remains whether one is justified in labeling these extra-rational factors with contemptuous terms and in denying to them, as Randall does, a rightful role in the drama of history, relegating them without further ado to the category of "artificial agitation" which can on no condition be reckoned among "fundamental causes."

Two histories—so says the Count de la Gorce in his striking little book on Louis XVIII—might be written about the Restoration. One would be the sober and serious history of the good services rendered by that regime to France from day to day and in an unsensational manner. The other one is the history of violent incidents, the execution of Ney, the expulsion of Manuel, et cetera, which, pictured in colorful prints, struck the popular imagination. And it is this second history that culminates in the revolution of 1830. You will notice here, in the writing of the French royalist, the same idea—merely indicated in passing, however—that the historian's rational criticism, working after the events, can detach from the total of what happened the emotions that brought about the catastrophe and that in the other sequence he will retain the real, the proper history. The suggestion is at least that this ought to have been the real history.

Now this idea is the basic idea of Randall's work. He constantly comes back to it. The Americans of the fifties both surprise and irritate him. An essay in which he recapitulates his grievances against them bears the title *A Blundering Generation*. How was it possible for these people to work up such excitement over trifles! All problems are distorted by them. Look how they made mountains out of mole hills and exaggerated matters which seen in their true

size would never have stood in the way of a peaceful settlement.

Take the Kansas-Nebraska Bill, with which Douglas in
1854 had set going so fateful a controversy. Randall is much
concerned to exculpate Douglas. Douglas is a man after his
own heart: a practical man, a man who wanted to do business, and with Northerners and Southerners alike. Can one
wonder if Douglas was astonished at the hubbub? Was it
such a crime that by his principle of popular sovereignty he
created the possibility of slavery in those territories situated
so far North? The very fact of the situation of Kansas and
Nebraska made it most improbable that slavery would ever
take root there. The raving in the North about a mere
theoretical possibility was therefore, according to Randall,
lacking in all sense of reality; it was an example of the hollowness of all that vehement quarreling.

But now let us try to picture to ourselves the state of
affairs. Shortly before, in 1850, the new Compromise had
been reached, intended to put an end to the dangerous tension that had been growing up over the disposal of the newly
acquired Western lands. The Compromise was worthless if
it did not confine the extension of slavery within limits accepted by both sides. But now, in effect, the demarcation
line of 1820, which had been looked upon as fixed, was
wiped out, among loud cheers from the South. Moreover,
what dominated the situation was Southern fears of the rapid
increase in power of the North, and Northern suspicions that
the South, to ward off that danger, was trying by all means
to fasten its grip on the Federal Government. Must one not
willfully blindfold one's historical imagination in order to
avoid seeing that the excitement was natural?

Besides, what happened? Had it been possible to apply
the principle of popular sovereignty honestly, as doubtless
Douglas had intended, then indeed neither Kansas nor
Nebraska would have thought of introducing slavery. But
the slaveholders from the neighboring slave states sent settlers with slaves to Kansas. A race developed between supporters of the two systems: a civil war in miniature. At last
an unrepresentative, tumultuous, armed assembly passed a

constitution admitting slavery and sent it to Washington. Douglas shrank from an approval which must have definitely alienated the North. In fact, the proceedings in Kansas were a mockery of his proudly proclaimed principle. His opposition to recognition roused much ill feeling against him among the Democrats in the South, with whom he had all along wanted to strengthen the ties. Meanwhile "Bleeding Kansas" had become a new slogan to arouse the North. But, Randall reflects, why is it that "squatter sovereignty" came to be a source of confusion? "Not so much because of genuine conflict of local interests, but because a minority of trouble makers, aided by outside agitators, made turbulence rather than reasonable pacification their business." And that is probably a fair statement of the case. But it does not in the least affect the fact that, in the circumstances, and with the public temper prevailing in the United States at that moment, the principle introduced by Douglas could not but be a new occasion for quarrel over the old point at issue, and that his policy was therefore a capital mistake. Douglas had wanted to do business, but he had underestimated the inflammable state of public opinion concerning that great point which he had thought he could safely use for a bargain. "Morally blind" is the way Morison describes him.[4]

In 1858, on the occasion of a senatorial election, the famous debates between Lincoln and Douglas were held up and down Illinois. Lincoln kept on, indefatigably, directing his attacks to the questions of Kansas, popular sovereignty, slavery in the Western territories. To Randall's mind it is but a foolish business. There might have been sense in it if the speakers had at least discussed the principle of slavery, but Lincoln, as everybody knows, was as little prepared to interfere in the internal affairs of the Southern States as was his opponent. So the debates ran on slaves in those regions where there were hardly any and where there were not likely ever to be many slaves. Was this really the only subject on which to claim the attention, for weeks at a stretch, of the electors of Illinois and the newspaper readers of the United States? Would not the time of the speakers have been better employed if they had dealt with such problems as immigration, tariff, international policy, promotion of education?

This is indeed a striking instance of Randall's somewhat masterful attitude toward his personages. In effect, he tells the speakers of 1858 what subjects they ought to have treated. Is it not the historian's more obvious line simply to conclude from their choice, and from the enormous impression they made, that the country's mood was strained to the utmost by the Kansas-Nebraska complication?

And this was indeed a great question. It did bring along, in spite of what Randall says, a discussion of the slavery question itself: Some of Lincoln's gravest, most profoundly moving utterances about the Negro's fate were made in those speeches. Douglas attacked him over his phrase, "A house divided cannot stand," in which he professed to read an incitement to civil war. Lincoln replied that he had only drawn attention to an undeniable danger. The generation of the Founding Fathers had believed that slavery was dying a natural death, so it had not been hard then to practice mutual forbearance and to compromise. Now, on the contrary, the "slave power" was full of self-confidence, or even of imperialistic ardor. Was not the recent verdict of the Supreme Court in the case of Dred Scott startling evidence of this? The Supreme Court, under its judicial mask, had always been a political body, and it was now, after nominations by a succession of Southern Presidents, dominated by the Southerners. The split of the churches, too, was touched upon. It is as if Lincoln is polemicizing with Randall when he says that here at least it is impossible to suspect the hand of "the politicians" or "the agitators." Furthermore, he commented on the restraints in the South laid upon freedom of speech, and on the Southern desire that the North should keep silent on slavery. But even silence was not enough. What they really wanted was express approval and admiration. The survival of democracy itself seemed concerned with the resistance to Southern arrogance; that is a point to which Lincoln frequently recurs. Does Randall, in earnest, want us to believe that the attention of Lincoln's audiences was thrown away on such questions as these?

Even the Fugitive Slave Law was, according to Randall,

all things considered, but a small matter. And, indeed, one can say: were a few hundred fugitives worth the risk of getting enmeshed in a destructive civil war? Answer: neither for the slaveholders nor for the Northerners, who had only on very rare occasions and in very few localities to look on when an unfortunate runaway was seized and forcibly carried back. Lincoln himself said that we must not act upon all our moral or theoretical preferences. "Ungodly," he exclaimed sadly, when once he came into contact with a case; "but it is the law of the land!" One can accept a personality in which deep moral feeling was united with caution, a sense of responsibility, and a capacity for weighing for and against in the scales of reason. But is it not as understandable that a crowd assembled when a captured fugitive in Boston was taken to the harbor and that a battalion of soldiers and a war vessel had to be commandeered to see that the law was executed? The Southerners clung to the law because they desired to have from the North an acknowledgment of their right, rather than because of the material advantage. A moral revulsion in the North[5] soon made the execution impracticable, and this in its turn created bad blood in the South. Seen in this way—and it seems a truer way than the merely statistical one—this was a considerable matter. It carried grist to the mills of the Abolitionists.

But Randall thinks himself entitled to brush aside the whole of that group as fundamentally insignificant—and here the Beards had set the example. Like the Beards, he always points to their small numbers and to the fact that their extreme position excluded them from practical politics. Their only significance, and a baleful one, he sees in the exaggerated importance attached in the South to their periodicals and speeches. Misunderstanding once again. Later, when the war resulted in making them more influential and they finally helped to decide the course taken by the North, he lays all stress on the disastrous effects of their intervention. Here again Randall is representative of a current in modern thought on these questions. The narrowness and cultivation of hatred characteristic of the puritan idealists during the Reconstruction period have given them a bad press with contemporary American historians. Nothing is more readily understandable. But should that lead us to overlook the dynamic strength which their ideas, in spite of their isolated position, had borne in the prewar years?

Not more than a generation before the Civil War, slavery was accepted in the North itself and the black man was despised. There the first struggle had to be waged. In those years the tendency in the North was to reassure the South on the great question, to meet it more than half way. The first Abolitionists, Lovejoy and Birney, had to endure violent persecution in their own North. It was in those days that Tocqueville wrote his *Démocratie en Amérique,* in which he shows so much concern about majority tyranny. Not without due cause, yet he now seems to have been lacking in a perception of the moral forces which defied that trend, often at the risk of being thrown into a river or hanged on a tree. There was something heroic about that struggle of a few men of conviction against their entire environment. Their ultimate success[6] shows that it is not sufficient to count noses. It shows the incalculable influence which may be exerted by an idea, by conscience, by individual moral strength, by passion in the service of an ethical cause. It shows, too, that America formed a part of the great Western civilization, which no longer tolerated slavery. The tremendous disturbance caused in American society by the question acquires a deeper meaning when this is clearly understood.

The spectacle of the dour fight put up by that small group of men, and even of the next generation who prepared for and lived through the Civil War—of Garrison, Wendell Phillips, Sumner—has a quality of greatness. I find encouragement in it. I know all about the unattractive characteristics of these men; the newer American books do not spare them.[7] I do not myself belong to their type and I have a keen perception, therefore, of the dangers which are inherent in it. Those heroes of the human conscience, who stand firm against the majority, and before whom the majority sometimes suddenly collapses, do not know half measures. To expect of them that they should combine the championship of their idea with any conception of the relative advantages of what they attack, or only with a recognition of the innocence of those who defend the old order as their rightful heritage; to expect that they should be alive to the disastrous consequences of a sudden upheaval—one may as well expect that the tiger will make his meal of grass.

Lincoln—yes. In Lincoln's case there is that rare combination of moderation with courage to stand alone; of detestation of the evil with understanding for the difficulties of the human agent or of the society in which the evil flourishes. But Lincoln was not an Abolitionist. He loathed slavery, but in abolitionism he perceived the defiance of the South and unconstitutionality. I admire that mentality and that temperament, but I wonder if, with that alone, the spiritual revolution in the North and the abolition of slavery in the South could have been achieved. A foolish question, I admit, for how can abolitionism, even in the imagination, be eliminated from the situation?

Lincoln's relationship to the Abolitionists reminds a Dutch historian of that between William the Silent and the Calvinists. The Calvinists caused a great deal of trouble to William the Silent, and their activities had at times disastrous consequences. But how could anyone write a history of the revolt of the Netherlands who saw in them nothing but eccentric enthusiasts, a minority who did nothing but keep on foot an artificial agitation? One has to begin by accepting their conviction as a profound historic reality and their dynamic strength as an element in the situation, which must at all times be taken into account very seriously. William the Silent, that master of expedients and of compromises, regarded them at first with disapproval and aversion. But when once the crisis had fairly set in, he could not do without their alliance. In fact, he was himself animated by so profound a sentiment that he was able to understand these men, and at times they were able to understand him. Nevertheless, he had every now and again to restrain them, mostly without result, and they paid him back with impatience, even with enmity. It was not until he was dead that his figure could be harmoniously integrated into the Calvinistic legend, so that in 1618 the forceful action of Maurice, so utterly opposed to his father's policy, could be undertaken under the auspices of the murdered martyr's name.

All this can be applied to Lincoln and the Abolitionists.

As long as there was a chance of a peaceable solution, which he pursued without sacrificing his detestation of slavery, he kept them at arm's length. When war had once broken out he could not possibly do without them any more, but even now he resisted their attempts to get hold of him, to push and to pester him beyond his purpose. So he never became the man after their hearts. The more violent spoke of the President with impatience, with scorn and contumely, with contempt and hatred. They worked against him, they tried to encompass his downfall. But once he was murdered, immediately after the conclusion of the great struggle and at the moment when his moderation, self-restraint, and capacity for seeing both sides might have proved a blessing in the work of healing and reconciliation, then the Abolitionists, even those who had been blind to his greatness, began glorifying Lincoln as a martyr. Yet in the same breath they advocated and forced through a policy of hatred and revenge, of humiliation and destruction of the vanquished South, a policy which was in the most flagrant contradiction of his spirit.

Many years previously, Lincoln—who was then a member of the Legislature of Illinois—had cast a look of concern on the turbulent conditions in what was in many ways still a primitive pioneer community. "Reason," he said, "unimpassioned reason, must furnish all the materials for our future support and defense." A most characteristic utterance, and a noble utterance. I know of no proposition that is more worthy of being followed as a directive for political action in a democratic community. But as a historian I know, too, that in its absolute form it lays down a rule which is beyond the capacity of man. Lincoln's own career furnishes striking proof that the fate of mankind is not from first to last governed by reason. Kindhearted as Lincoln was, lover of a rule of law, given to consultation and give-and-take, he had to school himself for the task of leadership in a civil war of unheard-of ferocity. And, being a man of full human capacity, he did not fail to draw the lesson.

In his Second Inaugural address he reminded his hearers of the circumstances in which, four years earlier, he had spoken as President for the first time. Then all thoughts were anxiously directed to an impending civil war. Both parties deprecated war, but, said Lincoln, the South tried to break the Union without war, while he himself had tried to save it without war. "*And the war came.*" A peculiar and powerful interest had grown up in the South around slavery, an interest which strove after expansion. "All knew that this interest was, somehow, the cause of the war. . . . Neither party expected for the war the magnitude or the duration which it has already attained. . . . Each looked for an easier triumph, and a result less fundamental and astounding. . . . The Almighty has his own purposes."

It is in this speech that Lincoln, a month before he was assassinated, announced his intentions with respect to the vanquished: "With malice toward none, with charity for all"—this is still the best-remembered passage. But the leading idea, expressed in religious terms, is that events had taken their course independently of human control. To me this humility in the face of the mighty happenings seems to be a truer proof of wisdom than Randall's rationalism. The conception in which it is founded may have its tragic implications; it has not, to anyone who accepts life in its entirety, anything depressing. What seems depressing is rather the attempt to show, over and over again, that those people could have been spared all their misfortunes if they had only been sensible. For do we not know at long last that man is not a sensible being? Moreover, the wisdom that Randall preaches to his fellow countrymen of three generations ago does not strike me as very convincing. Compromise; and when the seemingly final concessions have been made, for heaven's sake make short work of the remaining scruples. Deny contrasts which do not appear to have to do with the interest of the majority. Ignore moral facts. And, in short, cry peace where there is no peace. Could the conflict have been—I do not say postponed, but—solved in that way? One can easily imagine that out of a new Compromise, fabricated in 1861 in those feverish peace talks in Washington after the Compromises of 1820 and 1850, a new crisis would soon have sprung, and, who knows, an even worse war.

There is one solution which, if one holds the bloodshed and the distress of the war to be worse than anything, could perhaps be more easily tried out in the imagination—I mean that of a peaceable separation. But it seems as if for American writers the overriding importance of the maintenance of the Union allows of no discussion. Even Randall, argumentative as he is, and filled with loathing for the war, implicitly assumes that paramount necessity as an underlying axiom. It would throw this essay out of proportion if I tried, at the last moment, to deal thoroughly with that question, but I will not omit touching upon it. It is difficult for a European to suppress the reflection that the difference in civilization between the North and the South might have supplied a basis on which to establish two separate political entities, and that perhaps in that way a more natural and a more harmonious development would have been possible, without the ill feeling resulting from friction in too close a contact and without the subjection of the weaker party which followed in actual fact.[8]

Union sentiment was no doubt strong in the North, and once the conflict had broken out it created the sense of sacred obligation. Lincoln felt from the first that an appeal to this principle would have a rallying effect on Northern opinion, and it might even make an impression in the South, whereas the Abolitionist cry as a war aim would divide. The Dutch historian cannot help once more thinking of William the Silent, who for identical reasons kept *haec religionis causa* in the background and insisted on *haec libertatis causa*. For naturally the proposition that the revolt against Philip II was undertaken for the sake of the Protestant religion must have a chilling effect on the Catholic majority. It was ever his contention, therefore, that the fight was being waged for the sake of liberty, for political reasons, in other words. In Calvinistic ears this almost sounded like sacrilege, just as Lincoln's emphasis on the Union motif roused the scorn of the Abolitionists. But Lincoln, in speaking as he did, was not, any more than was William the Silent, guided by tactical considerations alone. His heart was set on the Union. The thought uppermost in his mind was the failure and loss of prestige of the democratic idea everywhere that must follow upon the disruption of the one big democratic republic which then existed.

That is indeed a great thought, and one is almost tempted to believe that it was inspired by a prophetic vision of our own times. The world role played by the United States today, and the role which no doubt it will be called upon to play in the future, would be impossible if the split of the sixties had not been averted. Lincoln was not the only one whose mind ran on these lines. The German-American Schurz and the visiting Frenchman Laboulaye both said that the Union must be preserved and must be strong in order to uphold the cause of democracy in the world. On the other hand, the conservatives in Europe hoped for the disruption, because a united American continent would in the long run mean a power which they feared would make itself a universal nuisance.[9] But if one asks—is the part in world affairs played by the United States today worth the sacrifices made by the generation of the Civil War; does it justify the subjection and permanent effacement of the South?—it is impossible to give an answer based on reason alone. Randall, therefore, convinced that he is proceeding critically and realistically all the time, constructs his argument from the bottom upward on a faith.

For the men of the sixties this too was a problem. A realization of that fact will intensify the feeling that the vision of "a blundering generation" does not do justice to the past. That vision belittles what had real greatness; it ignores the tragedy of that struggle with an overwhelming moral problem, slavery. For this was the struggle in which that generation engaged, after its fashion, that is to say, after a human fashion. The problem was never posed in absolute purity, and it could not be so posed. The Southerners knew the practical difficulties of abolition; the Northerners had no constitutional right of interference. Inextricably mixed up with the problem was that of Union and state rights, of the concepts of unity or of national diversity, and so were material interests on both sides. It is impossible, therefore, to say that in that painful crisis the South was wholly wrong and the North wholly right. This, too, Lincoln knew. In his Second Inaugural he represented the war as a just retribution for the evil of slavery, but North and South shared the punishment, because the offense had come by both.

The two main points on which the conventional conceptions of the origins of the war have of recent times been criticized, as I said at the outset, are that of slavery as the central issue, and that of the inevitability of the conflict. As regards the first, I have clearly enough expressed my opinion that neither with the one-sided attention to economic aspects of the Beards nor with Randall's determination to reduce everything to exclusively practical and reasonable terms can the importance of the moral problem be done justice.

As regards the second, I want to guard myself against a possible misunderstanding. I have not been arguing that the war was inevitable, not even—for that is what the discussion is mostly about—in the ten years preceding the outbreak. I have been arguing that Randall's argument in favor of the opposite contention is unconvincing. The question of evitable or inevitable is one on which, it seems to me, the historian can never form any but an ambivalent opinion. He will now stress other possibilities, then again speak in terms of a coherent sequence of causes and effects. But if he is wise, he will in both cases remain conscious that he has not been able to establish a definite equilibrium between the factors, dissimilar and recalcitrant to exact valuation as they are, by which every crisis situation is dominated.

And here I return to a point on which I find it possible to speak more positively. Randall's way of distinguishing between fundamental and artificial causes seems to me inadmissible. With his impressive scholarship and keen intelligence, schooled in historical dialectic, he counts among artificial causes everything that does not agree with the wishes of the majority or with its true interests, defined by himself in accordance with the best rational standards. But in the sequence of cause and effect, of which the human mind will never have complete command, the category of the *imponderabilia,* passion and emotion, conviction, prejudice, misunderstanding, have their organic function. No doubt it is this very fact which makes that command unattainable for us, but we are not therefore entitled to ignore those nonrational factors or to argue them away with the help of wisdom after the event.

XIII HISTORICAL INEVITABILITY
(*Isaiah Berlin*)[1]

History is often thought of as a study contentedly remote from the present, or as a hobby of scholars who have elected to fly from the world around them into the dead and gone past. The truth is rather that history is an active force in the struggles of every generation and that the historian by his interpretation of the past, consciously or half-consciously or even unconsciously, takes his part in them, for good or for evil.

History, then, is a factor to be reckoned with in the present. Some will maintain, the decisive one. Mr. Berlin, on the contrary, whose learned and subtle disquisition on Historical Inevitability is the occasion of my essay, argues with all the force that is in him against the doctrine of determinism, against the doctrine, that is, according to which we are helplessly caught in the grip of a movement proceeding from all that has gone before. I am with him wholeheartedly. But he himself admits, and it is the point that I want to stress now, that we cannot, while rejecting rigid determinism, represent man as being completely emancipated from the past. The social sciences have taught us to recognize that (as Mr. Berlin puts it) "the scope of human choice is a good deal more limited than we used to suppose." As I myself expressed it not long ago:

Man is both free and in bonds. *Free,* for he must always move on; old forms are all the time decaying; man must, and he can, use his will and choose. *In bonds,* for he cannot use his will indiscriminately, nor choose according to the dictates of his constructive cunning or his fancy. We are incessantly freeing ourselves from our past, but at the same time it maintains a sway over us.[2]

The past, however—what do I mean by the past? Is it the past which works upon our affairs directly? Is it not frequently rather through representations or interpretations, necessarily incomplete and subjective, that its sway is exercised; through what a generation, or a group of men, or a man, believe or imagine the past to be? And so we come back to history as an agent in the present.

For it is the historians who are the guardians of mankind's collective memory. It must be admitted that they often use (or abuse) their guardianship to help in creating the legends which substitute themselves for the reality, and many are the great writers of history whose immediate influence on their contemporaries and on the world's affairs has been due, more than to anything else, to the legendary or mythical features in their presentment of their subject. But criticism never slumbers, the argument without end that is history can never rest, and, indeed, to track down legend and to show up myth is the function that the professional historian today will look upon as his special contribution to society and to civilization; a contribution making for sanity, for clarity of vision, for a heightened sense of individuality, for balance and moderation of judgment.

Mr. Berlin's little book is a contribution in this sense, and an important one. It is not that he attacks any particular historian, or tries, by removing falsification or embellishment, to restore any particular historical character or historical episode to pristine truth. What he does is to demonstrate the fallacy as well as the danger of one method of interpreting the past; and one especially fertile in producing myths, myths especially potent for working on men's minds in the present. The method, as I told you before, is that of determinism.

The doctrine of determinism (so Mr. Berlin says) has owed most of its vogue in historical thought and writing to the example of the natural sciences and their enormous prestige in recent times. Their "success in classifying, correlating, and above all predicting" has made more "attractive the notion that one can discover large patterns or regularities in the procession of historical events." The statement seems to me incontrovertible, but although Mr. Berlin does occasionally refer to the metaphysical or religious sources of historical determinism, I think he might have insisted a good deal more on their importance.

He does not even mention the name of Augustine, and yet from *De Civitate Dei* might be traced an unbroken line of views of history in which it is reduced to the foreordained movement of impersonal forces. Hegel can be seen as St. Augustine secularized and rationalized, and even the notions of romanticism as represented by Vico and Herder and, in their different ways, by Ranke, Carlyle, Michelet—the notions in which Nations or Ideas are personified, or great men pictured as the instruments of some superhuman force—owe much more to the metaphysical tendency or craving that is an ineradicable feature of human nature, than to the example of the natural sciences. No doubt already during and even before Hegel's lifetime the latter factor was coming into play—it worked strongly on Montesquieu and on Condorcet —but it did not show itself in its strength until, not much more than a century ago, Auguste Comte elaborated his philosophy of Positivism.

Mr. Berlin's treatise is based on a lecture he gave at the London School of Economics for the Auguste Comte Memorial Trust. It is not without irony that the whole trend of his argument should be so directly opposed to the ruling tendency of Comte's system. He pays him a great tribute, and with obvious sincerity, for he does not in the least try to minimize the debt owed by history to modern sociological studies. Yet there can be no doubt that Positivism gave a tremendous support to the determinist outlook upon history.

To represent the historical process as a concatenation of events, one following upon the other inevitably, caused as they all are by a superhuman force or by impersonal forces working in society independently from the wishes or efforts of individuals—this is the fallacy. It can appear in many forms. Mr. Berlin enumerates teleological, metaphysical, mechanistic, religious, aesthetic, scientific. He distinguishes roughly between the optimistic school, among whose numerous representatives Comte, "with his fanatically tidy world of human beings joyfully engaged in fulfilling their functions," is prominent. Their tone is scientific, humanitarian, and enlightened. Over against them he places the pessimistic school, but when as its representatives he picks out Hegel and Marx, I must demur. For a true pessimist take, for instance, Spengler, but Hegel and Marx were not to my mind pessimists. Even though they envisaged catastrophes and destruction quite coolly—or, rather, according to Mr. Berlin, gloatingly—the main thing is that they saw them as inevitable stages of progress. To him their tone sounds furious, apocalyptic, and not a little sadistic—but Marx prided himself on his science, too.

Anyhow, all these various adherents of the theory

. . . agree in this: that the world has a direction and is governed by laws, and that the direction and the laws can in some degree be discovered by employing the proper techniques of investigation; and, moreover, that the working of these laws can only be grasped by those who realize that the lives, characters, and acts of individuals, both mental and physical, are governed by the larger "wholes" to which they belong, and that it is the independent evolution of those "wholes" that constitute the so-called "forces" in terms of whose direction truly "scientific" (or "philosophic") history must be formulated.

Several questions now present themselves. Mr. Berlin's mind is engaged upon all of them all the time and his answers, too, lie scattered over the whole of his treatise. I shall attempt, for clearness' sake, to deal with them under three headings.

First of all: Why is this theory a fallacy?

Note that the contention is not that *determinism* is a fallacy, but that *to apply determinism to history* is an impossible and necessarily misleading method. The ancient controversy between free will and determinism (this is how Mr. Berlin puts it) remains a genuine issue for theologians and philosophers; but for historians determinism is not a serious issue. If the affairs of mankind are indeed subject to laws and evolve in a closely knitted order in which every human action and every human thought is a factor, both determined and in its turn determining, it is only omniscience that will be able to discern the pattern and to assign to each human particle its place in it. The historian's knowledge is far removed indeed from omniscience, and even were every relevant fact within the reach of his investigating powers, the multitude and complexity would surpass his powers of comprehension.

The deterministic constructions which historians so often present—a historical process running on from one inevitable conclusion to another, down to the outcome, hidden from the actors in the drama but known to the historian—are really no more than constructions in the historian's mind, to which the unfathomable and unruly past has, by arbitrary selection and purposeful interpretation, been made to conform.

One of the most interesting points made by Mr. Berlin, and made with great ability and originality, is that the fallacy of historical determinism appears from its utter inconsistency with the commonsense and everyday way of looking at human affairs, which is so ingrained in our whole habit of thought that even the determinists cannot help using the terminology properly belonging to it. Consistent determinism in history, in other words, is unthinkable. If we held that theory in real earnest we should have to change our vocabulary for our ordinary life and our relations to our fellow human beings. Common sense alone shows that the inevitability of a demonstration in algebra is not applicable to human affairs, and human affairs are the subject matter of history.

Determinism as a historical method, then, is a fallacy. But why dangerous? This is the second question.

Mr. Berlin's answer is: because the spectacle of history thus presented saps the sense of individual responsibility. It engenders acquiescence and passive subjection to the mysterious and uncontrollable forces which are conjured up for the awed public as the masters of their destiny.

Among the creators of imposing theories or systems of this description he disposes rather lightly of Spengler and Toynbee. In their work, he suggests, "the frontier between facts and cosmic patterns" is effaced, a frontier which "is a central and objective concept for all those who take the problems of history seriously." He seems more gravely concerned about the sociologists of various schools who "advance scientific arguments for a historical determinism which excludes the notion of personal responsibility." The labors of these men, fertile in useful instruction as they may otherwise be, have created a new quasi-sociological mythology peopled with all but personified powers both good and bad—as "The Collectivist Spirit," or "The Myth of the Twentieth Century," or "The Contemporary Collapse of Values" (sometimes called "The Crisis of Faith"), or "Modern Man," or "The Last Stage of Capitalism." I shall quote from these brilliant pages one passage:

Cowed and humbled by the panoply of the new divinities, men are eager, and seek anxiously, for knowledge and comfort in the sacred books and in the new orders of priesthood which affect to tell them about the attributes and habits of their new masters. And the books and their expositors do speak words of comfort. . . . The discovery of the new, terrifying, impersonal forces may render life infinitely more dangerous, yet if they serve no other purpose, they do, at any rate, divest their victims from all those moral burdens which men in less enlightened days used to carry with so much labour and anguish. . . . Agonizing doubts about the conduct of individuals caught in historical crises and the feelings of hope and despair, guilt, pride, and remorse, which accompany such reflections, are taken from us. Like soldiers in an army driven by forces too great to resist, we lose those neuroses which depend on the fear of having to choose among alternatives. Where there is no choice, there is no anxiety; and a happy release from responsibility. Some human beings have always preferred the peace of imprisonment, a contented sense of security, a sense of having at last found one's proper place in the cosmos, to the painful conflicts and perplexities of the disordered freedom of the world beyond the walls.

Implicit in this passage we have the author's answer to a third question: the question as to what may be the appeal of this dangerous fallacy of a determinist interpretation of human affairs. And indeed he confirms it explicitly in his conclusion.

Principally it seems to me to spring from a desire to resign our responsibility, to cease from judging provided we be not judged ourselves and, above all, are not compelled to judge ourselves; from a desire to flee for refuge to some vast amoral, impersonal, monolithic whole, nature or history, or class, or race, or "the harsh realities of our time," or "the irresistible evolution of the social structure". . . . This is an image which has often appeared in the history of mankind, always at moments of confusion and inner weakness.

Now neither the second nor the third question (neither "Why dangerous?" nor "What is the appeal?") seems to me to have received from Mr. Berlin a complete answer. I agree about the paralyzing effect, and about the blessed sense of relief that many people will find in acquiescence. But I consider to be even more dangerous the fanaticizing effect that a determinist theory can have; and as for the sources in human nature from which these mythologies and systems spring, I should be inclined to bracket with the desire for relief from responsibility the desire for action unimpeded by doubts of success or by moral scruples.

The historical process conceived as an impersonal, irresistible, inevitable current may induce the feeling of passively floating along. But especially when the conception is reduced to some rigid system, this feeling may yield to one of being supported or driven, and an inhuman and amoral energy be imparted.

These sociological mythologies as we know them in our Western world are child's play compared with what we have seen happening in Russia. They have not, with us, succeeded —and I believe are a long way from succeeding—in nullifying the energy that we draw from a different source altogether, from free discussion, from criticism and the true scientific spirit.

Now in Russia they have triumphed, and the result is terrible enough, but it is something very different from apathy or weakness and confusion. That triumph is a challenge to us to cultivate our own traditions and resources of belief in the value of personality, and I welcome Mr. Berlin's spirited and valiant vindication of the true conception of history as a valuable contribution to that end.

NOTE OF ACKNOWLEDGMENT
TO FIRST EDITION, 1955

Of these essays, I, II, VII, IX and X were published in *From Ranke to Toynbee: Five Lectures on Historians and Historiographical Problems;* no. XXXIX of the *Studies in History,* Smith College, Northampton, Mass., 1952;

V in *Journal of the History of Ideas,* New York, 1948; and in *The Pattern of the Past* (together with Toynbee-Geyl B.B.C. discussion and an essay on Toynbee by Professor Sorokin), Boston, 1949;

VI in *Virginia Quarterly Review,* 1950;

VIII in *Journal of the History of Ideas,* New York, 1955;

XI and XIII in *The Listener,* Oct. 1953 and April 1955;

XII in *New England Quarterly,* 1951;

III and IV have not before been published in English.

Of the five lectures delivered at Smith College (some also at Pomona College and at Scripps College, Claremont, Calif.) in 1952 and published in the volume mentioned above, one (IX) had been written in 1949 and delivered at Princeton University.

VI was a lecture delivered at Stanford University, Calif., in 1949.

V was originally a lecture delivered at the Annual Meeting of the Historisch Genootschap te Utrecht, Nov. 1946, and published in its *Jaarverslag*.

X, written in 1944 during the occupation of Holland, was intended for the author's *Napoleon voor en tegen*, 1946 (*Napoleon For and Against*, 1949), but was not eventually included. It was used for a lecture at the Royal Dutch Academy at Amsterdam in 1950 and published in its *Jaarboek*.

XI and XIII were talks delivered in the B.B.C. Third Programme, 1953 and 1955.

XII is part of a paper published in *Mededelingen* of the Dutch Academy, 1949.

V and XII were reprinted in the author's *Tochten en Toernooien*, 1950.

Several of the other essays, some translated from the original English, some written originally in Dutch, appeared in the monthly review *De Gids* and were reprinted in the author's *Historicus in de tijd*, 1954.

NOTES

RANKE IN THE LIGHT OF THE CATASTROPHE

[1] He died two years after this essay was written, in 1954, at the age of ninety-one.

[2] For example, the pages devoted to Ranke in Veit Valentin's *Die deutsche Revolution*, 1930.

[3] I quote the following from a review in the *Times Literary Supplement* of February 18, 1955, of *The Third Reich*, published by the International Council for Philosophy and Humanistic Studies with the assistance of Unesco:

". . . Professor Vermeil, in a long introductory essay, sets out to prove that Hitler's Germany was no more than the logical culmination of Germany's political and intellectual heritage. Prussian militarism is traced back in an unbroken line to the fourteenth century. . . . The activities of the Hansa are described as 'the beginnings of the *Weltpolitik* which was to become Wilhelm II's dream.' By judicious selection from literary sources, Gobineau is mentioned only incidentally, Sorel and Pareto not at all, and by the inaccurate and tendentious use of historical illustrations Professor Vermeil reproduces the highly consistent and badly distorted view of Germany's past which he has already made familiar."

I had indeed heard the French historian set out this view in a lecture on the Origins of National Socialism at the International Congress on the Second World War, held at Amsterdam in 1950, and in the discussion had opposed him on these very lines.

MACAULAY IN HIS ESSAYS

[1] James Spedding, *Evenings with a Reviewer, or, Macaulay and Bacon*, 1881.

[2] Forster's and Paget's criticisms are mentioned later on in the text. See also Vol. I of Winston Churchill's *Life of Marlborough*.

[3] J. L. Hammond, *The Bleak Age*, 1934.

⁴ In Holland, Allard Pierson, who had in his younger days hailed the prophet of progress, in an essay of 1878 gave utterance to doubts and in 1881 (after reading Spedding) expressly renounced his allegiance.

⁵ Many writers dismiss the Essays as immature work and maintain that Macaulay should be judged on his *History*. Macaulay himself hesitated before allowing the Essays to be reprinted in book form, saying they were ephemeral productions, written on the spur of the moment and not to be taken seriously. I admit that no balanced view of Macaulay is possible without due attention to the *History*, and I hope to consider it later on. The *History* does not, however, show a mind essentially different from that which is revealed by the Essays. The light these throw may be so glaring as to be unflattering; it does not therefore falsify the picture.

CARLYLE: HIS SIGNIFICANCE AND REPUTATION

¹ See p. 22.

² *A Century of Hero Worship*, Philadelphia and New York. 1944.

³ Harrison here refers to the case of Governor Eyre who was recalled (1865) from his post on account of the panic-stricken and blind savageness with which he had put down a Negro rising in Jamaica, or, rather, exacted revenge after it had been put down. Carlyle headed a committee for the rehabilitation and compensation of the ex-governor. The affair has some of the same interest that the Dreyfus case was to have a generation later in France in that it shows us some of the leading intellectuals of the day ranged on opposite lines. Tennyson, Kingsley, Ruskin, even Dickens, sided with Carlyle; against Eyre was first of all Mill, supported by Herbert Spencer, Huxley, Goldwin Smith.

⁴ *Life and Letters*, 1930. He takes the same line in the introduction to his recent *Carlyle, an Anthology* (1952).

⁵ An interesting account of Carlyle's influence as a herald of the imperialistic spirit was given in 1903 by J. Gazeau in a doctoral *thèse: L'impérialisme anglais*. A most remarkable sketch of that spirit in its unreasoning self-confidence and its sense of mission all cloaked in religious terms is to be found in yet another French book, *Etudes anglaises*, by André Chevrillon (1903): especially the essay "L'opinion anglaise et la guerre du Transvaal" (1900) and the essay on Rudyard Kipling (1899). No more than Cazamian do Gazeau and Chevrillon give any sign of having understood that what they described was no more than a phase. It is a curious experience for the present-day

reader who knows another England to note how glibly contemporaries transpose their impressions of the fleeting moment into a conception of "typically English," "the English national character," with which they go on lightheartedly to operate.

6 "What fails you is confidence in the divine guidance of our present day godless world": quoted by Dr. J. B. Manger, *Thorbecke en de Historie* (1938), p. 99.

7 It occurs in a letter to his brother: Froude, *Carlyle, Life in London*, II, p. 360.

8 *Letters of M. Arnold to A. H. Clough* (1932), p. 111 and p. 151.

9 Reprinted in her *Nineteenth Century Teachers*, 1909.

10 The father of Frederick the Great.

11 Mr. Bentley does not, I think, do justice to Carlyle's style.

12 The academic and expert public, however, were reserved. See W. Bussmann, *Treitschke, Sein Welt- und Geschichtsbild* (1952), pp. 371 *seq.* The German Liberals (and Treitschke was originally a Liberal) were suspicious on general grounds, too, of this exalting of great men at the expense of currents of opinion or movements.

MICHELET AND HIS HISTORY OF THE FRENCH REVOLUTION

1 In his letters from Paris (*Lutèce*, ed. 1882, p. 353): quoted by O. A. Haac, *Les principes inspirateurs de Michelet*, Yale U. P., Presses Universitaires, 1951, p. 184.

2 It should be remembered that the term "federation" is here strictly confined to the movement of 1789-90 tending to a closer relationship, ultimately on a national basis, between the various localities and regions. The movement of resistance to the unitary government imposed by the Convention two or three years later, and which also goes by the name of Federalism, represented, of course, a directly opposite tendency.

3 "*Ego sum via et veritas*, Messiah, Duce, Fuehrer." Thus G. J. Renier in his striking little book *Robespierre* (1936), p. 119.

4 In 1868 Michelet, who twenty years earlier had announced that war was imminent, asserted with his customary assurance that the period of wars was over! (*Préface de 1868;* Walter's edition, I, p. 9 ff.) For details of the statement of 1846, see p. 77.

5 Alphonse Aulard, 1849-1928; wrote *Histoire politique de la Révolution française*, 1901; edited, from 1881 on, the review *La Révoluton française*. In opposition to this Albert Mathiez (1874-1932) founded in 1908 *Les annales révolutionnaires;* he, too, in addition to numerous monographs, wrote a complete summary, in the Collection Colin, 1922-27: *La Révolution française.*

[6] Ch. Seignobos, 1854-1942, e.g.: *Histoire sincère de la nation française*, 1933. G. Pariset, e.g.: vol. II of Lavisse's *Histoire de la France contemporaine*, *La Révolution, 1792-99*, 1920. Georges Lefebvre, born 1874, contributed the first books to the volume on the Revolution in the *Peuples et civilisations* series; second edition, 1938.

[7] See my *Napoleon, For and Against*, pp. 356 ff.

[8] Jean Jaurès, *Histoire socialiste de la Révolution française*, 1901-1904.

[9] E.g.: *Histoire de la terreur*, 1938; *Robespierre*, 1946.

[10] So says, for instance, E. Fueter, *Geschichte der neueren Historiographie*, 1911, p. 454, who himself, however, puts the Revolution part higher: 453. Of older historians there is also Camille Jullian, who in an anthology of French historical writing (1896) extols M.'s *Révolution*. Lanson, Thibaudet, Gooch, all prefer the medieval portion.

[11] *Michelet*. It contains an anthology from the *Introduction à l'histoire universelle* (1831), preceded by an important introduction.

[12] *Notions d'historiographie moderne*, in *Cours de Sorbonne* (stencilled edition), 1952.

[13] S.-B.'s real opinion about Michelet is to be found, together with slighting or downright murderous comments on many others, in a volume published long after his death and appropriately called *Mes poisons* (ed. by V. Giraud, 1929). A poet? he says; "by the sweat of his brow;" it was all will and ambition; "a vulgar mind."

[14] A few years earlier (April 11, 1866) De Goncourt had noted the far-reaching influence Michelet was exercising. *"Michelet s'est emparé de la pensée contemporaine."*

[15] This leading idea was not of course entirely new. It had been clearly formulated in 1844 by Thorbecke, the Leyden professor who was to become the *auctor intellectualis* of the 1848 revision in a literal sense of the Dutch constitution and Prime Minister. See his *Historische Schetsen*, p. 85.

[16] Quoted by G. Kalff, *De verklaring de Fransche Revolutie bij haar vornaamste geschiedschryvers*, 1921.

[17] In his eight-volume *L'Europe et la Révolution française;* the first volume appeared in 1885.

[18] Quoted by D. Halévy in *Histoire d'une histoire* (1939), p. 49.

[19] See *La réforme intellectuelle et morale de la France*, 1871.

[20] *Les origines de la France contemporaine;* first volume, 1875.

[21] Aulard, *Taine: Historien de la Révolution française*, appeared in 1907, fourteen years after Taine's death. Augustin Cochin, who soon afterward was killed in the First World War, replied in 1909 with *La Crise de l'Histoire révolutionnaire*.

[22] 1939; D.H. was born in 1872.

[23] I must apologize for speaking the language of the supporters of Dreyfus, in which the personifying metaphors undeniably have the usual effect of effacing transitionary shadings or exceptions.

[24] 1867-1930. The book alluded to in the text is *La doctrine officielle de l'Université,* 1913. Lasserre soon afterward broke away from the *Action française* and wrote a five-volume work, *La jeunesse de Renan.* In his doctoral thesis, *Le Romantisme français,* which created quite a stir in 1907, L. devoted to Michelet a merciless chapter, exposing, not his apology for the Revolution, but, more generally, his abandonment of the reasoning faculty to follow the dictates of his intuition, or his fancy.

TOYNBEE'S SYSTEM OF CIVILIZATIONS

[1] See footnote 21.

[2] III, p. 192.

[3] II, p. 31.

[4] II, p. 260.

[5] I draw attention to what in II, p. 108, is said about the respective positions of France, Germany and England at the moment when that volume was written (1931). Perhaps it is unfair to pick on that passage, because the fifteen years which have since elapsed supply us with so convenient a standard of criticism; here is at least proof how little guarantee of objectivity there is in Toynbee's so-called empirical method.—Take II, p. 70, where the New Englanders' success in the struggle with their Spanish, Dutch, French, and Southern rivals for the North American continent is said to throw light on the question of the different degrees of hardness in the physical environment of human existence and their stimulating effect. As if the assistance given or not given by the various mother countries had not been really decisive, not to speak of various other factors! This point has received special treatment in a later essay, pp. 170 ff. But there would be no end if one went on to discuss particular cases.

[6] III, p. 346.

[7] III, p. 351.

[8] III, p. 366. According to G. M. Trevelyan as well, *History of England,* these two events "saved the British Constitution," a curious way of putting it: in those times the *British* constitution still lay hidden in the womb of the future.

[9] IV, p. 105.

[10] IV, p. 114.

[11] How unmethodical is his treatment of national as distinct from "civilization" phenomena will be discussed later.

[12] IV, pp. 131 ff.

[13] IV, pp. 278-289.

[14] IV, p. 287.

[15] G. M. Trevelyan, *Manin and the Venetian Republic of 1848*, p. 139.

[16] Henri Hauvette, *Littérature Italienne* (1914), p. 383.

[17] II, pp. 400-401.

[18] VI, p. 177.

[19] V, pp. 2-22.

[20] *Geschonden Wereld*, published posthumously in 1945. Huizinga is here arguing against the believers in a continuous progress of our own civilization, a group to which Professor Toynbee does not of course belong. But his remarks are relevant also against Toynbee's pretension to indicate (as he attempts to do in Volume VI) the exact rhythm of all civilizations.

[21] These tables—four in all—are to be found among the appendices to Volume VI, pp. 327 ff. The way in which Western civilization is there dealt with might give rise to an extensive critical discussion. I shall do no more than make a few remarks on the first table. The first thing that strikes one is that Western civilization is there unquestioningly drafted into a table particularizing the disintegration process. It is surprising, and not in agreement with remarks made elsewhere in the book, to see the Time of Troubles fixed for the Western half between 1378 and 1797 and for the Eastern half between 1128 and 1528. Two universal states are indicated, the Napoleonic empire and the Danubian monarchy. When in connection therewith one sees a *pax œcumenica* assigned to the years 1797-1814 and 1528-1918 respectively, one is inclined to ask if words have the same meaning for Professor Toynbee as they have for the rest of us. Of the other tables I shall only say that they too seem to show to excess the author's gift of observing parallels and of building constructions on them.

[22] V, pp. 89, 153.

[23] VI, p. 321.

[24] Professor Romein in *De Nieuwe Stem* (1946), p. 44.

[25] For this and preceding utterances, cf. IV, pp. 221, 225, 228.

[26] V, pp. 193-194.

[27] V, p. 138.

[28] IV, p. 295.

[29] There is in particular a passage in which Afrikaans as a cultural language is belittled in comparison with Dutch: V, pp. 493-494. It is amusing to see so completely misinformed a statement delivered so positively. Of course not even Professor Toynbee can know everything. It is useful, nevertheless, quite apart from the

considerations built upon them in the text, to note such mistakes. The conclusion may be drawn that it is not imperative to believe him unreservedly when he speaks with the same assurance about peoples or ages unfamiliar to us and constructs his towering conclusions on facts which we cannot so easily check.

[50] VI (published in 1939), p. 57, footnote.

TOYNBEE ONCE MORE: EMPIRICISM OR APRIORISM?

[1] See the two preceding essays. The reader should bear in mind that this paper was originally a lecture delivered at Smith College, Northampton, Mass., where I resided, in the spring of 1952, as W. A. Neilson Research Professor.

[2] Thus it was that the translator of Oswald Spengler's *Untergang des Abendlandes* tried to render the title of that book. *Decline* does not, however, do full justice to the force of the word *Untergang*, which means *ruin, dissolution, extinction*.

[3] *Civilization on Trial*, 1949, p. 9.—I had not seen that statement when I referred to the relationship between T. and Sp. before; cf. above, pp. 114-15, 156 ff.

[4] Vol. II, pp. 65-72, in the original edition.

[5] See p. 148.

TOYNBEE THE PROPHET (THE LAST FOUR VOLUMES)

[1] I remind the reader that the essay "Toynbee's System of Civilizations" (No. V of this volume), which did not appear in English until January, 1948, was originally a paper read for the Annual Meeting of the Utrecht Historical Society in November, 1946.

[2] See p. 176.

[3] VIII, pp. 290-291.

[4] IX, p. 502.

[5] IX, p. 409.

[6] Even when specifically discussing "The Value of Diversity" (VII, p. 442), Toynbee will disappoint the reader who is looking for some recognition of the uses of mankind's being divided into nationalities. His treatment of diversity remains confined within the sphere of religion and his basic conception of it is purely individualistic.

[7] IX, pp. 406 *seq.*

[8] IX, p. 409.

[9] VII, p. 748.

[10] VII, p. 428.

[11] VII, p. 445.

[12] VII, p. 422.

282 NOTES

[13] IX, p. 411.

[14] He has, it is true, a passage where he distinguishes between the beneficent possibilities inherent in a knowledge of the laws of nature and the destructive effects due to human sin; IX, p. 172.

[15] IX, p. 644.

[16] VII, p. 428, footnote.

[17] VII, p. 384.

[18] I have read the front-page article (anonymous) of the *Times Literary Supplement* of October 22, 1954; articles by A. J. P. Taylor in *The New Statesman* of October 16th; Geoffrey Barraclough in *The Listener* of October 14th; Hugh Trevor-Roper in *The Sunday Times* of October 17th. Only Noel Annan in *The Manchester Guardian Weekly* of October 21st takes the work seriously and seems to regard the strictures passed on it by "the academic" or "professional" historians with distrust. But see note 26, below.

[19] X, p. 35.

[20] One might, of course, also mention Ranke and his famous dictum about every epoch being immediate to God.

[21] IX, p. 210.

[22] Jacob Burckhardt's phrase used in a letter.

[23] It is rather extraordinary to observe that in Vol. IX, pp. 297 ff., there is another passage about territorial developments in the North American continent during the seventeenth and eighteenth centuries, in which what was the leading motif in Vol. II—the poverty of the soil and rigor of the climate in New England—is not even mentioned. It is true that the matter is here dealt with from a somewhat different angle, yet there is an insoluble contradiction between the two passages. In Vol. IX all the emphasis falls on the contest between the mother countries which I complained had been entirely overlooked in Vol. II.—Not that the new passage is any more satisfactory. It is "History" which is now represented as having decided the course of events, History, or Clio, "paying a passing tribute to a physiography whose political requirements" (unity) "she was evidently bent on defying" (the survival of Canada as a separate entity). History "permits," History "reasserts her ascendancy," History "keeps a watchful eye" or indulges in a "caprice," History "led the people of the U.S. to lose a desire." "History," in short, solving all his problems for him, dispenses the historian from the trouble of looking for rational or factual explanations. It is obvious that rational or factual criticism can have no meaning for a man privileged to share the confidence of this self-willed Muse and that no discussion with him is possible.

[24] X, p. 139.

[25] Professor G. J. Renier, in his *History, Its Purpose and Method,* 1950, p. 218, has an acute remark on "the Dutch theorist Romein" as presenting a typical instance of the mentality that comes under the spell of *A Study of History.*—The tendency to seek the reality of history in formulas or phrases, the suspicion that scholarly research will only result in "a pulverizing of the image" (*Het vergruisde beeld* was the title of Professor Romein's inaugural oration in 1939), and the carping, almost inimical attitude toward Western civilization (born in Romein's case, as has been pointed out by several critics of his latest book *De aera van Europa,* from a feeling of guilt, from an emotion rather than from an attempt at understanding)—these are all strands of the bond uniting this at first sight curiously ill-assorted couple. (1955)

[26] Since writing this article I have received from a friend in England an advertisement page cut from the *New York Times Book Review.* "Have you seen what they're saying about Arnold Toynbee?" I quote some of the headings of the seventeen extracts from reviews (among which I spotted only one written by a trained historian— who, on reading this remark when the essay was republished in 1955 wrote to me to show how his words had been torn from their context for purposes of advertisement): "Amazing and monumental. . . . An immortal masterpiece. . . . The greatest work of our time. . . . A literary and intellectual phenomenon. . . . Probably the greatest historical work ever written. . . . A landmark, perhaps even a turning point."

This chorus of praise is a chastening reminder of the very restricted influence exercised by professional criticism. The effect it had on me was nevertheless a heartening one. I have sometimes felt the uncomfortable thought stirring: "Is it still worth while?" Apparently it *is* worth while. For we must never abdicate misdirected popular enthusiasm (1955).

THE NATIONAL STATE AND THE WRITERS
OF NETHERLANDS HISTORY

[1] Apart from a considerable shift in the extreme west to the detriment of Dutch, which occurred in the early Middle Ages, there have been only very small movements. Brussels has in recent times come to constitute a semi-French linguistic island north of the boundary.

[2] In three lectures delivered at University College, London, in 1919, published under the title: *Holland and Belgium: Their Common History and Their Relations.*

³ *Tien Jaren uit den Tachtigjarigen Oorlog,* sixth edition, 1904, p. 342.

⁴ Reprinted in *Verspreide Geschriften,* I en III.

⁵ A selection of the polemical essays, which had before been collected in various volumes, was published in 1946 in *Eenheid en tweeheid in de Nederlanden.* Two parts of the unfinished *Geschiedenis van de Nederlandse Stam,* those covering the periods 1555-1609 and 1609-1648, have appeared in English: *The Revolt of the Netherlands,* and *The Netherlands Divided* (London, 1932 [3rd impression, 1946] and 1936).

⁶ Nor has it been so accepted. When I said earlier in this essay that my views are today finding a large measure of acceptance I did not mean to suggest that the larger questions of Dutch-Flemish or Dutch-Belgian relationship, or of the natural delimitation of Dutch or Netherlands history, have passed beyond the controversial stage. "History," I wrote in *Napoleon, For and Against,* "is an argument without end." In 1948 there appeared the first volume of a twelve-volume co-operative *History of the Netherlands, Algemene Geschiedenis der Nederlanden.* Dutch and Flemish historians are the contributors, but by "the Netherlands" is understood the old seventeen provinces, or Holland and Belgium combined—Benelux, one might say. The work marks the passage of the old "Little Netherlands" and "Belgicist" conceptions, but it will attempt to operate on a dual-state basis, taking in both the Dutch-speaking and the Walloon regions.

THE FRENCH HISTORIANS AND TALLEYRAND

¹ D. C. 1953; his *Talleyrand* appeared in 1939; Guglielmo Ferrero's *Réconstruction* in French in 1940; English translation 1941. I must confess that I read Crane Brinton's brilliant book *The Lives of Talleyrand* (1937) only after having written this lecture. Had I known it, I might have adduced it in confirmation of my argument. For although Professor Brinton is concerned more to bring out the elusive quality of Talleyrand's genius than his consistency, his view of him and of his policy is decidedly sympathetic.

² Jonathan Cape and Yale University Press, 1949. This paper was originally intended to be a chapter in that book. The Dutch version was written under the German occupation, in 1944, and published by the Kon. Nederl. Akademie, of Amsterdam, in 1950. Only the passage relating to Mr. Churchill's *War Memoirs,* IV, 1951 (see p. 235-36) was inserted in 1952.

³ In fact this is sometimes admitted by French writers. Marshal Lyautey, for instance, in commemorating, on the occasion of his reception into the French Academy, the member whose place he

was taking—Henry Houssaye, a Napoleon worshipper of the truest brand—spoke very sensibly of the service rendered by Talleyrand to France in 1814 and made the further very just observation that he and the monarchy were to be judged by the treaty of 1814, not by that of 1815, which was in fact the ransom paid by France for Napoleon's adventure of the Hundred Days.—Quoted in Ch. Maurras, *Jeanne d'Arc, Louis XIV, Napoléon*, 1937.

⁴ Vol. IV, 1951. p. 574. Cf. footnote 2.

LATTER-DAY NAPOLEON WORSHIP

¹ A Third Programme (London) broadcast on "Napoleon at St. Helena: Memoirs of General Bertrand, January-May, 1821," deciphered and annotated by Paul Fleuriot de Langle. Translated by Frances Hume, London, 1953.

THE AMERICAN CIVIL WAR AND THE PROBLEM OF INEVITABILITY

¹ A third volume appeared after this essay was written. Professor Randall died in 1953, leaving his great work unfinished.

² That the same might be said about the Northern people is brought out very clearly by David M. Potter in his *Lincoln and His Party in the Secession Crisis* (1942). Lincoln and the Republicans generally never took the secession talk in the South seriously; they looked upon it as blackmail. Not until the very last moment, well after the election at any rate, did they realize that the war danger was an awful reality.

³ To quote the words used by Lincoln in his Second Inaugural.

⁴ Allan Nevins entitles the chapter of his *Ordeal of the Union* in which he introduces the story of the Kansas-Nebraska Bill, "Disaster: 1854." His account throughout differs radically from that of Randall. He quotes with approval the utterance of an Abolitionist, Quincy, who had characterized the situation as early as 1852 by the biblical phrase which Lincoln was to use six years later: A house divided against itself cannot stand. In 1852, so shortly after the Compromise of 1850, peace might seem safe enough. But Nevins judges that "the Compromise had laid over the erupting lava of 1849-50" only a thin crust (II, p. 79). "The slavery question was in fact irrepressible." Indeed, the account in this work of 1947 does not differ in essence from the traditional view which I briefly summarized at the outset of my argument. It is full with the fullness of life, it does not try to skip over the complications or to slur the multiple shadings of reality, but it places the moral issue of slavery in the very center. Randall had been led by his aversion to, or misunderstanding of, the passions aroused by the

measure to attempt the whitewashing of Douglas. Nevins is severe on the man who tore "open all the wounds of 1848-50" (p. 21), and though he admits that "circumstances" may have had their share in the "disaster," he does not try to dispose of the reactions as merely due to agitators or politicians.

[5] Nevins connects this immediately with the Kansas-Nebraska Bill.

[6] Although this success stands in need of qualification. Even when the tide seemed to be running with the Abolitionists, there was in the North more fervor for abolition of slavery in the abstract than willingness to accept the Negro as a citizen on an equal footing. Indeed the Free Soil agitation in the West was largely due to fear of the black man's low wage competition, and the lot of the free Negro was in most of the Northern states far from being a happy one. The Southerners were not entirely without justification when they railed at the element of hypocrisy in the attitude of their Northern critics, who moreover seemed to be forgetting the wretched conditions under which their own white factory workers had to labor. (A. Nevins, I, pp. 518 ff.) The anti-Negro outbreak in New York at the height of the Civil War shows that actual contact between the races could still rouse ugly feelings in the North.

[7] Nevins discriminates admirably between those among them who, while attacking the institution of slavery, refrained from reviling the slaveholders, and the bitter spirits, so wrapped up in their feeling of rectitude or warped by their detestation of the black man's wrong, that they seemed to take pleasure in antagonizing Southern opinion. It was especially Garrison and Sumner who did a great deal of harm in that way, although again they were very dissimilar and Sumner at one time disapproved of Garrison's extremism. *Ordeal of the Union*, I, pp. 144, 146; II, p. 438.

[8] Nevins ends his second volume with a chapter entitled "Contrast of Cultures."

[9] The fear is not so surprising when one remembers the overbearing tone and spirit as well as the actual violence which had of late years characterized American foreign policy. When conservative Europeans wished that the Civil War might lead to a permanent break-up of the Union (striking utterances are for instance to be found in a leading article of the London *Dispatch*, quoted by Sandburg, *Abraham Lincoln, The War Years*, II, p. 68, or in *Aus dem Leben Th. von Bernhardis*, VI, p. 194), this does not necessarily denote sympathy with slavery or with an aristocratic slaveholding class. Gladstone's well-known utterance about Jefferson Davis having succeeded in creating a nation proceeded from a different line of thought altogether. I am inclined to regard it as

meaning exactly what it said and as evidence of Gladstone's keen interest in national movements, however mistaken the application may have been in this case. See Paul, *A History of Modern England*, II, p. 340. When the Beards interpolate in connection with Gladstone's indiscretion the remark that his "family fortune contained profits from the slave trade," they only reveal the dangers inherent in a preconceived opinion that everything must be explained by economic factors or motives of self-interest.

HISTORICAL INEVITABILITY (ISAIAH BERLIN)

[1] A Third Programme (London) broadcast on Isaiah Berlin, "Historical Inevitability," Auguste Comte Memorial Trust Lecture; 1954.

[2] This passage from a speech held on the anniversary day of the University of Utrecht in 1953 is here given as quoted in *Use and Abuse of History,* being the Terry Lectures delivered by me at Yale University in October 1954 and published by the Yale University Press.

Pieter Geyl

Pieter Geyl, who was bo[rn]
of the world's distinguished livin[g]
most of his work is written in Dutch
history, he has achieved an enviable
and style. This is not unaccoun[t]
Professor Geyl was London corre[s]
newspaper from 1914 to 191[?]
History at University Colle[ge]
His works include, besid[es]
of the Netherlands (1932), [?]
Napoleon For and Against (194[9])
at Yale University, *The Use and Abuse*
counters in History (1961, Meridian Books, [N?])
Geyl has just retired as Professor of Modern Hist[ory]
University of Utrecht.